## What Readers Are Saying About
### *The Cucumber for Java Book*

This book is not just for programmers but for testers as well. It goes beyond using Cucumber; it gives testing guidelines as well and hints and tips to avoid bad tests.

➤ **Janet Gregory**
    Author, *Agile Testing: A Practical Guide for Testers* (with Lisa Crispin)

If you read this book in the morning, then find a stakeholder quickly enough, you'll be writing effective scenarios with that person in the afternoon. Start today.

➤ **J.B. Rainsberger**
    Author, *JUnit Recipes*

The best thing about this book: it will help you identify WHY you may want to use Cucumber, and it will guide you to good ways to do it in collaboration with your whole team.

➤ **Lisa Crispin**
    Author, *Agile Testing: A Practical Guide for Testers* (with Janet Gregory)

This is an excellent introduction to using Cucumber on the JVM that guides the reader clearly through the complexities of the API and away from common pitfalls in its application to real projects.

➤ **Nat Pryce**
    Author, *Growing OO Software Guided By Tests* (with Steve Freeman)

Not only does [this book] go deep on the technical details of using Cucumber effectively in a Java environment, it also covers the broader issues of how to succeed in driving software implementation through readable examples of system behavior, and as such it will be a valuable reference for the whole team.

➤ **David Evans**

Author, *Fifty Quick Ideas to Improve Your User Stories* (with Gojko Adžić)

[If you] implement an application in a test-first manner, taking small and careful steps and alternating implementation and refactoring phases, your tests will tell you what to do next. So listen to your tests and listen to this book!

➤ **Gáspár Nagy**

Creator of *SpecFlow - Cucumber for .NET*

This book will teach you all you need to know to get started with Cucumber on the Java platform...although the authors make sure that nonprogrammers can follow along. It will find its place on my bookshelf and in the book recommendations I give out in my training classes.

➤ **Markus Gaertner**

Author, *ATDD by Example*

This is a great reference guide for software project builds maintainers, because the authors carefully address the integration of Cucumber with other Java platform favorites such as JDBC, databases, dependency injection containers such as CDI and Spring Framework, and REST server-side endpoints.

➤ **Peter Pilgrim**

Author, *The Java EE 7 Developer Handbook*

# The Cucumber for Java Book

Behaviour-Driven Development
for Testers and Developers

Seb Rose
Matt Wynne
Aslak Hellesøy

The Pragmatic Bookshelf

Dallas, Texas • Raleigh, North Carolina

Our Pragmatic courses, workshops, and other products can help you and your team create better software and have more fun. For more information, as well as the latest Pragmatic titles, please visit us at *https://pragprog.com*.

The team that produced this book includes:

Jacquelyn Carter (editor)
Potomac Indexing, LLC (indexer)
Liz Welch (copyeditor)
Dave Thomas (typesetter)
Janet Furlow (producer)
Ellie Callahan (support)

For international rights, please contact *rights@pragprog.com*.

Printed in the United States of America.
ISBN-13: 978-1-941222-29-4
Printed on acid-free paper.
Book version: P1.0—February 2015

# Contents

## Part II — A Worked Example

# Part III — More Techniques

# Foreword

OK, before we do anything else, let's be sure we're talking about the testing tool. Right? Cucumber. The acceptance testing tool. I mean, you wouldn't have picked this book up if you didn't know something about it already. Right? I mean, you're a software person, right?

So, you're probably wondering, since Cucumber is so simple to use and all, just how much this book could possibly teach you. I mean, you've probably seen, or even written, some Gherkin scenarios, and you've probably seen some Cucumber tests run. You've probably watched a video or two, so you know what Cucumber is like. So perhaps you're looking at the page count, or just looking at how thick the book is, and you're wondering: "Is there really that much to talk about?" You might be suspicious that this book is like all those early SOA books: full of fluffy descriptions, vacuous advice, and tedious repetition just to fill up space and make it look thick and important.

Well, put those thoughts out of your mind—because, trust me, this book may be thick, but it's also dense. (Uh…This just isn't coming out right…But you know what I mean.)

What you're looking at here is a book about acceptance testing—a *deep* book about acceptance testing. It happens to use Cucumber as the tool, and Gherkin as the language for writing those acceptance tests—and make no mistake you'll learn every nook and cranny of that tool and that language. However, Cucumber and Gherkin is the *least* that you'll learn. Even if you never intend to use Cucumber and Gherkin, this book has a lot to teach you.

The first few chapters might not convince you of this, because they're mostly about the syntax and semantics of the tool and language. They walk you through setting up simple acceptance tests, features, and scenarios. They show you how to construct step files and where to put them. They show you how to execute the tests, and how to deal with the error messages. Think of these early chapters as the appetizer—a light and tasty tease with just a hint of the meat that is to come.

And then, hold on to your hats, because when the meat comes, *it comes*! I mean, these authors put you in the passenger seat, take you on a nice gentle ride once or twice around the track, and then, just when you're thinking that the ride should be over, they look at you, smile with an evil grin, and floor it.

And what a dizzying ride it is! You'll learn what acceptance tests are, what they're good for, who should write them, who should read them, what can go wrong, how to fix what can go wrong, how to avoid making it go wrong—and (pant, pant) that's just the first lap.

The next laps include things like how to deal with race conditions, how to test and manage concurrent operations, and what to do with intermittently flickering tests. They talk about how to write tests that use databases, and why and when that's a good idea, and why and when it's not. They talk about complex configurations, dependency injection, continuous integration, and (get this) legacy code!

And, just to prove that no topic is out of bound for these guys, they talk about organizational structure, team structure, and the sociology of programmers, testers, managers, customers, and product owners.

And every time you think that they're about to slow down for their last lap so you can get out of this crazy ride, you turn the page and there's another whirlwind lap full of deep knowledge, genuine experience, and solid advice.

For those of you who are experienced in acceptance testing, you might find parts in the middle of the book a bit annoying because they seem to break all the rules you thought were golden. But they're just teasing you, because as you read on you find not only that they've got those bases covered but that they have a better set of solutions and a better perspective than you thought —maybe better even than your own.

So, here's my advice. Get ready to study! Get ready for a really meaty meal that will take a long time to eat, and an even longer time to digest. You won't be disappointed. This one is worth the time and effort.

*Robert C. Martin (Uncle Bob)*

# Acknowledgments

The first people we want to thank are the hundreds of you who contribute to the Cucumber community. Whether you're sharing ideas, experiences, and opinions on the mailing list, helping people in the IRC channel, or contributing new features and bug fixes to the codebase, it all helps. Without your contribution, there would be no Cucumber and therefore no book.

Writing this book has taken much more effort than any of us had anticipated. Throughout it all, our editor Jackie Carter has patiently been there at our side, cajoling us when we needed it, chiding us when we deserved it, and giving us thoughtful feedback at every opportunity. Jackie has made a massive contribution to the quality of what you're reading, and her name fully deserves its place on the cover.

Thanks to our reviewers:

| | | |
|---|---|---|
| Nat Pryce | Marton Meszaros | Tim Pizey |
| Roberto Lo Giacco | Gáspár Nagy | Craig Harrison |
| Kev McCabe | Paolo Ambrosio | Simon Spencer |
| Leslie Brooks | Jim Speakman | Sten Aksel Heien |

Your suggestions and encouragement were greatly appreciated.

Special thanks go to Paolo Ambrosio and Krzysztof Jelski, for their help coping with the evolving Spring integration, and to Ulises Cerviño Beresi, for his timely Clojure-fu.

Thanks to all the beta readers who left us feedback, helping us iron out the little mistakes we would never have seen ourselves.

We're hugely grateful to Uncle Bob for his powerful (and hilarious) foreword. You might think, given the glowing nature of what he's written, that we've influenced him with payment or threats of blackmail—but we haven't. Honest. We're very proud that he likes our book almost as much as we like his.

From Seb: To Claire, Megan, and Angus, thank you for putting up with my constant absences over the past year—this might not be the end of the absences, but I'll need a new excuse from now on. Without the success of *The Cucumber Book* there would have been nothing to rewrite for Java, so thanks to Matt and Aslak for that. And without the port of Cucumber from Ruby to the JVM there would have been no need for this book at all, so extra thanks to Aslak and the whole Cucumber-JVM team.

From Matt: I want to thank the team at Songkick, especially Sabrina Leandro, Niko Felger, Dan Lucraft, Phil Cowans, and Matt Johnson. Many of the lessons in this book I learned with you. Greatest thanks go to my wonderful wife Anna, for believing in this project and giving me the support I needed to actually get it done. Imagine all the things we'll be able to do now that it's finished!

From Aslak: Dad, thanks for having the foresight to buy me a Commodore 64 in 1981. Patricia, my dear wife—thank you for the countless hours of patience and encouragement. And for coming up with the silly but catchy name Cucumber!

# Preface

Companies often have huge issues with trust—the customer doesn't trust the supplier, the business doesn't trust the developers, the developers don't trust the testers, and the testers don't trust anyone. Cucumber gives the business, developers, and testers a way to collaborate and specify, in plain English, how the system should work. We've seen how these conversations over a simple Cucumber specification can begin the process of recuperation.

Out of these conversations grow a set of specifications that all stakeholders could understand. Cucumber enables the direct automation of the specification, which means that anyone can see, at a glance, what functionality has been implemented and what hasn't. It also gives the development team a safety net so that they get early feedback if a change they're working on has broken any existing functionality. And it frees your testers up to do interesting, creative work instead of regularly running through a repetitive, manual regression pack.

Cucumber has now been used by thousands of teams who have derived benefit from it in different ways. Those of us who were drawn to Cucumber from the beginning instinctively realized that it's more than a test automation tool; it's a collaboration tool. Let's be clear about this—Cucumber can be used for test automation—but this was not the intent of its creators, and some of our design choices reflect this. By writing this book, we hope to show you not just how to use Cucumber but how to use it well.

Cucumber was originally written in Ruby. Over the years it has become incredibly popular and has been ported to plenty of other languages. This book is a Java version of *The Cucumber Book*, containing the same great advice about how to deliver rock-solid applications collaboratively, but with all code completely rewritten in Java and new chapters that cover features unique to the Java version of Cucumber.

# Who This Book Is For

Cucumber is designed to help build bridges between the technical and non-technical members of a software team, and we've tried to consider both of those readers. The majority of the book is written to the technical reader, someone who is interested in test automation and already has some programming skill. However, several of the chapters—especially in the first part of the book where we explain how to write specifications—are written with the nontechnical reader very much in mind. Specifically, those chapters are:

- Chapter 1, *Why Cucumber?*, on page 3
- Chapter 3, *Gherkin Basics*, on page 31
- Chapter 5, *Expressive Scenarios*, on page 69
- Chapter 6, *Keeping Your Cucumbers Sweet*, on page 91
- Chapter 16, *Working with Legacy Applications*, on page 285

As the book develops, we'll look at more complex testing situations, and the level of technical know-how required to read the chapters will increase.

## You Don't Need to Be a Java Expert

Java[1] is a programming language that can be installed and run on all major operating systems. Cucumber has been ported to many programming languages, but this book is about the version written in Java.

That doesn't mean the system you're testing has to be written in Java. Java has many libraries that enable it to talk to other languages and platforms, and we'll show you how to use them to test web-based systems that could be written in any language. Additionally, since the Java Virtual Machine (JVM) supports many programming languages, the Java version of Cucumber works well with programs written in other JVM languages (such as Groovy, Scala, and Clojure).

To follow along with the coding examples in the technical chapters, it will help if you're familiar with Java. Java is not the easiest language to learn, but neither is it the hardest, and the Java examples we'll use are deliberately simple.

## It's OK if You're Not Test-Driven

We've had our greatest success with Cucumber as part of an *outside-in* approach, starting with a failing Cucumber test and using that to drive our

---

1. http://java.com

development work on the application code. As developers, this way of working helps us stay honest and avoid the temptation to build in functionality that nobody asked us for, just in case it might be needed one day in the future.

Cucumber is a tool that facilitates this way of working, but it doesn't force it on you. Some teams use Cucumber to automate tests for the work that developers have already done. This can often be a first step toward adopting an outside-in approach, as Cucumber's readable tests start to attract the attention of the team's nontechnical stakeholders, drawing them into the process. Even if you're using Cucumber to write tests against existing code, you'll still get a great deal of benefit from Cucumber over alternatives like QTP and Selenium IDE, and we think you'll still get a lot out of this book. We're not here to preach to you about process, but we will share our insights about what has worked for us and why.

## Why You Should Listen to Us

All the authors have been building software for a living for a very long time, and using automated tests for the last ten years. Aslak created Cucumber in 2008, Matt has been one of its most active users from day one, and Seb came to the party a little later, while Cucumber was being ported to Java.

We've used Cucumber to test all kinds of systems: from Ruby on Rails web applications, through Flash games, to enterprise Java web services. We've also trained hundreds of developers in how to use Cucumber, teaching the material in this book at events and companies around the world.

The Cucumber community is full of lively debate, and we've spent many hours of our spare time having our ideas challenged and honed in discussions with other users. We hope we've distilled as much of that knowledge and experience as possible in this book.

## How This Book Is Organized

The book is in three parts. In Part I, we'll take you through the core concepts you need to know in order to make use of Cucumber. Novice readers will learn everything they need to know to get up and running, and readers already experienced with Cucumber should pick up plenty of useful detail too.

Part II works through a practical example of developing a new application using Cucumber. You'll pair with us as we build a simple application from scratch, giving you a chance to experience how we like to build software using Cucumber and to consolidate what you've learned in Part I. We'll also teach you some advanced features of Cucumber that are easier to learn in the context of an example.

In Part III, you'll learn techniques for using Cucumber in situations that weren't covered in the previous worked example, as well as looking in more detail at how to configure Cucumber for Java.

## What Is Not in This Book

Although it is possible to test Flash and mobile applications using Cucumber, the details are sadly beyond the scope of this edition. This book covers the Java version of Cucumber that runs natively on the JVM, but using it with other JVM languages will not be covered. Cucumber's wire protocol (a protocol for driving remote systems over a TCP socket) is also out of scope.

## Running the Code Examples

This book is full of practical examples, and we encourage you to follow along with them to get the most out of the book. You'll learn the most if you type them in by hand as you read along, but if you'd prefer, you can always download the code examples from the book's website.[2] To run the examples, you'll need to install the Java language itself as well as the Maven software project management tool. You can find the full instructions in Appendix 1, *Installing Cucumber*, on page 293.

### Windows Users

Most of the code examples work just the same on Windows and *nix operating systems. On the rare occasions that they differ, you'll find the Windows version in a sidebar nearby, with a note in the body of the text pointing you there.

You'll soon notice that we've used the $ symbol for the command prompt. This is familiar to Linux or Mac users but might feel a little unfamiliar to Windows users. So, when you're looking at something like this:

```
$ mvn clean test
```

try to imagine you're seeing this instead:

```
C:\> mvn clean test
```

Other than that, everything should work just the same for everyone.

---

2.   http://pragprog.com/titles/srjcuc/source_code

## Online Resources

The apps and examples shown in this book can be found at the Pragmatic Programmers website for this book.[3] You'll also find the community forum, for help if you're stuck on one of the exercises in this book, and the errata-submission form, where you can report problems with the text or make suggestions for future versions.

If you have a general question about Cucumber, the Cucumber community will welcome you to their mailing list.[4] Cucumber is an open source tool, which means that everyone contributing to the group is volunteering their time, so please make sure you've researched your question as thoroughly as you can before you ask for help on the mailing list. People will be much more likely to help you if they can see you're trying to help yourself.

**Seb Rose, Matt Wynne, and Aslak Hellesøy**
February 2015

---

3.  http://pragprog.com/book/sjrcuc
4.  https://groups.google.com/forum/#!forum/cukes

# Part I

# Cucumber Fundamentals

*In this first part of the book, we start by talking about behaviour-driven development (BDD) and why organizations all over the world find it helps them deliver more value to their customers. There will be a few simple examples to introduce you to how Cucumber helps teams work in a behavior-driven way, but nothing too technical. In fact, this part of the book is ideal for the whole team—including product owners, managers, designers, and customers.*

*It's important to understand that BDD is not a "silver bullet" solution, so we'll also spend some time looking at how things can go wrong. We've seen BDD help all sorts of organizations and, once you're able to recognize (and correct) the common symptoms that teams new to Cucumber suffer from, we're confident that it will help your team too.*

# CHAPTER 1

# Why Cucumber?

Software starts as an idea.

Let's assume it's a good idea—an idea that could make the world a better place, or at least make someone a bit of money. The challenge of the software developer is to take the idea and make it real, into something that actually delivers that benefit.

The original idea is perfect, beautiful. If the person who has the idea happens to be a talented software developer, then we might be in luck: the idea could be turned into working software without ever needing to be explained to anyone else. More often, though, the person with the original idea doesn't have the necessary programming skill to make it real. Now the idea has to travel from that person's mind into other people's. It needs to be *communicated*.

Most software projects involve teams of several people working collaboratively together, so high-quality communication is critical to their success. As you probably know, good communication isn't just about eloquently describing your ideas to others; you also need to solicit feedback to ensure you've been understood correctly. This is why Agile software teams have learned to work in small *increments*, using the software that's built incrementally as the feedback that says to the stakeholders, "Is this what you mean?"

Even this is not enough. If the team spends a two-week iteration implementing a misunderstanding, not only have they wasted two weeks of effort, but they've corrupted the integrity of the codebase with concepts and functionality that do not reflect the original idea. Other developers may have already innocently started to build more code on top of those bad ideas, making it unlikely that the codebase will ever reflect the business domain correctly.

We need a kind of filter to protect our codebase from these misunderstood ideas.

## Automated Acceptance Tests

The idea of *automated acceptance tests* originates in extreme programming[1] (XP), specifically in the practice of test-driven development[2] (TDD).

Instead of a business stakeholder passing requirements to the development team without much opportunity for feedback, the developer and stakeholder collaborate to write automated tests that express the outcome that the stakeholder wants. We call them acceptance tests because they express what the software needs to do in order for the stakeholder to find it *acceptable*. The test fails at the time of writing, because no code has been written yet, but it captures what the stakeholder cares about and gives everyone a clear signal as to what it will take to be *done*.

These tests are different from *unit tests*, which are aimed at developers and help them to drive out and check their software designs. It's sometimes said that unit tests ensure you *build the thing right*, whereas acceptance tests ensure you *build the right thing*.

Automated acceptance testing has been an established practice among good XP teams for years, but many less experienced Agile teams seem to see TDD as being a programmer activity only. As Lisa Crispin and Janet Gregory point out in *Agile Testing: A Practical Guide for Testers and Agile Teams [CG08]*, without the business-facing automated acceptance tests, it's hard for the programmers to know which unit tests they need to write. Automated acceptance tests help your team to focus, ensuring the work you do each iteration is the most valuable thing you could possibly be doing. You'll still make mistakes—but you'll make a lot less of them—meaning you can go home on time and enjoy the rest of your life.

## Behaviour-Driven Development

Behaviour-driven development[3] (BDD) builds upon test-driven development (TDD) by formalizing the good habits of the best TDD practitioners. The best TDD practitioners work from the *outside-in*, starting with a failing customer acceptance test that describes the behavior of the system from the customer's point of view. As BDD practitioners, we take care to write the acceptance tests as *examples* that anyone on the team can read. We make use of the process of writing those examples to get feedback from the business stakeholders

---

1. *Extreme Programming Explained: Embrace Change [Bec00]*
2. *Test Driven Development: By Example [Bec02]*
3. http://behaviour-driven.org/

about whether we're setting out to build the right thing before we get started. As we do so, we make a deliberate effort to develop a shared, *ubiquitous language* for talking about the system.

## Ubiquitous Language

As Eric Evans describes in his book *Domain Driven Design [Eva03]*, many software projects suffer from low-quality communication between the domain experts and programmers on the team:

> "A project faces serious problems when its language is fractured. Domain experts use their jargon while technical team members have their own language tuned for discussing the domain in terms of design...Across this linguistic divide, the domain experts vaguely describe what they want. Developers, struggling to understand a domain new to them, vaguely understand."

With a conscious effort by the team, a ubiquitous language can emerge that is used and understood by everyone involved in the project. When the team uses this language consistently in their conversations, documentation, and code, the friction of translating between everyone's different little dialects is gone, and the chances of misunderstandings are greatly reduced.

Cucumber helps facilitate the discovery and use of a ubiquitous language within the team by giving the two sides of the linguistic divide a place where they can meet. Cucumber tests interact directly with the developers' code, but they're written in a medium and language that business stakeholders can understand. By working together to write these tests—*specifying collaboratively*—not only do the team members decide what behavior they need to implement next, but they learn how to describe that behavior in a common language that everyone understands.

When we write these tests before development starts, we can explore and eradicate many misunderstandings long before they ooze their way into the codebase.

## Examples

What makes Cucumber stand out from the crowd of other tools is that it has been designed specifically to ensure the acceptance tests can easily be read —and written—by anyone on the team. This reveals the true value of acceptance tests as a communication and collaboration tool. The easy readability of Cucumber acceptance tests draws business stakeholders into the process, helping you explore and understand their requirements.

Here's an example of a Cucumber acceptance test:

```
Feature: Sign-up

  Sign-up should be quick and friendly.

  Scenario: Successful sign-up

    New users should get a confirmation email and be greeted
    personally by the site once signed in.

    Given I have chosen to sign up
    When I sign up with valid details
    Then I should receive a confirmation email
    And I should see a personalized greeting message

  Scenario: Duplicate email

    Where someone tries to create an account for an email address
    that already exists.

    Given I have chosen to sign up
    When I sign up with an email address that has already registered
    Then I should be told that the email is already registered
    And I should be offered the option to recover my password
```

Notice how the test is specified as *examples* of the way we want the system to behave in particular scenarios. Using examples like this has an unexpectedly powerful effect in enabling people to visualize the system before it has been built. All the team members can read a test like this and tell you whether it reflects their understanding of what the system should do, and it may well spark their imagination into thinking of other scenarios that you'll need to consider too. Gojko Adzic's book *Specification by Example [Ad 11]* contains many case studies of teams who have discovered this and used it to their advantage.

Acceptance tests written in this style become more than just tests; they become *executable specifications*.

## Living Documentation

Cucumber *feature files* share the benefit of traditional specification documents in that they can be written and read by business stakeholders, but they have a distinct advantage in that a computer can understand them too. In practice, this means that your documentation, rather than being something that's written once and then gradually goes out of date, becomes a living thing that reflects the true state of the project.

### Source of Truth

For many teams, the Cucumber feature files become the definitive *source of truth* as to what the system does. Having a single place to go for this information saves a lot of time that is often wasted trying to keep requirements documents, tests, and code all in sync. Having a single source of truth also helps to build trust within the team, because different parts of the team no longer have their own personal versions of the truth.

## How Cucumber Works

Before we dive into the meat of the book, let's give you some context with a high-level overview of a typical Cucumber test suite. This structure, from features down to automation library, is illustrated in the figure.

Cucumber was originally created as a command-line tool by members of the Ruby community. It has since been translated into several development environments, including Java, to allow more of us to enjoy its benefits. When you run Cucumber, it reads in your specifications from plain-language text files called *features*, examines them for *scenarios* to test, and runs the scenarios against your system. Each scenario is a list of *steps* for Cucumber to work through. So that Cucumber can understand these feature files, they must follow some basic syntax rules. The name for this set of rules is *Gherkin*.

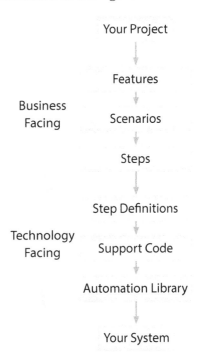

Along with the features, you give Cucumber a set of *step definitions*, which map the business-readable language of each step into code (written in Java throughout this book) to carry out whatever action is being described by the step. In a mature test suite, the step definition itself will probably just be one or two lines of code that delegate to a library of *support code*, specific to the domain of your application, that knows how to carry out common tasks on the system. Sometimes that may involve using an *automation library*, like the browser automation library Selenium, to interact with the system itself.

If the code in the step definition executes without error, Cucumber proceeds to the next step in the scenario. If it gets to the end of the scenario without any of the steps raising an error, it marks the scenario as having passed. If any of the steps in the scenario fail, however, Cucumber marks the scenario as having failed and moves on to the next one. As the scenarios run, Cucumber prints out the results showing you exactly what is working and what isn't.

That's it in a nutshell. There are many other advantages to Cucumber that make it an excellent choice: you can write your specifications in more than forty different spoken languages, you can use tags to organize and group your scenarios, and you can easily integrate with a host of high-quality automation libraries to drive almost any kind of application. All that and more will become clear as you read the rest of this book.

## What We Just Learned

Let's review what we've covered so far.

Software teams work best when the developers and business stakeholders are communicating clearly with one another. A great way to do that is to collaboratively specify the work that's about to be done using automated acceptance tests.

When the acceptance tests are written as examples, they stimulate people's imaginations and help them see other scenarios they hadn't previously considered.

When the team members write their acceptance tests collaboratively, they can develop their own ubiquitous language for talking about their problem domain. This helps them avoid misunderstandings.

Cucumber was designed specifically to help business stakeholders get involved in writing acceptance tests.

Each test case in Cucumber is called a *scenario*, and scenarios are grouped into features. Each scenario contains several steps.

The business-facing parts of a Cucumber test suite, stored in feature files, must be written according to syntax rules—known as Gherkin—so that Cucumber can read them.

Under the hood, step definitions translate from the business-facing language of steps into code.

To illustrate these concepts, in the next chapter we're going to dive right in and build a very simple application, using Cucumber to drive the development.

## Try This

Cucumber has its own ubiquitous language. Can you list the terms about Cucumber's domain you've learned in this chapter and describe what you think each of them means?

# CHAPTER 2

# First Taste

We figured you'd be eager to start playing with your shiny new toy right away, so we're going to work through a simple example that will give you a feel for what it's like to work with Cucumber. You might not quite understand everything that happens here just yet, but try not to let that worry you. We'll come back and fill in the details over the next few chapters.

We're going to build a simple class from the outside-in, driving our development with Cucumber. Watch how we proceed in baby steps, going back to run Cucumber after we make each change. This patient rhythm is an important characteristic of working effectively with Cucumber, but it's much easier to demonstrate than to explain.

Assuming you want to follow along with the action in this chapter (it'll be a lot more fun if you do), you'll need to have Cucumber installed.[1] Eventually we'll end up using build and dependency management tools (such as Maven, Ant, Gradle, or Ivy) as described in Appendix 1, *Installing Cucumber*, on page 293, but for this first example we'll do things by invoking Cucumber directly so that you can see exactly what's going on.

Right...shall we get started then?

## Understanding Our Goal

Our goal is to write a Java library that calculates the cost of your groceries at the supermarket. Some people might call this a checkout.

We have an incredible vision of what this checkout will one day power: a traditional checkout till, a portable scanner that you carry around while you shop, or even a cloud-based service that uses the camera on your mobile

---

1.  http://cukes.info/install-cucumber-jvm.html

phone to scan the barcodes. We're pragmatic business people, though, so the first release of our library has to be as simple as possible. The first release will be a Java library. It will take two inputs: the prices of available items and the notification of items as they are scanned at the checkout.

The checkout will keep track of the total cost. So, for example, if the prices of available items looks like this:

```
banana 40c
apple  25c
```

and the only item you scan at the checkout is this:

```
1 banana
```

then the output will be 40c.

Similarly, if you scan multiple items:

```
3 apple
```

then the output will be 75c.

You get the idea.

## Creating a Feature

Cucumber tests are grouped into *features*. We use this name because we want them to describe the features that a user will be able to enjoy when using our program. The first thing we need to do is make a directory where we'll store our new program along with the features we'll be writing for it.

```
$ mkdir checkout
$ cd checkout
```

The next thing we need is to get a couple of JARs that contain the bare minimum for running Cucumber. Create a new folder to place them in:

```
$ mkdir jars
```

Download the latest versions of the following JARs from the public Maven repository[2] and copy them into the jars folder. This is enough for us to use Cucumber with Java.

• cucumber-core  • cucumber-java  • cucumber-jvm-deps  • gherkin

---

2.    http://repo1.maven.org/maven2/info/cukes/

We're going to let Cucumber guide us through the development of our checkout program, so let's start right away by running cucumber from the checkout folder:

```
$ java -cp "jars/*" cucumber.api.cli.Main -p pretty .
No features found at [.]

0 Scenarios
0 Steps
0m0.000s
```

There's a lot going on here, so let's take a closer look at the command line. First off, we invoke the java interpreter, with a specified classpath to execute the entry point contained within the cucumber.api.cli.Main class. This class contains the code that implements the Cucumber *command-line interface* (CLI), which allows us to control how Cucumber searches for tests to run. In this case, we're passing two things to Cucumber:

- -p pretty tells cucumber to use the *pretty formatter* plugin (you'll see why later)
- a path that points to where our feature files are located

We haven't written any feature files yet, which is why, when we run Cucumber, it gives us the helpful error message No features found at [.].

This is also quite a lot to type, so let's put it into a shell file. In the project root (called /checkout), use your favorite text editor to create a file called cucumber (or cucumber.bat if you're using Windows). Enter the following text:

**first_taste/00/cucumber**
```
java -cp "jars/*" cucumber.api.cli.Main -p pretty .
```

If you're working on a Unix-style operating system, you may need to make the cucumber file executable before running the new shell script:

```
$ chmod u+x cucumber
$ ./cucumber
```

If you're working on Windows, then simply run the batch file (from now on use this command whenever you see ./cucumber in the text):

```
C:\checkout> cucumber.bat
```

Whichever operating system you are using, you should get exactly the same output as we did the first time:

```
No features found at [.]

0 Scenarios
0 Steps
0m0.000s
```

Now it's time to create our first feature. We could create it in the current folder, but that would quickly get confusing, so let's create a folder:

```
$ mkdir features
```

Now let's create an empty feature file in the features folder. If you're running Windows, you can use these commands:

```
C:\checkout> cd features
C:\checkout\features> type nul > checkout.feature
```

On other operating systems, issue these commands:

```
$ cd features
$ touch checkout.feature
```

Then we modify our shell file to tell Cucumber where to find our feature files:

first_taste/01/cucumber
```
java -cp "jars/*" cucumber.api.cli.Main -p pretty features
```

Now, let's run cucumber again:

```
$ ./cucumber
No features found at [features]

0 Scenarios
0 Steps
0m0.000s
```

Each Cucumber test is called a *scenario*, and each scenario contains *steps* that tell Cucumber what to do. This output means that Cucumber is happily scanning the features directory, but it didn't find any scenarios to run. Let's create one.

Our user research has shown us 67 percent of all shoppers buy bananas, so that's what we'll start with. In your favorite editor, edit the empty feature file that you just created, checkout.feature:

first_taste/02/features/checkout.feature
```
Feature: Checkout
  Scenario: Checkout a banana
    Given the price of a "banana" is 40c
    When I checkout 1 "banana"
    Then the total price should be 40c
```

This .feature file contains the first scenario for our checkout class. We've translated one of the examples we were given at the beginning of the chapter into a Cucumber scenario that we can ask the computer to run, over and over again. You can probably see that Cucumber expects a bit of structure in this file. The keywords Feature, Scenario, Given, When, and Then are the structure, and everything else is documentation. Although some of the keywords are highlighted here in the book—and they may be in your editor too—it's just a plain-text file. The structure is called *Gherkin*.

When you save this file and run cucumber, you should see a great deal more output than the last time:

```
$ ./cucumber
Feature: Checkout

  Scenario: Checkout a banana               # checkout.feature:2
    Given the price of a "banana" is 40c
    When I checkout 1 "banana"
    Then the total price should be 40c

1 Scenarios (1 undefined)
3 Steps (3 undefined)
0m0.000s

You can implement missing steps with the snippets below:

@Given("^the price of a \"(.*?)\" is (\\d+)c$")
public void the_price_of_a_is_c(String arg1, int arg2) throws Throwable {
    // Write code here that turns the phrase above into concrete actions
    throw new PendingException();
}

@When("^I checkout (\\d+) \"(.*?)\"$")
public void i_checkout(int arg1, String arg2) throws Throwable {
    // Write code here that turns the phrase above into concrete actions
    throw new PendingException();
}

@Then("^the total price should be (\\d+)c$")
public void the_total_price_should_be_c(int arg1) throws Throwable {
    // Write code here that turns the phrase above into concrete actions
    throw new PendingException();
}
```

Wow, that's a lot of output all of a sudden! Let's take a look at what's going on here. First, we can see that Cucumber has found our feature and is trying to run it. We can tell this because Cucumber has repeated the content of the feature back to us. You might also have noticed that the summary output 0 scenarios has changed to 1 scenario (undefined). This means that Cucumber has read the scenario in our feature but doesn't know how to run it yet.

Second, Cucumber has printed out three code snippets. These are sample code for *step definitions*, written in Java, which tell Cucumber how to translate

**Seb says:**
## Colored Console Output in Windows

If you're working in Windows, then you'll probably be seeing strange control characters in the output. That's because Cucumber is using ANSI control sequences to print colored text in the console. Windows doesn't recognize these automatically, so you'll need to install a small application to render them correctly. See Appendix 1, *Installing Cucumber*, on page 293 for further details.

the plain English steps in the feature into actions against our application. Our next step will be to put these snippets into a Java file where we can start to flesh them out. But first, since we're following Java coding standards we notice that these step definitions are using *snake case*[3] rather than camel case. Don't worry—we don't need to edit them by hand; we just need to tell Cucumber that's what we want:

first_taste/03/cucumber
```
java -cp "jars/*" cucumber.api.cli.Main -p pretty --snippets camelcase features
```

Now when we run ./cucumber it generates snippets with method names that conform to the Java standard:

```
You can implement missing steps with the snippets below:

@Given("^the price of a \"(.*?)\" is (\\d+)c$")
public void thePriceOfAIsC(String arg1, int arg2) throws Throwable {
    // Write code here that turns the phrase above into concrete actions
    throw new PendingException();
}

@When("^I checkout (\\d+) \"(.*?)\"$")
public void iCheckout(int arg1, String arg2) throws Throwable {
    // Write code here that turns the phrase above into concrete actions
    throw new PendingException();
}

@Then("^the total price should be (\\d+)c$")
public void theTotalPriceShouldBeC(int arg1) throws Throwable {
    // Write code here that turns the phrase above into concrete actions
    throw new PendingException();
}
```

---

3.   http://en.wikipedia.org/wiki/Snake_case

Before we explore beneath the layer of business-facing Gherkin features, it's worth taking a quick look at the map in case anyone is feeling lost. The figure reminds us how things fit together. We start with features, which contain our scenarios and steps. The steps of our scenarios call step definitions that provide the link between the Gherkin features and the application being built.

Now we'll implement some step definitions so that our scenario is no longer undefined.

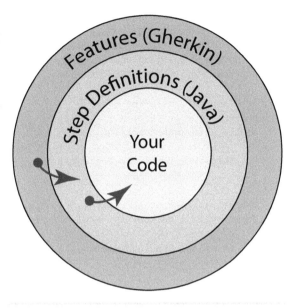

Figure 1—The main layers of a Cucumber test suite

## Creating Step Definitions

Without thinking too much about what they mean, let's just copy and paste the snippets from Cucumber's last output into a new Java file. Let's create a new folder to keep our step definitions in:

```
$ mkdir step_definitions
```

Now create a Java file called CheckoutSteps.java in step_definitions. Cucumber won't mind what you call it as long as it's a Java file, but this is a good name to use. Open it in your text editor and enter the following class definition:

**first_taste/04/step_definitions/CheckoutSteps.java**
```
package step_definitions;

import cucumber.api.java.en.*;
import cucumber.api.PendingException;

public class CheckoutSteps {
}
```

Now paste in those snippets:

```
first_taste/04/step_definitions/CheckoutSteps.java
package step_definitions;

import cucumber.api.java.en.*;
import cucumber.api.PendingException;

public class CheckoutSteps {
    @Given("^the price of a \"(.*?)\" is (\\d+)c$")
    public void thePriceOfAIsC(String arg1, int arg2) throws Throwable {
        // Write code here that turns the phrase above into concrete actions
        throw new PendingException();
    }

    @When("^I checkout (\\d+) \"(.*?)\"$")
    public void iCheckout(int arg1, String arg2) throws Throwable {
        // Write code here that turns the phrase above into concrete actions
        throw new PendingException();
    }

    @Then("^the total price should be (\\d+)c$")
    public void theTotalPriceShouldBeC(int arg1) throws Throwable {
        // Write code here that turns the phrase above into concrete actions
        throw new PendingException();
    }
}
```

What we'd like to do now is run Cucumber so that it can tell us what to do next, but before we can do that we have to compile the new CheckoutSteps class and add it to our classpath. This is work that we normally don't bother with when working in our favorite IDE, but since we're doing this from the command line, we'll now edit our cucumber shell file so that it compiles our Java code as well as invoking Cucumber.

```
first_taste/04/cucumber
javac -cp "jars/*" step_definitions/CheckoutSteps.java
java -cp "jars/*:." cucumber.api.cli.Main -p pretty --snippets camelcase \
                        -g step_definitions features
```

Line 1 compiles the CheckoutSteps class that we've just created. Then line 2 invokes Cucumber. There are two slight additions to Cucumber's invocation:

1. We've added the current directory "." to the classpath.

2. We've added the -g step_definitions command-line argument to tell Cucumber where to look for the step definitions that it will need to "glue" the steps in the feature file to the checkout application (which we haven't written yet).

Now, let's execute ./cucumber again and see what we need to do next:

**Seb says:**
## Classpath Separators

The syntax of the Java classpath is dependent on the underlying operating system. For *nix operating systems the separator is a colon (:) whereas for Windows operating systems the separator is a semicolon (;).

We're showing the cucumber script in this chapter, which is for *nix users. You'll also find the cucumber.bat batch file in the downloadable code, which contains exactly the same operations but formatted for Windows.

```
Feature: Checkout

  Scenario: Checkout a banana               # checkout.feature:2
    Given the price of a "banana" is 40c # CheckoutSteps.thePriceOfAIsC(String,int)
      cucumber.api.PendingException: TODO: implement me
        at step_definitions.CheckoutSteps.thePriceOfAIsC(CheckoutSteps.java:12)
        at *.Given the price of a "banana" is 40c(checkout.feature:3)
    When I checkout 1 "banana"               # CheckoutSteps.iCheckout(int,String)
    Then the total price should be 40c    # CheckoutSteps.theTotalPriceShouldBeC(int)

1 Scenarios (1 pending)
3 Steps (2 skipped, 1 pending)
0m0.138s

cucumber.api.PendingException: TODO: implement me
        at step_definitions.CheckoutSteps.thePriceOfAIsC(CheckoutSteps.java:12)
        at *.Given the price of a "banana" is 40c(checkout.feature:3)
```

The scenario has graduated from undefined to pending. This is good news, because it means Cucumber is now running the first step, but as it did so, it hit the call to throw new PendingException() inside our copied-and-pasted step definition code, which tells Cucumber that this scenario is still a work in progress. We need to replace throwing this exception with a real implementation.

Notice that Cucumber reports the two other steps as skipped. As soon as it encounters a failed or pending step, Cucumber will stop running the scenario and skip the remaining steps.

Let's implement the first step definition.

## Implementing Our First Step Definition

We've decided this first release of our checkout is going to be a class that takes the price list and the items being bought as arguments to a method. So, our job in the step definition for Given the price of a banana is 40c is just to remember the price of bananas. In the step_definitions folder, edit the Checkout-Steps.java file so that the first step definition looks like this:

first_taste/05/step_definitions/CheckoutSteps.java
```java
@Given("^the price of a \"(.*?)\" is (\\d+)c$")
public void thePriceOfAIsC(String name, int price) throws Throwable {
    int bananaPrice = price;
}
```

Great, that was easy. Now, where were we again? Well, we've written some Java code so we'll need to compile the CheckoutSteps class and run Cucumber again by running ./cucumber.

```
Feature: Checkout

  Scenario: Checkout a banana                # checkout.feature:2
    Given the price of a "banana" is 40c # CheckoutSteps.thePriceOfAIsC(String,int)
    When I checkout 1 "banana"             # CheckoutSteps.iCheckout(int,String)
      cucumber.api.PendingException: TODO: implement me
        at step_definitions.CheckoutSteps.iCheckout(CheckoutSteps.java:17)
        at *.When I checkout 1 "banana"(checkout.feature:4)
    Then the total price should be 40c   # CheckoutSteps.theTotalPriceShouldBeC(int)


1 Scenarios (1 pending)
3 Steps (1 skipped, 1 pending, 1 passed)
0m0.126s

cucumber.api.PendingException: TODO: implement me
        at step_definitions.CheckoutSteps.iCheckout(CheckoutSteps.java:17)
        at *.When I checkout 1 "banana"(checkout.feature:4)
```

Yay! Our first step passed! The scenario is still marked as pending, of course, because we still have the other two steps to implement, but we're starting to get somewhere.

## Changing Cucumber's Output

It can be distracting to look at the whole content of the feature in Cucumber's output each time we run it. Let's switch to use the progress *plugin* to get a more focused output. Edit cucumber so that the line that runs Cucumber looks like this:

first_taste/06/cucumber
```
java -cp "jars/*:." cucumber.api.cli.Main -p progress --snippets camelcase \
                                    -g step_definitions features
```

Now when you run ./cucumber you should see the following output:

```
.P-
```

```
1 Scenarios (1 pending)
3 Steps (1 skipped, 1 pending, 1 passed)
0m0.081s
```

```
cucumber.api.PendingException: TODO: implement me
        at step_definitions.CheckoutSteps.iCheckout(CheckoutSteps.java:17)
        at *.When I checkout 1 "banana"(checkout.feature:4)
```

Instead of printing the whole feature, the progress plugin has printed three characters in the output, one for each step. The first . character means the step passed. The P character means the second step, as we know, is pending. The final - character means that the last step has been skipped. Cucumber has several different plugins that produce output in different formats; you'll learn more about them through the course of the book.

> ## Plugins
>
> Cucumber plugins allow you to customize how the tool behaves. The plugins that ship with Cucumber produce various output formats that record what happened in a test run. There are plugins that produce HTML reports, plugins that produce JUnit XML for continuous integration servers like Jenkins, and many more. Use this command to see the different plugins that are available and try some out for yourself:
>
> ```
> java -cp "jars/*" cucumber.api.cli.Main --help
> ```
>
> We'll explain more about plugins in Chapter 14, *Controlling Cucumber*, on page 259.

That was an interesting little diversion, but let's get back to work. We have a pending test to fix!

## Testing Our Checkout Class

To implement the next step, edit step_definitions/CheckoutSteps.java so that the second step definition looks like this:

first_taste/07/step_definitions/CheckoutSteps.java
```java
@When("^I checkout (\\d+) \"(.*?)\"$")
public void iCheckout(int itemCount, String itemName) throws Throwable {
    Checkout checkout = new Checkout();
    checkout.add(itemCount, bananaPrice);
}
```

This code attempts to call an add() on an instance of our Checkout class, passing it the number of items being bought and their price.

This time when we run ./cucumber, we should get a compile error because we haven't created a Checkout class yet:

```
step_definitions/CheckoutSteps.java:15: error: cannot find symbol
        Checkout checkout = new Checkout();
        ^
  symbol:   class Checkout
  location: class CheckoutSteps
```

Our step is failing, because we don't have a Checkout class to use yet.

You might well think it's a bit odd that we've written and run code that tries to run our Checkout class, knowing perfectly well that the Checkout class doesn't even exist yet. We do this deliberately, because we want to make sure we have a fully functioning test in place before we drop down to working on the solution. Having the discipline to do this means we can trust our tests, because we've seen them fail, and this gives us confidence that when the tests pass, we're really done. This gentle rhythm is a big part of what we call *outside-in development*, and though it might seem strange at first, we hope to show you throughout the book that it has some great benefits.

Another benefit of working from the outside-in is that we've had a chance to think about the command-line interface to our checkout class from the point of view of a user, without having made any effort to implement it yet. At this stage, if we realize there's something we don't like about the interface, it's very easy for us to change it.

Now we create a folder to hold our implementation:

```
$ mkdir implementation
```

Now create a Java file in implementation, called Checkout.java. Open it in your text editor and enter the following class definition:

first_taste/08/implementation/Checkout.java
```
package implementation;

public class Checkout {
    public void add(int count, int price) {
    }
}
```

We'll need to add this to our compile step in our script cucumber, as well as modify the classpath to include the root of the project:

first_taste/08/cucumber
```
javac -cp "jars/*:." step_definitions/CheckoutSteps.java \
                   implementation/Checkout.java
```

We import the Checkout class into CheckoutSteps:

first_taste/08/step_definitions/CheckoutSteps.java
```
import implementation.Checkout;
```

And we run Cucumber again:

```
step_definitions/CheckoutSteps.java:19: error: cannot find symbol
        checkout.add(itemCount, bananaPrice);
                                ^
  symbol:   variable bananaPrice
  location: class CheckoutSteps
1 error
```

We still have a syntax error. The variable bananaPrice is local to thePriceOfAIsC(), but we're trying to use it in iCheckout(). Let's move it to be an instance variable so that it can be shared by all step definitions in CheckoutSteps:

first_taste/09/step_definitions/CheckoutSteps.java
```
public class CheckoutSteps {
    int bananaPrice = 0;

    @Given("^the price of a \"(.*?)\" is (\\d+)c$")
    public void thePriceOfAIsC(String name, int price) throws Throwable {
        bananaPrice = price;
    }
```

We now have two passing steps and a skeleton implementation of Checkout.

## Adding an Assertion

To get the last step working, change the last step definition in step_definitions/CheckoutSteps.java to look like this:

first_taste/10/step_definitions/CheckoutSteps.java
```
@Then("^the total price should be (\\d+)c$")
public void theTotalPriceShouldBeC(int total) throws Throwable {
    assertEquals(total, checkout.total());
}
```

We're using a JUnit assertion to check that the expected total specified in the feature matches the total from our checkout. If it doesn't, JUnit will raise an error. Before this can compile, we'll need to add an import statement to step_definitions/CheckoutSteps.java:

first_taste/10/step_definitions/CheckoutSteps.java
```
import static org.junit.Assert.*;
```

We'll also need to download the latest JUnit JAR[4] and put it in the jars folder.

---

4.   https://github.com/junit-team/junit/wiki/Download-and-Install

Now add an implementation of total() to Checkout:

first_taste/10/implementation/Checkout.java
```
public int total() {
    return 0;
}
```

When we run ./cucumber, we get another compile error:

```
step_definitions/CheckoutSteps.java:31: error: cannot find symbol
        assertEquals(total, checkout.total());
                            ^
  symbol:   variable checkout
  location: class CheckoutSteps
1 error
```

The local variable checkout that we created in iCheckout() has gone out of scope by the time we get to call total() later in theTotalPriceShouldBeC(). What we need to do is make it an instance variable of CheckoutSteps:

first_taste/11/step_definitions/CheckoutSteps.java
```
public class CheckoutSteps {
    Checkout checkout;
    @When("^I checkout (\\d+) \"(.*?)\"$")
    public void iCheckout(int itemCount, String itemName) throws Throwable {
        checkout = new Checkout();
        checkout.add(itemCount, bananaPrice);
    }
}
```

This is a common way we share information between different step definitions that are implemented in the same Java class. Later, you'll see other ways to do this, but this is a simple approach that you'll use often.

Now when we run ./cucumber, we have ourselves a genuine failing test:

```
..F

1 Scenarios (1 failed)
3 Steps (1 failed, 2 passed)
0m0.099s

java.lang.AssertionError: expected:<40> but was:<0>
        at org.junit.Assert.fail(Assert.java:92)
        at org.junit.Assert.failNotEquals(Assert.java:646)
        at org.junit.Assert.assertEquals(Assert.java:127)
        at org.junit.Assert.assertEquals(Assert.java:471)
        at org.junit.Assert.assertEquals(Assert.java:455)
        at step_definitions.CheckoutSteps.theTotalPriceShouldBeC
        at *.Then the total price should be 40c(checkout.feature:5)
```

Great! Now our test is failing for exactly the right reason: it's using Checkout, examining the total, and telling us just what the total should look like. This is a natural point to pause for a break. We've done the hard work for this release: when we come back to this code, Cucumber will be telling us exactly what we need to do to our program to make it work. If only all our requirements came ready-rolled with a failing test like this, building software would be easy!

### Try This

Can you write an implementation of Checkout.java that makes the scenario pass? Remember, at this stage we have only a single scenario to satisfy, so you might be able to get away with a simple solution.

We'll show you our solution in the next section.

  **Joe asks:**
## I Feel Weird: You're Making Tests Pass but Nothing Works!

We've implemented a step that uses the Checkout class and passes, even though the "class" just contains method implementations that don't do anything useful. What's going on here?

Remember that a step isn't a test in itself. The test is the whole scenario, and that isn't going to pass until all of its steps do. By the time we've implemented all of the step definitions, there's going to be only one way to make the whole scenario pass, and that's to build a checkout that can total items!

When we work outside-in like this, we often use temporary *stubs* like the empty Checkout class as placeholders for details we need to fill in later. We know that we can't get away with leaving that as an empty file forever, because eventually Cucumber is going to tell us to come back and make it do something useful in order to get the whole scenario to pass.

This principle, *deliberately doing the minimum useful work the tests will let us get away with*, might seem lazy, but in fact it's a discipline. It ensures that we make our tests thorough: if the test doesn't drive us to write the right thing, then we need a better test.

## Making It Pass

So, now that we have our solid failing Cucumber scenario in place, it's time to let that scenario drive out a solution.

There is a very simple solution that will make the test pass, but it's not going to get us very far. Let's try it anyway, for fun:

```
first_taste/12/implementation/Checkout.java
package implementation;

public class Checkout {
    public void add(int count, int price) {
    }

    public int total() {
        return 40;
    }
}
```

Try it. You should see the scenario pass at last:

```
. . .

1 Scenarios (1 passed)
3 Steps (3 passed)
0m0.116s
```

Hooray! So, what's wrong with this solution? After all, we already said that we want to do the minimum work that the tests will let us get away with, right?

Actually, that's not quite what we said. We said we want to do the minimum *useful* work that the tests will let us get away with. What we've done here might have made the test pass, but it isn't very useful. Apart from the fact that it certainly isn't going to function as a checkout yet, let's look at what we've missed out on testing with our smarty-pants one-liner solution:

- We haven't used either of the inputs.
- We haven't tried to total anything up.

In *Crystal Clear: A Human-Powered Methodology for Small Teams [Coc04]*, Alistair Cockburn advocates building a *walking skeleton* as early as possible in a project to try to flush out any potential problems with your technology choices. Obviously, our checkout is trivially simple, but it's still worth considering this principle: why don't we build something more useful that passes this scenario *and* helps us learn more about our planned implementation?

If you're unconvinced by that argument, try looking at it as a problem of duplication. We have a hard-coded value of 40 in two places: once in our scenario and once in our Checkout. In a more complex system, this kind of duplication might go unnoticed, and we'd have a brittle scenario.

Let's force ourselves to fix this, using what Kent Beck calls *triangulation* (*Test Driven Development: By Example [Bec02]*). We'll add another scenario to our feature, using a new keyword called a Scenario Outline:

first_taste/13/features/checkout.feature
```
Feature: Checkout

  Scenario Outline: Checkout bananas
    Given the price of a "banana" is 40c
    When I checkout <count> "banana"
    Then the total price should be <total>c

    Examples:
    | count | total |
    | 1     | 40    |
    | 2     | 80    |
```

We've turned our scenario into a Scenario Outline, which lets us specify multiple scenarios using a table. We could have copied and pasted the whole scenario and just changed the values, but we think this is a more readable way of expressing the examples, and we want to give you a taste of what's possible with Gherkin's syntax. Let's see what the output looks like now:

```
$ ./cucumber
.....F

2 Scenarios (1 failed, 1 passed)
6 Steps (1 failed, 5 passed)
0m0.155s

java.lang.AssertionError: expected:<80> but was:<40>
        at org.junit.Assert.fail(Assert.java:92)
        . . .
        at step_definitions.CheckoutSteps.theTotalPriceShouldBeC
        at *.Then the total price should be 80c(checkout.feature:6)
```

We can see from the summary 2 scenarios (1 failed, 1 passed) that Cucumber has run two scenarios. Each row in the Examples table is expanded into a scenario when Cucumber runs the scenario outline. The first example—where the result is 40—still passes, but the second example is failing.

Now it definitely makes sense to reimplement our program with a more realistic solution:

first_taste/14/implementation/Checkout.java
```
package implementation;

public class Checkout {
    private int runningTotal = 0;
```

```
    public void add(int count, int price) {
        runningTotal += (count * price);
    }

    public int total() {
        return runningTotal;
    }
}
```

First we create an instance variable, runningTotal, to keep track of the running total. Then we increment this in the add. Finally, we return the runningTotal in the total method.

Try that. Do both scenarios pass? Great! You've just built your first program with Cucumber.

## What We Just Learned

We've taken a quick skim over a lot of different things in this chapter, all of which will be covered again in more detail later. Let's recap and highlight some of the most important points.

### Directory Structure

Cucumber needs you to specify where your features and step definition are kept.

### Baby Steps

As we progressed through the example, did you notice how often we ran ./cucumber?

One of the things we love about working outside-in with Cucumber is how it helps us to stay focused. We can let Cucumber guide us through the work to be done, leaving us free to concentrate on creating an elegant solution. By running Cucumber every time we make a change, any mistakes we make are found and resolved quickly, and we get plenty of feedback and encouragement about our progress.

### Gherkin

Cucumber tests are expressed using a syntax called Gherkin. Gherkin files are plain text and have a .feature extension. We'll talk more about Gherkin in Chapter 3, *Gherkin Basics*, on page 31.

## Step Definitions

Step definitions are the glue that binds your Cucumber tests to the application you're testing. When the whole thing plays together, it looks a bit like Figure 1, *The main layers of a Cucumber test suite*, on page 17.

You'll learn more about step definitions in Chapter 4, *Step Definitions: From the Outside*, on page 45.

After that whistle-stop tour of Cucumber's features, we're going to slow down and get into a bit more depth. We'll work our way in through the layers over the next few chapters, starting with a look at Gherkin, the language we use to write Cucumber features.

## Try This

See whether you can add more scenarios to drive out a more complete implementation.

For instance, what if we were to checkout a banana twice?

**first_taste/15/features/checkout.feature**
```
Scenario: Two bananas scanned separately
  Given the price of a "banana" is 40c
  When I checkout 1 "banana"
  And I checkout 1 "banana"
  Then the total price should be 80c
```

And then we should think about selling apples too:

**first_taste/15/features/checkout.feature**
```
Scenario: A banana and an apple
  Given the price of a "banana" is 40c
  And the price of a "apple" is 25c
  When I checkout 1 "banana"
  And I checkout 1 "apple"
  Then the total price should be 65c
```

# CHAPTER 3

# Gherkin Basics

Now that you've gained some confidence with how Cucumber works, it's worth stepping back for a few moments and doing a little studying. We're going to look at Gherkin, the language we use for writing Cucumber features.

By the end of this chapter you'll understand how to write specifications for your software that can be both read by your stakeholders and tested by Cucumber. You'll learn what each of the Gherkin keywords does and how they all fit together to make readable, executable Cucumber specifications.

## What's Gherkin For?

When we build software for people (let's call them *stakeholders*), it's notoriously difficult to figure out exactly what they want us to build. In his famous essay, *No Silver Bullet [Bro95]*, Fred Brooks says:

> "The hardest single part of building a software system is deciding precisely what to build."

We've all worked on projects where, because of a misunderstanding, code that we'd worked hard on for several days or more had to be thrown away. Better communication between developers and stakeholders is essential to help avoid this kind of wasted time. One technique that really helps facilitate this communication is the use of *concrete examples* to illustrate what we want the software to do.

### Concrete Examples

By using real-world examples to describe the desired behavior of the system we want to build, we stay grounded in language and terminology that makes sense to our stakeholders: *we're speaking their language*. When we talk in terms of these examples, they can really imagine themselves using the system, and that means they can start to give us useful feedback and ideas before a single line of code has been written.

To illustrate this, let's imagine you're building a credit card payment system. One of the requirements is to make sure users can't enter bad data. Here's one way of expressing that:

> *Customers should be prevented from entering invalid credit card details.*

This is an example of what Agile teams often call *acceptance criteria* or *conditions of satisfaction.*[1] We use the word *acceptance* because they tell us what the system must be able to do in order for our stakeholders to find it acceptable.

The previous requirements statement is useful, but it leaves far too much room for ambiguity and misunderstanding. It lacks *precision*. What exactly makes a set of details invalid? How exactly should the user be prevented from entering them? We've seen too many projects get dragged into the tar pit[2] by these kind of worthy but vague statements. Let's try illustrating this requirement with a concrete example:

> *If a customer enters a credit card number that isn't exactly 16 digits long, when they try to submit the form, it should be redisplayed with an error message advising them of the correct number of digits.*

Can you see how much more specific this second statement is? As a developer implementing this feature, we know almost everything we need to be able to sit down and start working on the code. As a stakeholder, we have a much clearer idea of what the developer is going to build.

In fact, a stakeholder reading this might point out that there are certain types of cards that are valid with fewer than 16 digits and give us another example. This is the real power of examples: they stimulate our imagination, enabling us to explore and discover edge cases we might otherwise not have found until much later.

By giving an example to illustrate our requirement, we've turned an acceptance criterion into an *acceptance test*. Now we have something unambiguous that we can use to test the behavior of the system, either manually or by using an automated test script.

---

1. *Agile Estimating and Planning [Coh05]*
2. The tar pit metaphor comes from the seminal book by Fred Brooks, *The Mythical Man Month: Essays on Software Engineering [Bro95].*

Try This

Think about a feature you're working on right now or have worked on recently. Can you write down three concrete examples of the behavior needed for that feature to be acceptable?

## Executable Specifications

Another advantage of using concrete examples is that they're much easier to validate against the running system than vague requirement statements. In fact, if we're neat and tidy about how we express them, we can get the computer to check them for us. We call this *automated acceptance testing*.[3]

The challenge with writing good automated acceptance tests is that, for them to be really effective, they need to be readable by not only the computer but also by our stakeholders. It's this human readability that allows us to get feedback about what we're building while we're building it. This is where Gherkin comes in.

Gherkin gives us a lightweight structure for documenting examples of the behavior our stakeholders want, in a way that can be easily understood both by the stakeholders and by Cucumber. Although we can call Gherkin a programming language,[4] its primary design goal is human readability, meaning you can write automated tests that read like documentation. Here's an example:

**gherkin_basics/sample.feature**
```
Feature: Feedback when entering invalid credit card details

  In user testing we've seen a lot of people who made mistakes
  entering their credit card. We need to be as helpful as possible
  here to avoid losing users at this crucial stage of the
  transaction.

  Background:
    Given I have chosen some items to buy
    And I am about to enter my credit card details

  Scenario: Credit card number too short
    When I enter a card number that's only 15 digits long
    And all the other details are correct
    And I submit the form
    Then the form should be redisplayed
    And I should see a message advising me of the correct number of digits
```

3. *Extreme Programming Explained: Embrace Change [Bec00]*
4. A note for the pedantic reader: The Gherkin language does have a grammar enforced by a parser, but the language is not Turing Complete.

```
Scenario: Expiry date must not be in the past
  When I enter a card expiry date that's in the past
  And all the other details are correct
  And I submit the form
  Then the form should be redisplayed
  And I should see a message telling me the expiry date must be wrong
```

One interesting feature of Gherkin's syntax is that it is not tied down to one particular spoken language. Each of Gherkin's keywords has been translated into more than forty different spoken languages, and it is perfectly valid to use any of them to write your Gherkin features. No matter if your users speak Norwegian or Spanish, med Gherkin kan du beskrive funksjonalitet i et språk de vil forstå. (Gherkin lets you to write your features in a language they will understand.) Tocino grueso! (Chunky Bacon!) More on that later.

## Format and Syntax

Gherkin files use the .feature file extension. They're saved as plain text, meaning they can be read and edited with simple tools. In this respect, Gherkin is very similar to file formats like Markdown, Textile, and YAML.

### Keywords

A Gherkin file is given its structure and meaning using a set of special keywords. There's an equivalent set of these keywords in each of the supported spoken languages, but for now let's take a look at the English ones:

- Feature
- Background
- Scenario
- Given
- When
- Then
- And
- But
- *
- Scenario Outline
- Examples

We'll spend the rest of this chapter exploring how to use the most common of these keywords, which will be enough to get you started writing your own Cucumber features. We'll come back to look at the remaining keywords later in Chapter 5, *Expressive Scenarios*, on page 69.

## Dry Run

All of the examples in this chapter are valid Gherkin and can be parsed by Cucumber. If you want to play around with them as we go through the chapter, just create a features/test.feature working file. Then run it with the following:

```
$ java -cp ".:jars/*" cucumber.api.cli.Main -g step_definitions --dry-run features
```

The --dry-run switch tells Cucumber to parse the file without executing it. It will tell you if your Gherkin isn't valid.

# Feature

Each Gherkin file begins with the Feature keyword. This keyword doesn't really affect the behavior of your Cucumber tests at all; it just gives you a convenient place to put some summary documentation about the group of tests that follow.

Here's an example:

```
Feature: This is the feature title
  This is the description of the feature, which can
  span multiple lines.
  You can even include empty lines, like this one:

  In fact, everything until the next Gherkin keyword is included
  in the description.
```

The text immediately following on the same line as the Feature keyword is the *name* of the feature, and the remaining lines are its *description*. You can include any text you like in the description except a line beginning with one of the words Scenario, Background, or Scenario Outline. The description can span multiple lines. It's a great place to wax lyrical with details about who will use the feature, and why, or to put links to supporting documentation such as wireframes or user research surveys.

It's conventional to name the feature file by converting the feature's name to lowercase characters and replacing the spaces with underscores. So, for example, the feature named User logs in would be stored in user_logs_in.feature.

In valid Gherkin, a Feature must be followed by one of the following:

- Scenario
- Background
- Scenario Outline

Although `Background` is a handy keyword to know once you've written a few scenarios, we don't need to worry about it just yet. It's covered later in Chapter 5, *Expressive Scenarios*, on page 69. Right now all we need is the Scenario.

### A Template for Describing a Feature

Although feature descriptions are often helpful documentation, they're not mandatory. If you're struggling to work out what to say, the following template can be a great place to start:

```
In order to <meet some goal>
As a <type of stakeholder>
I want <a feature>
```

By starting with the goal or value that the feature provides, you're making it explicit to everyone who ever works on this feature why they're giving up their precious time. You're also offering people an opportunity to think about other ways that the goal could be met. Maybe you don't actually need to build this feature at all, or you could deliver the same value in a much simpler way.

This template is known as a *Feature Injection* template, and we are grateful to Chris Matts and Liz Keogh for sharing it with us.

## Scenario

To actually express the behavior we want, each feature contains several scenarios. Each scenario is a single concrete example of how the system should behave in a particular situation. If you add together the behavior defined by all of the scenarios, that's the expected behavior of the feature itself.

When Cucumber runs a scenario, if the system behaves as described in the scenario, then the scenario will pass; if not, it will fail. Each time you add a new scenario to your Cucumber test suite and make it pass, you've added some new functionality to the system, and that's time for a high-five.

Each feature typically has somewhere between five and twenty scenarios, each describing different examples of how that feature should behave in different circumstances. We use scenarios to explore edge cases and different paths through a feature.

Scenarios all follow the same pattern:

1. Get the system into a particular state.
2. Poke it (or tickle it, or...).
3. Examine the new state.

So, we start with a *context*, go on to describe an *action*, and then finally check that the *outcome* was what we expected. Each scenario tells a little story describing something that the system should be able to do.

## Given, When, Then

In Gherkin, we use the keywords Given, When, and Then to identify those three different parts of the scenario:

```
Scenario: Successful withdrawal from an account in credit
  Given I have $100 in my account  # the context
  When I request $20               # the event(s)
  Then $20 should be dispensed     # the outcome(s)
```

So, we use Given to set up the context where the scenario happens, When to interact with the system somehow, and Then to check that the outcome of that interaction was what we expected.

## And, But

Each of the lines in a scenario is known as a *step*. We can add more steps to each Given, When, or Then section of the scenario using the keywords And and But:

```
Scenario: Attempt withdrawal using stolen card
  Given I have $100 in my account
  But my card is invalid
  When I request $50
  Then my card should not be returned
  And I should be told to contact the bank
```

Cucumber doesn't actually care which of these keywords you use; the choice is simply there to help you create the most readable scenario. If you don't want to use And or But, you could write the previous scenario like this, and it would still work exactly the same way:

```
Scenario: Attempt withdrawal using stolen card
  Given I have $100 in my account
  Given my card is invalid
  When I request $50
  Then my card should not be returned
  Then I should be told to contact the bank
```

But that doesn't read as nicely, does it?

## Replacing Given/When/Then with Bullets

Some people find Given, When, Then, And, and But a little verbose. There is an additional keyword you can use to start a step: * (an asterisk). We could have written the previous scenario like this:

```
Scenario: Attempt withdrawal using stolen card
  * I have $100 in my account
  * my card is invalid
  * I request $50
  * my card should not be returned
  * I should be told to contact the bank
```

To Cucumber, this is exactly the same scenario. Do you find this version easier to read? Maybe. Did some of the meaning get lost? Maybe. It's up to you and your team how you want to word things. The only thing that matters is that everybody understands what's communicated.

## Stateless

When writing scenarios, here's a really important concept you need to grasp:

*Each scenario must make sense and be able to be executed independently of any other scenario.*

That means you can't put some money into the account in one scenario and then expect that money to be there in the next scenario. Cucumber won't stop you from doing this, but it's extremely bad practice: you'll end up with scenarios that fail unexpectedly and are harder to understand.

This might seem a little dogmatic, but trust us, it really helps keep your scenarios simple to work with. It avoids building up brittle dependencies between scenarios and also gives you the flexibility to run just the scenarios you need to when you're working on a particular part of the system, without having to worry about getting the right test data set up. We explain these problems in depth in Chapter 6, *Keeping Your Cucumbers Sweet*, on page 91.

When writing a scenario, always assume that it will run against the system in a default, blank state. Tell the story from the beginning, using Given steps to set up all the state you need for that particular scenario.

## Name and Description

Just like a Feature, a Scenario keyword can be followed by a name and description. Normally you'll probably just use the name, but it's valid Gherkin to follow the name with a multiline description—everything up until the first Given, When, or Then will be slurped up into the description of the scenario.

Stale scenario names can cause confusion. When modifying existing scenarios (or copying and pasting them), take care to check that the name still makes sense. Since the scenario name is just documentation, Cucumber won't fail the scenario even if its name no longer has anything to do with what's actually going on in the steps. This can be really confusing for anyone reading the scenario later.

 **Matt says:**
## Take Care with Your Naming Scenarios

Even though they can't make your tests pass or fail, scenario names are surprisingly important to get right. Here are some reasons why it's a good idea to pay attention to them:

- When your tests break, it's the failing scenario's name that will give you the headline news on what's broken. A concise, expressive name here can save everyone a lot of time.

- Once you have a few scenarios in a feature file, you don't want to have to read the detail of the steps unless you really need to do so. If you're a programmer, think of it a bit like method naming. If you name the method well, you won't need to read the code inside it to work out what it does.

- As your system evolves, your stakeholders will quite often ask you to change the expected behavior in an existing scenario. A well-composed scenario name will still make sense even if you add an extra Then step or two.

A good tip is to avoid putting anything about the outcome (the Then part) of the scenario into the name and concentrate on summarizing the context and event (Given and When) of the scenario.

## Try This

- Now that you understand how to write Gherkin scenarios, try converting some of the concrete examples you wrote down earlier for your own project into Gherkin.

- Show them to someone who knows nothing about your project, and ask them what they think your application does.

- Practice describing what you're doing with Given/When/Then while you're doing everyday things such as starting your car, cooking breakfast, or switching channels on the TV. You'll be surprised how well it fits.

## Comments

As well as the description fields that follow Feature and Scenario keywords, Cucumber allows you to precede these keywords with comments.

Comments start with a # character and have to be the first and only thing on a line (well, apart from whitespace).

Here's an example:

```
gherkin_basics/comments_example.feature
# This feature covers the account transaction and hardware-driver modules
Feature: Withdraw Cash
  In order to buy beer
  As an account holder
  I want to withdraw cash from the ATM

  # Can't figure out how to integrate with magic wand interface
  Scenario: Withdraw too much from an account in credit
    Given I have $50 in my account
    # When I wave my magic wand
    And I withdraw $100
    Then I should receive $100
```

You can also put comments within a scenario. The most common use for this is to comment out a step, as we've shown in the previous example.

As in any programming language, comments can quickly go stale and become meaningless or downright confusing. When this happens, the comment causes more harm than good. We advise you to use them as sparingly as you can and put the important stuff into scenarios where it can be tested.

Here's how we think about this: the description, which you can put after each keyword, is part of the structured Gherkin document and is the right place to put documentation for your stakeholders.

Comments, on the other hand, can be used more to leave notes for testers and programmers who are working with the features. Think of a comment as something more temporary, a bit like a sticky note.

Don't forget that programmers and testers need documentation too. If there are technical details that need to be documented with the feature, you should feel free to put them into the description too, provided that the business-facing members of your team are comfortable with them being there.

# Spoken Languages

Remember earlier we said that you can write your Gherkin features in the spoken language of your stakeholders? Here's how.

Putting a # language: comment on the first line of a feature file tells Cucumber which spoken language that feature is written in. If you omit this header, Cucumber will default to English, as you've already seen.

Here's an example of a feature written in Norwegian:

```
# language: no
Egenskap: Summering
  For å unngå at firmaet går konkurs
  Må regnskapsførerere bruke en regnemaskin for å legge sammen tall

  Scenario: to tall
    Gitt at jeg har tastet inn 5
    Og at jeg har tastet inn 7
    Når jeg summerer
    Så skal resultatet være 12
```

If you're wondering whether Cucumber knows how to speak your language, you can ask it for the list of all valid languages with this command:

```
$ ./cucumber --i18n help
```

When you're working with a particular language, you can discover the keywords by passing the language code (as listed by the previous command) to the --i18n switch. Here's Japanese, for example:

```
$ ./cucumber --i18n ja
```

The --i18n option only became available in Cucumber-JVM 1.2.0. Prior to that, the easiest way to find out what languages were supported was to look in the Gherkin project at lib/i18n.json.[5]

One of the greatest benefits of working with a tool like Cucumber is the conversations you have with your stakeholders as you write the scenarios. These conversations can help you find gaps and misunderstandings that otherwise might have emerged only after you'd spent days or even weeks working on the code. So, even if you never run the tests, just writing them can help make you go faster.

---

5.  https://github.com/cucumber/gherkin/blob/master/lib/gherkin/i18n.json

> \\//  **Joe asks:**
>
> ﾠ﹖ﾠ  **So, Can I Mix Spoken Languages in My Features?**
>
> A project can have a mix of features that use different spoken languages, yes. However, remember that the setting is for a *feature*, so all the scenarios in a feature have to use the same spoken language.

## What We Just Learned

Let's review what we've talked about in this chapter:

- We saw how the core Gherkin keywords Feature, Scenario, Given, When, and Then can be used to describe the behavior your stakeholders want as concrete examples.

- There is a fundamental pattern to each Gherkin scenario, with a context (Given), an event (When), and an outcome (Then).

- Each scenario must be capable of being run on its own and should not depend on data set up by other scenarios. This means every scenario has to include enough Given steps to set up all the data it needs.

- You can add descriptions and comments to your .feature files to turn them into useful documentation of your system.

- Using the #language: header, you can write your features in different spoken languages.

At this point you have all the knowledge you need to get started writing your own Gherkin features. Even though there are some keywords we haven't covered yet, there's a huge amount of value in what you already know. Just pretend you have a machine that can turn your Cucumber scenarios into perfect working code, and play the game of working with your team to create the best descriptions you can of what you want the software to do.

In the next chapter, we'll start to explore step definitions, the layer beneath the Gherkin features where you interact with your application, and bring your scenarios to life.

## Try This

Here are some exercises for you to try.

### Practice Given/When/Then

Let's build a robot! Here's a scenario:

```
Scenario: Tickle a happy robot
  Given I am in a good mood
  When you tickle me
  Then I will giggle
```

What happens if you change the context in which this scenario happens? Write another scenario where the first step puts the robot into a bad mood. Leave the action the same. What will be the outcome when you tickle a grumpy robot?

Now try changing the action:

```
Scenario: Attack a happy robot
  Given I am in a good mood
  When you kick me in the shins
  Then I will ...
```

What will the outcome be now?

### Your First Scenario

Write the first formal Gherkin scenario for your project. Pick a feature you're working on right now, and try to describe the way the system should behave when you're done. Notice when you have questions about the precise language you should use, or the precise behavior, and write down those questions. Try to get some time with the right people on your team to answer those questions. Show them the scenario: does it make sense to them? How would they have worded it?

# CHAPTER 4

# Step Definitions: From the Outside

Now that you know how to use Gherkin to describe *what* you want your tests to do, the next task is to tell them *how* to do it. Whether you choose to drive your acceptance tests from Cucumber scenarios or simple JUnit tests, there's no escaping the fact that you're going to need to write some code eventually. It's about that time.

Step definitions sit right on the boundary between the business's domain and the programmer's domain. You can write them in many JVM languages (for now we'll show examples in Java) and their responsibility is to translate each plain-language step in your Gherkin scenarios into concrete actions in your code. As an example, take this step from the ATM scenario in the previous chapter:

```
Given I have $100 in my Account
```

This step definition needs to make the following things happen:

- Create an account for the protagonist in the scenario (if there isn't one already).

- Set the balance of that account to be $100.

How exactly those two goals are achieved depends a great deal on your specific application. Automated acceptance tests generally try to simulate user interactions with the system, and the step definitions are where you'll tell Cucumber how you want it to poke around with your system. That might involve clicking buttons on a user interface or reaching beneath the covers and directly inserting data into a database, writing to files, or even calling a web service. We think of step definitions themselves as distinct from the automation code that does the actual poking so that the layers separate out, as shown in the following figure:

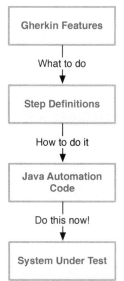

There are two sides to a step definition. On the outside, it translates from plain language into code, and on the inside it tells your system what to do using automation code. The JVM has an incredibly rich set of libraries for automating a whole variety of systems, from JavaScript-heavy web applications to REST web services. We're not going to show you how to use all of those libraries in this chapter; that will come later in the book. Here we're going to concentrate on the main responsibility of this layer of your Cucumber tests, which is to interpret a plain-language Gherkin step and decide what to do.

We're going to start by explaining some of the mechanics of how step definitions match up to plain-language steps and then work through an example of how to write a single step definition that can handle many different steps. We'll finish by explaining how Cucumber executes step definitions and deals with their results. When we're done, you should understand enough to start writing and running your own step definitions.

## Steps and Step Definitions

Let's start by clarifying the distinction between a *step* and a *step definition*.

Each Gherkin scenario is made up of a series of steps, written in plain language. On its own, a step is just documentation; it needs a step definition to bring it to life. A step definition is a piece of code that says to Cucumber, "If you see a step that looks like this…, then here's what I want you to do…."

When Cucumber tries to execute each step, it looks for a matching step definition to execute. So, how does Cucumber match a step definition to a step?

### Matching a Step

Gherkin steps are expressed in plain text. Cucumber scans the text of each step for patterns that it recognizes, which you define using a *regular expression*. If you haven't used regular expressions before, then just think of them like a slightly more sophisticated version of the wildcards you'd use to search for a file. Although they can look intimidating at first, you need only a small number of patterns to get a great deal of mileage out of them. All of those patterns will be covered in this chapter; if you're already well familiar with regular expressions, you might want to skim over the next few sections, up until *Returning Results*, on page 58.

Let's take the ATM example from the previous chapter:

```
step_definitions/intro/features/cash_withdrawal.feature
Feature: Cash withdrawal
  Scenario: Successful withdrawal from an account in credit
    Given I have $100 in my account
    When I request $20
    Then $20 should be dispensed
```

As Cucumber executes this feature, it will come to the first step of the scenario, Given I have $100 in my Account and say to itself, *Now, do I have any step definitions that match the phrase I have $100 in my Account?*

A simple regular expression that will match this step would look like this:

```
"I have \\$100 in my Account"
```

Notice that we've had to escape the dollar sign with a double backslash. That's because the dollar sign can have a special meaning in a regular expression, but in this case we want to interpret it literally. To make life even more complicated, the backslash has a special meaning within a Java string, so we need to use a double backslash. We'll come back to these special characters a bit later in the chapter.

If Cucumber sees a step definition with this regular expression, it will execute it when it comes to the first step of our scenario. So, how do we create a step definition?

## Creating a Step Definition

Step definitions live in ordinary files. To create a step definition in Java, you use a special Cucumber annotation, such as @Given, like this:

```
@Given("I have \\$100 in my Account")
public void iHave$100InMyAccount() throws Throwable {
    // TODO: code that puts $100 into User's Account goes here
}
```

You'll typically put several step definitions like this together in the same source file. Since you have to tell Cucumber where to find your step definitions it's really up to you how exactly you want to organize them. We suggest keeping a separate file per domain entity so that step definitions that work with similar parts of the system are kept together. (For more details on how Cucumber knows where to find your step definitions, see *How Cucumber Finds Our Step Definitions*, on page 260.)

Let's examine the step definition in detail. This is a Java file, and we're using the special Cucumber annotation @Given, which tells Cucumber that we want

## Dependency Management—Part 1

So far, we've been running Cucumber using a small shell script. As we continue, we'll see the complexity of this script grow as our examples start using more components. Rather than manage these dependencies by hand, it's time to start using one of the dependency management tools provided by the development community. We're going to use Maven[a] from the Apache Foundation.

Maven is incredibly powerful, but we're only going to use a small subset to help manage the dependencies in our examples. At the heart of Maven is a configuration file, called pom.xml by default. The main contents of our POM file simply express the dependencies that were described in our cucumber script in XML format:

```
expressive_scenarios/01/pom.xml
<properties>
    <cucumber.version>1.2.0</cucumber.version>
    <junit.version>4.11</junit.version>
</properties>

<dependencies>
    <dependency>
        <groupId>info.cukes</groupId>
        <artifactId>cucumber-java</artifactId>
        <version>${cucumber.version}</version>
        <scope>test</scope>
    </dependency>
    <dependency>
        <groupId>info.cukes</groupId>
        <artifactId>cucumber-junit</artifactId>
        <version>${cucumber.version}</version>
        <scope>test</scope>
    </dependency>
</dependencies>
```

---

a.    http://maven.apache.org

to register a step definition. We pass the @Given annotation a regular expression to match one or more steps (the bit between the double quotes), and we define a Java method that will execute when it does match. Cucumber stores a mapping between regular expression and the method, so it can call the method later if it comes across a matching step.

You can also use the annotations @When or @Then to create a step definition in just the same way.

## Given, When, Then Are the Same

It doesn't actually matter which of the three methods you use to register a step definition, because Cucumber ignores the keyword when matching a step. Under the hood, all of the annotations are aliases for StepDefAnnotation.

## Dependency Management—Part 2

An extra section needs to be added to include the Surefire plugin,[a] which contains the code necessary to allow Maven to find and run our JUnit tests:

```
expressive_scenarios/01/pom.xml
<plugin>
  <groupId>org.apache.maven.plugins</groupId>
  <artifactId>maven-surefire-plugin</artifactId>
  <version>2.12.2</version>
  <configuration>
      <argLine>-Duser.language=en</argLine>
      <argLine>-Xmx1024m</argLine>
      <argLine>-XX:MaxPermSize=256m</argLine>
      <argLine>-Dfile.encoding=UTF-8</argLine>
      <useFile>false</useFile>
  </configuration>
</plugin>
```

From now on, when we want to build our projects and run our tests, we'll use Maven:

```
mvn clean test
```

The first time you run this command it may take quite a while to download the dependencies from the Internet to a local *repository*. The next time you use Maven to build your project it will use the copies in the repository.

---

a.   http://maven.apache.org/surefire

The annotations are really just there for extra documentation to help you express the intent of each step or step definition.

This means that, whether it was created with the method @Given, @When, or @Then, a step definition will match any Gherkin step as long as the regular expression matches the main text of the step. This figure highlights what Cucumber sees when it scans a scenario for matching step definitions.

This flexibility can be really handy, as we'll show you later, but there is one gotcha to watch out for. Let's take a look at an example.

```
Feature: Cash Withdrawal
  Scenario: Attempt withdrawal using stolen card
    Given I have $100 in my account
    But my card is invalid
    When I request $50
    Then my card should not be returned
    And I should be told to contact the bank
```

Imagine you have already implemented your ATM withdrawal scenario, including writing a step definition for Given I have $100 in my Account. So, you have a step definition that matches the text I have $100 in my Account and creates an account with $100 in it. A few weeks later that scenario is a dim and distant memory, and you get a new requirement to give all new accounts a $1 gift. You sit down with your domain expert and write the following scenario:

```
Scenario: New accounts get a $1 gift
  Given I have a brand new Account
  And I deposit $99
  Then I have $100 in my Account
```

That looks reasonable, doesn't it? We set up the new account, deposit some money, and then check that the new balance is what we'd expect it to be. But can you see what's going to happen if we run this new scenario together with our original ATM withdrawal scenario?

Let's look at our original step definition again:

```
@Given("I have \\$100 in my Account")
void iHave$100InMyAccount() {
  // TODO: code that puts $100 into User's Account goes here
}
```

Now that we've learned that Cucumber ignores the @Given/@When/@Then annotation when matching a step, we can see that this original step definition is also going to match the last step of our new scenario, Then I have $100 in my Account. Surprise! We expected that step to check the balance of the account, but instead it's going to put $100 *into* the account!

We obviously need to be careful in this situation, because we could easily have had a scenario that was giving us a *false positive*: passing when it should have been failing. It might not seem like it, but Cucumber's flexibility has actually helped us here by exposing some quite subtle ambiguity in the language used in each of the steps. The best way we've found to avoid this kind of problem is to pay careful attention to the precise wording in your steps. You could change both steps to be less ambiguous:

```
Given I have deposited $100 in my Account
Then the balance of my Account should be $100
```

By rewording the steps like this, you've made them better at communicating exactly what they will do when executed. Learning to spot and remove this kind of ambiguity is something that takes practice. Paying attention to the distinction in wording between two steps like this can also give you hints about concepts that may not be expressed in your code but need to be. It might seem pedantic, but we've found that teams who pay this much careful attention to detail write much better software, faster.

## Speaking in Tongues

If you're using a different spoken language than English in your features, you can still use the same language when registering step definitions. Cucumber creates an alias of each annotation for every spoken language, so a team working in Spain, for example, could use the following:

```
@Dado("tengo \\$100 en mi Cuenta")
public void tengo$100EnMiCuenta() {
  // TODO: code that puts $100 into User's Account goes here
}
```

# Capturing Arguments

You'll notice that in the step we've been using as an example, we've talked about the sum of $100 the whole time. What if we had another scenario where we needed to deposit a different amount of money into the account? Would we need another step definition, like this?

```
@Given("I have deposited \\$100 in my Account")
public void iHaveDeposited$100InMyAccount() {
  // TODO: code goes here
}

@Given("I have deposited \\$250 in my Account")
public void iHaveDeposited$250InMyAccount() {
  // TODO: code goes here
}
```

Happily, we don't. This is where the flexibility of regular expressions comes into play. We can use two of regular expressions' most useful features here to capture any dollar amount as an *argument* to the step definition. Those features are *capture groups* and *wildcards*.

## Capture Groups

When you surround part of a regular expression with parentheses, it becomes a capture group. Capture groups are used to highlight particular parts of a pattern that you want to lift out of the matching text and use. In a Cucumber step definition, the text matched within each capture group is passed to the code block as an argument:

```
@Given("I have deposited \\$(100) in my Account")
public void iHaveDeposited$100InMyAccount(int amount) {
  // TODO: code goes here
}
```

Here the method argument `amount` will receive the string value 100 when this step definition matches. The previous example is a bit silly, because this regular expression is still only ever going to match steps that talk about the amount of $100. We need to use a wildcard inside the capture group to open it up to other values.

## Alternation

We can specify a wildcard in a regular expression using a few different approaches. One of the simplest is *alternation*, where we express different options separated by a pipe character |, like this:

```
@Given("I have deposited \\$(100|250) in my Account")
public void iHaveDeposited$InMyAccount(int amount) {
  // TODO: code goes here
}
```

This step definition will now match a step with either of the two values 100 or 250 in it, and the number will be captured and passed to the method as an argument. Alternation can be useful if there are a fixed set of values that you want to accept in your step definition, but normally you'll want something a little looser.

## The Dot

The dot is a *metacharacter*, meaning it has magical powers in a regular expression. Literally, a dot means *match any single character*. So, we can try this instead:

```
@Given("I have deposited \\$(...) in my Account")
public void iHaveDeposited$InMyAccount(int amount) {
  // TODO: code goes here
}
```

That will now match a step with any three-figure dollar sum and send the matched amount into the method. This is definitely a step in the right direction, but there are a couple of problems with what we've done. For one, remember that the dot matches *any character*, so we could end up capturing letters in here instead of numbers. More importantly, what if we wanted a step that deposits just $10 in the account, or $1,000? This step definition won't match those steps because it's always looking for three characters. We can fix this by using a *modifier*.

## The Star Modifier

In regular expressions, a *repetition modifier* takes a character (or metacharacter) and tells us how many times over it can appear. The most flexible modifier is the star:

> **Joe asks:**
> # What If I Actually Want to Match a Dot?
>
> Any of the metacharacters like the dot can be escaped by preceding them with a backslash. So, if you wanted to specifically match, say 3.14, you could use "3\\.14".
>
> You might have noticed that there's a backslash in front of the dollar amount in the step definition we're using. That's because $ itself is a metacharacter (it's an anchor, which we'll explain later), so we need to escape to make it match a normal dollar sign.

```
@Given("I have deposited \\$(.*) in my Account")
public void iHaveDeposited$InMyAccount(int amount) {
  // TODO: code goes here
}
```

The star modifier means *any number of times*. So, with .* we're capturing *any character, any number of times*. Now we're getting somewhere—this will allow us to capture all those different amounts. But there's still a problem.

The star modifier is a bit of a blunt instrument. Because we're using it with the dot that matches *any character*, it will gobble up any text at all up until the phrase in my Account. This is why, in regex terminology, the star modifier is known as a *greedy* operator. For example, it would happily match this step:

```
Given I have deposited $1 and a cucumber in my Account
```

The amount captured by our regular expression in this case would be 1 and a cucumber. We need to be more specific about the characters we want to match and just capture numbers. Instead of a dot, we can use something else.

## Character Classes

Character classes allow you to tell the regular expression engine to match one of a range of characters. You just place all of the characters you would accept inside square brackets:

```
@Given("I have deposited \\$([01234567890]*) in my Account")
public void iHaveDeposited$InMyAccount(int amount) {
  // TODO: code goes here
}
```

For a continuous range of characters like we have, you can use a hyphen:

```
@Given("I have deposited \\$([0-9]*) in my Account")
public void iHaveDeposited$InMyAccount(int amount) {
  // TODO: code goes here
}
```

Now we've restricted the character we'll accept to be numeric. We're still modifying the character with the star to accept any number of them, but we're now being specific that we'll accept only a continuous string of numbers.

## Shorthand Character Classes

For common patterns of characters like [0-9], there are a few *shorthand character classes* that you can use instead. You may find this just makes your regular expressions more cryptic, but there are only a few to learn. For a digit, you can use \d as a shorthand for [0-9]:

```
@Given("I have deposited \\$(\\d*) in my Account")
public void iHaveDeposited$InMyAccount(int amount) {
  // TODO: code goes here
}
```

Here are the most useful shorthand character classes:

\d  stands for *digit*, or [0-9].

\w  stands for *word character*, specifically [A-Za-z0-9_]. Notice that underscores and digits are included but not hyphens.

\s  stands for *whitespace character*, specifically [ \t\r\n]. That means a space, a tab, or a line break.

\b  stands for *word boundary*, which is a lot like \s but actually means the opposite of \w. Anything that is not a word character is a word boundary.

You can also negate shorthand character classes by capitalizing them, so for example, \D means *any character except a digit*.

Back to matching our amount. It looks like we're done, but there's one last problem to fix. Can you see what it is?

## The Plus Modifier

The star is one example of a repetition modifier, but there are others. A subtle problem with the star is that *any number of times* can mean zero.

So, this step would match:

```
Given I have deposited $ in my Account
```

That's no good. To fix this, we can use the + modifier, which means *at least once*:

```
@Given("I have deposited \\$(\\d+) in my Account")
public void iHaveDeposited$InMyAccount(int amount) {
  // TODO: code goes here
}
```

There we go. We took a rambling route to get to the answer, but on the way we've visited almost every one of the features of regular expressions that are useful to us when building Cucumber step definitions. We have only a couple more to cover.

### Try This

Imagine you're building a system for airport departure lounge screens. You need to be able to capture examples of flight codes from the Cucumber scenarios. Can you write a single step definition that can capture the flight codes from all of these steps?

```
Given the flight EZY4567 is leaving today
...
Given the flight C038 is leaving today
...
Given a flight BA01618 is leaving today
```

Start by writing a step definition that works for the first step, and then make it more and more generic so that it works with the other steps too.

## Multiple Captures

You don't have to stop at capturing just a single argument. Cucumber will pass an argument to your method for every capture group in your regular expression, so you can grab as many details as you like from a step.

Here's an example. Let's imagine our bank wants to start offering its customers savings accounts as well as their regular checking account. Customers can use the ATM to transfer money between their accounts. Here's one of the scenarios for this new feature:

```
Scenario: Transfer funds from savings into checking account
  Given I have deposited $10 in my Checking Account
  And I have deposited $500 in my Savings Account
  When I transfer $500 from my Savings Account into my Checking Account
  Then the balance of the Checking Account should be $510
  And the balance of the Savings Account should be $0
```

Let's try to write a step definition that can handle the first two steps. As well as the amount deposited, we need to capture the type of account so that we know where to put it.

We can use a modified version of the regular expression we used previously to capture the type of account:

```
@Given("I have deposited \\$(\\d+) in my (\\w+) Account")
public void iHaveDeposited$InMyAccount(int amount, String accountType) {
  // TODO: code goes here
}
```

We use the shorthand character class \w, modified with the plus to mean *any word character, at least once*, effectively capturing a single word. That word is then passed to the method we named accountType in the second argument.

### Try This

Write a step definition for the next step in the scenario, When I transfer $500 from my Savings Account into my Checking Account. The step definition should capture three arguments:

- The amount of money being transferred
- The type of account being debited in the transfer
- The type of account that receives the credit in the transfer

Test it by writing simple System.out.println statements in your step definition to print the value captured in each argument to the console.

## Flexibility

The readability of Cucumber features helps teams learn to use a ubiquitous language when talking about the system they're building. This is a really important benefit, because that consistent use of terminology helps reduce misunderstandings and allow communication to flow more smoothly between everyone on the team.

So, we want to encourage our feature authors to be consistent about the nouns and verbs they use in the Cucumber features, because it helps make features that can be readily understood by anyone on the team. Equally, we also want feature authors to be able to express themselves as naturally as possible, which means they may often use slightly different phrasing to mean exactly the same thing. This is fine; in fact, it's to be encouraged. Cucumber features are all about communicating with business users in their language, and it's important that we don't force them to sound like robots.

To keep the features readable and natural, it's useful to develop the skill to make your step definitions flexible enough to match the different ways something might be expressed by a feature author. This isn't as hard as you might think.

## The Question Mark Modifier

When matching business-facing Gherkin text, you'll often want to indicate that you don't care about the odd character in your match, such as when a word could be singular or plural:

```
Given I have 1 cucumber in my basket
Given I have 256 cucumbers in my basket
```

Like the star and the plus, the question mark modifies the character that precedes it, specifying how many times it can be repeated. The question mark modifier means *zero or one times*; in other words, it makes the preceding character optional. In step definitions, it's particularly useful for plurals:

```
@Given("I have (\\d+) cucumbers? in my basket")
public void iHaveCucumbersInMyBasket(int number) {
  // TODO: code goes here
}
```

By putting a question mark after the s in cucumbers, we're saying that we don't care whether the word is singular or plural. So, this step definition will match both of the previous steps.

Another useful technique is to use a *noncapturing group*.

## Noncapturing Groups

Remember back in *Alternation*, on page 52 we showed how you can list a set of possible values for part of a regular expression, separated by a pipe symbol. We can use this same technique to add flexibility to our step definitions, letting feature authors say the same thing in slightly different ways. There's one little change we'll need to make, but we'll get to that in a minute.

Take this extremely common step for a web application:

```
When I visit the homepage
```

Suppose someone comes along and writes another step that looks like this:

```
When I go to the homepage
```

Both of these steps have identical meaning to the reader, but unfortunately a step definition for the first one won't match the second one without some modification. It would be helpful to have a step definition to recognize both phrases, because it really doesn't matter whether you say visit or go to—they both mean the same thing. We can use an *alternate* to relax the step definition to accept this slightly different phrasing:

```
@When("I (?:visit|go to) the homepage")
public void iVisitTheHomepage() {
  // TODO: code goes here
}
```

Notice that we've had to prefix the list of alternates with another bit of regular expression magic. The ?: at the start of the group marks it as *noncapturing*, meaning Cucumber won't pass it as an argument to our block.

## Anchors

You might have noticed that the step definition snippets that Cucumber prints for undefined steps start with a ^ and end with a $. Perhaps you've become so used to seeing them that you've stopped noticing them altogether. These two metacharacters are called *anchors*, because they're used to tie down each end of the regular expression to the beginning and end of the string that they match on.

You don't have to use them, and we deliberately left them out of the example up to this point because we wanted to wait until we'd explained what they do. If you omit one or both of them, you'll find you end up with a much more flexible step definition—perhaps too flexible. As a silly example, suppose we add the ^ anchor to the beginning but omit the $ at the end of our bank account step definition:

```
@Given("^I have deposited \\$(\\d+) in my Account")
public void iHaveDeposited$InMyAccount(int amount) {
  // TODO: code goes here
}
```

This allows a particularly creative feature author to write something like:

```
Given I have deposited $100 in my Account from a check my Grandma gave to me
```

Generally, it's best to keep your regular expressions as tight as you can so that there's less chance of two step definitions clashing with each other. That's why the snippets that Cucumber generates for undefined steps always include the anchors. Still, leaving off the anchors is a trick worth knowing about that can sometimes come in handy.

# Returning Results

Cucumber is a testing tool, and it's in the Java code of a step definition where our tests find out whether a step has succeeded in whatever it set out to do. So, how does a step definition tell Cucumber whether it passed or failed?

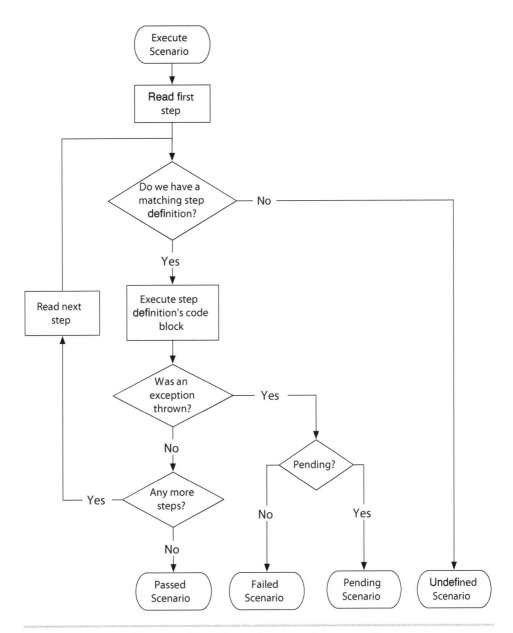

**Figure 2—How Cucumber executes a scenario**

Like most other testing tools, Cucumber uses exceptions to communicate the failure of a test. As it executes a scenario, one step at a time, Cucumber assumes that a step has passed unless its step definition throws an exception. If the exception thrown is a PendingException, then the step is marked as pending —all other exceptions cause the step to fail. If a step passes, Cucumber moves on to the next step. Figure 2, *How Cucumber executes a scenario*, on page 59 shows how this plays out.

In Cucumber, results are a little more sophisticated than a simple pass or fail. A scenario that's been executed can end up in any of the following states:

- Failed
- Pending
- Undefined
- Skipped
- Passed

These states are designed to help indicate the progress that you make as you develop your tests. Let's run through an example of automating the ATM withdrawal scenario to illustrate what we mean.

## Undefined Steps

When Cucumber can't find a step definition that matches a step, it marks the step as undefined (yellow) and stops the scenario. The rest of the steps in the scenario will be either skipped or marked as undefined too if they don't have a matching step definition themselves.

To show you how this works, we can run our ATM withdrawal scenario. Create a file called resources/cash_withdrawal.feature, and put the following into it:

```
step_definitions/00/src/test/resources/cash_withdrawal.feature
Feature: Cash Withdrawal
  Scenario: Successful withdrawal from an account in credit
    Given I have deposited $100 in my account
    When I request $20
    Then $20 should be dispensed
```

We haven't written any step definitions yet, so when we run this feature, we should see the steps all come up as undefined:

```
---------------------------------------------------------
 T E S T S
---------------------------------------------------------
Running RunCukesTest
Feature: Cash Withdrawal
```

```
  Scenario: Successful withdrawal from an account in credit
    Given I have deposited $100 in my account
    When I request $20
    Then $20 should be dispensed

1 Scenarios (1 undefined)
3 Steps (3 undefined)
0m0.000s

You can implement missing steps with the snippets below:

@Given("^I have deposited \\$(\\d+) in my account$")
public void iHaveDeposited$InMyAccount(int arg1) throws Throwable {
    // Write code here that turns the phrase above into concrete actions
    throw new PendingException();
}

@When("^I request \\$(\\d+)$")
public void iRequest$(int arg1) throws Throwable {
    // Write code here that turns the phrase above into concrete actions
    throw new PendingException();
}

@Then("^\\$(\\d+) should be dispensed$")
public void $ShouldBeDispensed(int arg1) throws Throwable {
    // Write code here that turns the phrase above into concrete actions
    throw new PendingException();
}

Tests run: 5, Failures: 0, Errors: 0, Skipped: 4, Time elapsed: 0.382 sec
```

You should see each step is yellow, indicating that it's neither failing (red) nor passing (green) but somewhere in between. Notice also that Cucumber has printed out a snippet for each missing step definition. We can use these as a starting point for implementing our own step definitions.

## Pending Steps

When Cucumber discovers a step definition that's halfway through being implemented, it marks the step as pending (yellow). Again, the scenario will be stopped, and the rest of the steps will be skipped or marked as undefined.

How does Cucumber know whether a step definition has been implemented?

Of course, you have to tell it, by throwing a PendingException.

When you throw a PendingException from within a step definition, this tells Cucumber's runtime that the step has failed but in a particular way: the step definition is still being worked on. You'll probably have noticed that the

## Assertions and Exceptions

Even if you're used to using a testing library like JUnit, you might not have realized that the assertions in those libraries work by raising exceptions.

You can prove this to yourself by writing a little Java program that runs a failing assertion:

```
step_definitions/assertions_sidebar/AssertionExample.java
import org.junit.*;
import static org.junit.Assert.*;

public class AssertionExample {

  public static void main(String[] args) {
    try {
      assertTrue(false);
    } catch (AssertionError e) {
      System.out.print("Exception was raised was ");
      System.out.println(e.getClass().getName());
    }
  }
}
```

When you run it, you should find that this program raises an exception of type java.lang.AssertionError.

---

snippets Cucumber generates for undefined steps throw a PendingException in them; now you understand why.

Let's get back to our ATM withdrawal scenario to show you what we mean.

Create a file called step_definitions/Steps.java and paste in this step definition:

```
step_definitions/01/src/test/java/nicebank/Steps.java
package nicebank;

import cucumber.api.java.en.*;
import cucumber.api.PendingException;

public class Steps {

  @Given("^I have deposited \\$(\\d+) in my account$")
  public void iHaveDeposited$InMyAccount(int amount) throws Throwable {
    // Write code here that turns the phrase above into concrete actions
    throw new PendingException();
  }
}
```

Now when we run mvn clean test, we'll see that it has only tried to execute the first step and has marked it as pending. All the rest are still undefined:

```
--------------------------------------------------------
 T E S T S
--------------------------------------------------------
Running RunCukesTest
Feature: Cash Withdrawal

  Scenario: Successful withdrawal from an account in credit
    Given I have deposited $100 in my account
      cucumber.api.PendingException: TODO: implement me
        at nicebank.Steps.iHaveDeposited$InMyAccount(Steps.java:11)
        at *.Given I have deposited $100 in my account(cash_withdrawal.feature:3)
    When I request $20
    Then $20 should be dispensed

1 Scenarios (1 undefined)
3 Steps (1 pending, 2 undefined)
0m0.121s

cucumber.api.PendingException: TODO: implement me
        at nicebank.Steps.iHaveDeposited$InMyAccount(Steps.java:11)
        at *.Given I have deposited $100 in my account(cash_withdrawal.feature:3)
```

The pending status is a bit like those *under construction* signs you used to see all over the Internet in the 1990s. You can use it as a temporary signpost to your teammates that you're in the middle of working on something.

When we're developing a new scenario from the outside-in like this, we'll tend to work right across the same layer before diving into the next one. Right now we're concentrating on adding step definitions, so let's do that for each of the other steps and add a pending call in each one:

**step_definitions/02/src/test/java/nicebank/Steps.java**
```java
package nicebank;

import cucumber.api.java.en.*;
import cucumber.api.PendingException;

public class Steps {

  @Given("^I have deposited \\$(\\d+) in my account$")
  public void iHaveDeposited$InMyAccount(int amount) throws Throwable {
    // Write code here that turns the phrase above into concrete actions
    throw new PendingException();
  }

  @When("^I request \\$(\\d+)$")
  public void iRequest$(int arg1) throws Throwable {
      // Write code here that turns the phrase above into concrete actions
      throw new PendingException();
  }
```

```
@Then("^\\$(\\d+) should be dispensed$")
public void $ShouldBeDispensed(int arg1) throws Throwable {
    // Write code here that turns the phrase above into concrete actions
    throw new PendingException();
}

}
```

As we do this, we can check to see whether there are any existing step definitions we could use and, if not, just create a new one that throws a PendingException. The pending scenarios become our to-do list for the work we'll do when
we drop down to the next layer and start implementing the step definitions.

> ## Strict Mode
>
> If you use the --strict command-line option in your shell script, ./cucumber, then it will
> return an exit code of 1 (to indicate an error) if there are any undefined or pending
> steps.
>
> This can be useful in a continuous integration build to spot any half-finished features
> that have been accidentally checked in or when you've refactored your step definitions
> and some of your steps are no longer matching.

## Failing Steps

If the block of code executed by a step definition raises an exception,
Cucumber will mark that step as failed (red) and stop the scenario. The rest
of the steps in the scenario will be skipped.

In practice, a step definition will fail for one of two reasons:

- The scenario couldn't finish because you have a bug in your step definition
  code, or in the system under test, that has caused it to throw an error.
  You'll get used to seeing these failures all the time during development if
  you use Cucumber to drive your development from the outside-in. Each
  failure message tells you what you need to do next.

- The step definition has used an *assertion* to check something about the
  state of the system, and the check didn't pass. You'll typically get these
  errors right at the end of your outside-in cycle or long after the feature
  has been implemented if someone accidentally introduces a bug.

An assertion is a check in your tests that describes some condition that you
expect to be satisfied. Failures because of assertions tend to happen in Then
steps, whose job is to check things about the state of the system. These are

the alarm bells you're fitting to the system that will go off if it starts to behave in unexpected ways. Either way, Cucumber will show you the exception message and backtrace in its output, so it's up to you to investigate.

We're almost done with this chapter, but we want to show you an example of a failing step first. We're at the point where we need to start designing the interface between our tests and our system. Let's start with something simple and imagine an Account class that we can use to create a bank account for the actor in our scenario. We can modify the step definition like this:

```
step_definitions/03/src/test/java/nicebank/Steps.java
@Given("^I have deposited \\$(\\d+) in my account$")
public void iHaveDeposited$InMyAccount(int amount) throws Throwable {
    new Account(amount);
}
```

What's going to happen when we run this? We don't actually have an Account class yet, so it's going to fail during compilation. So, let's create a skeleton Account class inside our Steps.java. Notice that we're defining the class right here in our steps file. Don't worry—it's not going to stay here forever, but it's most convenient for us to create it right here where we're working. Once we have a clear idea of how we're going to work with the class, then we can refactor and move it to a more permanent home.

```
step_definitions/04/src/test/java/nicebank/Steps.java
class Account {
  public Account(int openingBalance) {
  }
}
```

Now when we run mvn clean test we get the following failure:

```
-------------------------------------------------------
 T E S T S
-------------------------------------------------------
Running RunCukesTest
Feature: Cash Withdrawal

  Scenario: Successful withdrawal from an account in credit
    Given I have deposited $100 in my account
    When I request $20
      cucumber.api.PendingException: TODO: implement me
        at nicebank.Steps.iRequest$(Steps.java:24)
        at *.When I request $20(cash_withdrawal.feature:4)
    Then $20 should be dispensed

1 Scenarios (1 pending)
3 Steps (1 skipped, 1 pending, 1 passed)
0m0.100s
```

```
cucumber.api.PendingException: TODO: implement me
        at nicebank.Steps.iRequest$(Steps.java:24)
        at *.When I request $20(cash_withdrawal.feature:4)

Tests run: 5, Failures: 0, Errors: 0, Skipped: 3, Time elapsed: 0.739 sec
```

As you've seen, our first step definition is now succeeding. Cucumber has caught the PendingException thrown by the second step definition and displayed it to us just beneath the step. In the summary at the bottom we can see that one step passed, one step failed, and one was skipped.

## What We Just Learned

It's useful to think of a step definition as being a special kind of method. Unlike a regular method, whose name has to match exactly, a step definition can be invoked by any step that matches its regular expression. Because regular expressions can contain wildcards, this means you have the flexibility to make the Gherkin steps nice and readable, while keeping your Java step definition code clean and free of duplication.

- Step definitions provide a mapping from the Gherkin scenarios' plain-language descriptions of user actions into Java code, which simulates those actions.

- Step definitions are registered with Cucumber by using @Given, @When, @Then, or one of the aliases for your spoken language.

- Step definitions use regular expressions to declare the steps that they can handle. Because regular expressions can contain wildcards, one step definition can handle several different steps.

- A step definition communicates its result to Cucumber by raising, or not raising, an exception.

Now that you've seen how Gherkin and step definitions fit together, you're ready to start using Cucumber to test your own applications. To get your step definitions talking to the application, you'll need to learn how to use one of Java's automation libraries, many of which are covered in the recipes part of this book. If you're testing a web application, for example, see Chapter 12, *Working with Web Applications*, on page 225. Web services are covered in Chapter 15, *Working with a REST Web Service*, on page 273.

Over here in the fundamentals part, we're going to start putting some more flesh on the bones of your Cucumber knowledge. There's much more to

Gherkin than the basic keywords we taught you in the previous chapter, and that's what we'll explore next.

## Try This

At the end of the previous chapter, we suggested that you write some scenarios for your own project. Now try running them with Cucumber and use the snippets to create your first step definitions. Think about which domain entity each step is working with, and use that to decide which file to put the step definition into. Look for places you can use what you've learned about regular expressions to make the step definitions more flexible.

# CHAPTER 5

# Expressive Scenarios

In Chapter 3, *Gherkin Basics*, on page 31, we deliberately didn't give you the whole story and showed you just a core set of keywords instead. They're the fundamental building blocks you need to get started working with Cucumber, and we wanted to get you started as quickly as possible. Now it's time to refine your skills.

When you're writing Cucumber features, make readability your main goal. Otherwise, a reader can easily feel more like they're reading a computer program than a specification document, which is something we want you to try to avoid at all costs. After all, if your features aren't easy for nonprogrammers to read, you might as well just be writing your tests in plain old code.

The real key to expressive scenarios is having a healthy vocabulary of domain language to use to express your requirements. That said, using only the basic set of Gherkin keywords can often make your features repetitive, making them cluttered and awkward to read. By the end of this chapter you'll know everything there is to know about Gherkin's syntax, giving you all the tools you need to write clear, readable Cucumber acceptance tests. We'll also show you how to use tags and folders to stay organized as you write more features for your project.

First we want to concentrate on helping you remove that repetitive clutter. We're going to show you how to use *scenario outlines* and *data tables* to help make your Gherkin scenarios more readable, but we'll start with a new keyword called Background.

## Background

A *background* section in a feature file allows you to specify a set of steps that are common to every scenario in the file. Instead of having to repeat those steps over and over for each scenario, you move them up into a Background element. Here are a couple of advantages to doing this:

- If you ever need to change those steps, you have to change them in only one place.

- The importance of those steps fades into the background so that when you're reading each individual scenario, you can focus on what is unique and important about that scenario.

To show you what we mean, let's take an existing scenario that uses only the basic Gherkin Scenario element and improve its readability by *refactoring* it to use a Background. Here's our feature before the refactoring starts:

```
Feature: Change PIN

  Customers being issued new cards are supplied with a Personal
  Identification Number (PIN) that is randomly generated by the
  system.

  In order to be able to change it to something they can easily
  remember, customers with new bank cards need to be able to
  change their PIN using the ATM.

  Scenario: Change PIN successfully
    Given I have been issued a new card
    And I insert the card, entering the correct PIN
    When I choose "Change PIN" from the menu
    And I change the PIN to 9876
    Then the system should remember my PIN is now 9876

  Scenario: Try to change PIN to the same as before
    Given I have been issued a new card
    And I insert the card, entering the correct PIN
    When I choose "Change PIN" from the menu
    And I try to change the PIN to the original PIN number
    Then I should see a warning message
    And the system should not have changed my PIN
```

You can see that there are two scenarios here, but without reading them carefully, it's quite hard to see what exactly is going on in each one. The first three steps in each scenario, while necessary to clarify the context of the scenario, are completely repeated in both scenarios. That repetition is distracting, making it harder to see the *essence* of what each scenario is testing.

Let's factor out the three repeated steps into a Background, like this:

```
Feature: Change PIN

  As soon as the bank issues new cards to customers, they are
  supplied with a Personal Identification Number (PIN) that
  is randomly generated by the system.

  In order to be able to change it to something they can easily
  remember, customers with new bank cards need to be able to
  change their PIN using the ATM.

  Background:
    Given I have been issued a new card
    And I insert the card, entering the correct PIN
    And I choose "Change PIN" from the menu

  Scenario: Change PIN successfully
    When I change the PIN to 9876
    Then the system should remember my PIN is now 9876

  Scenario: Try to change PIN to the same as before
    When I try to change the PIN to the original PIN number
    Then I should see a warning message
    And the system should not have changed my PIN
```

Our refactoring hasn't changed the behavior of the tests at all: at runtime, the steps in the background are executed at the beginning of each scenario, just as they were before. What we have done is made each individual scenario much easier to read.

You can have a single Background element per feature file, and it must appear before any of the Scenario or Scenario Outline elements. Just like all the other Gherkin elements, you can give it a name, and you have space to put a multiline description before the first step. For example:

```
Feature: Change PIN

  In order to be able to change it to something they can easily
  remember, customers with new bank cards need to be able to
  change their PIN using the ATM.

  Background: Insert a newly issued card and sign in

    Whenever the bank issues new cards to customers, they are supplied
    with a Personal Identification Number (PIN) that is randomly
    generated by the system.

    Given I have been issued a new card
    And I insert the card, entering the correct PIN
    ...
```

Using a Background element isn't always necessary, but it's often useful to improve the readability of your features by removing repetitive steps from individual scenarios. Here are some tips for using it well:

- Don't use Background to set up complicated state unless that state is something the reader actually needs to know. For example, we didn't mention the actual digits of the system-generated PIN in the previous example, because that detail wasn't relevant to any of the scenarios.

- Keep your Background section short. After all, you're expecting the user to actually remember this stuff when reading your scenarios. If the background is more than four lines long, can you find a way to express that action in just one or two steps?

- Make your Background section vivid. Use colorful names and try to tell a story, because your readers can keep track of stories much better than they can keep track of dull names like User A, User B, Site 1, and so on. If it's worth mentioning at all, make it really stand out.

- Keep your scenarios short, and don't have too many. If the Background is more than three or four steps long, think about using higher-level steps or splitting the feature file in two. You can use a background as a good indicator of when a feature is getting too long: if the new scenarios you want to add don't fit with the existing background, consider splitting the feature.

- Avoid putting technical details such as clearing queues, starting back-end services, or opening browsers in a background. Most of these things will be assumed by the reader, and there are ways to push those actions down into your *support code* that we'll explain later in the book, such as in *Tagged Hooks*, on page 157.

Backgrounds are useful for taking Given (and sometimes When) steps that are repeated in each scenario and moving them to a single place. This helps keep your scenarios clear and concise.

## Data Tables

Sometimes steps in a scenario need to describe data that doesn't easily fit on a single line of Given, When, or Then. Gherkin allows us to place these details in a table right underneath a step. *Data tables* give you a way to extend a Gherkin step beyond a single line to include a larger piece of data.

For example, consider these steps:

**Refactoring to Background**

Refactoring[a] is the process of changing code to improve its readability or design without changing its behavior. This technique applies to Gherkin features just as well as it does to the rest of your codebase. As your understanding of your domain grows through the course of the project, you'll want to reflect that learning by updating your features.

Often you don't see a background immediately. You might start out by writing one or two scenarios, and it's only as you write the third that you notice some common steps. When you spot a feature where the same or similar steps are repeated in several scenarios, see whether you can refactor to extract those steps into a background. It can take a little bit of courage to do this, because there's a risk you might make a mistake and break something, but this is a pretty safe refactoring. Once you're done, you should end up with the feature doing exactly the same thing as it did before you started but easier to read.

---

a.    *Refactoring: Improving the Design of Existing Code [FBBO99]*

```
Given a User "Michael Jackson" born on August 29, 1958
And a User "Elvis" born on January 8, 1935
And a User "John Lennon" born on October 9, 1940
...
```

Boring! We wouldn't tolerate this kind of repetitive stuff in a traditional specification document, and we don't have to tolerate it in a Cucumber specification either. We can collect those steps together into a single step that uses a table to express the data:

```
Given these Users:
  | name            | date of birth    |
  | Michael Jackson | August 29, 1958  |
  | Elvis           | January 8, 1935  |
  | John Lennon     | October 9, 1940  |
```

That's much clearer. The table starts on the line immediately following the step, and its cells are separated using the pipe character: |. You can line up the pipes using whitespace to make the table look tidy, although Cucumber doesn't mind whether you do; it will strip out the values in each cell, ignoring the surrounding whitespace.

In the previous table, we've used a heading for each column in the table, but that's only because it made sense for that particular step. You have the freedom to specify data in different ways, such as putting the headings down the side:

```
Then I should see a vehicle that matches the following description:
  | Wheels      | 2                        |
  | Max Speed   | 60 mph                   |
  | Accessories | lights, shopping basket  |
```

Or just to specify a list:

```
Then my shopping list should contain:
  | Onions    |
  | Potatoes  |
  | Sausages  |
  | Apples    |
  | Relish    |
```

To explain how to work with these different shaped tables, we need to take a short dive down into the step definition layer. If you're not interested in writing Java step definition code, feel free to skip this bit.

## Working with Data Tables in Step Definitions

We'll illustrate how to use a data table in your step definitions with a quick game of tic-tac-toe. Let's imagine we're building a tic-tac-toe game and we've started working on the basic feature for making moves on the board. We start with a scenario like this:

```
expressive_scenarios/01/src/test/resources/tic_tac_toe/tic_tac_toe.feature
Feature:
  Scenario:
    Given a board like this:
      |   | 1 | 2 | 3 |
      | 1 |   |   |   |
      | 2 |   |   |   |
      | 3 |   |   |   |
    When player x plays in row 2, column 1
    Then the board should look like this:
      |   | 1 | 2 | 3 |
      | 1 |   |   |   |
      | 2 | x |   |   |
      | 3 |   |   |   |
```

We'll show you how to grab the table from the first step, manipulate it in the second, and finally compare the expected board from the scenario with the actual one.

Run ./cucumber to generate the step definition snippets, and paste them into step_definitions/BoardSteps.java:

expressive_scenarios/01/src/test/java/tic_tac_toe/BoardSteps.java
```java
package tic_tac_toe;

import cucumber.api.java.en.*;
import cucumber.api.PendingException;
import cucumber.api.DataTable;

public class BoardSteps {
    @Given("^a board like this:$")
    public void aBoardLikeThis(DataTable arg1) throws Throwable {
        // Write code here that turns the phrase above into concrete actions
        // For automatic transformation, change DataTable to one of
        // List<YourType>, List<List<E>>, List<Map<K,V>> or Map<K,V>.
        // E,K,V must be a scalar (String, Integer, Date, enum etc)
        throw new PendingException();
    }

    @When("^player x plays in row (\\d+), column (\\d+)$")
    public void playerXPlaysInRowColumn(int arg1, int arg2) throws Throwable {
        // Write code here that turns the phrase above into concrete actions
        throw new PendingException();
    }

    @Then("^the board should look like this:$")
    public void theBoardShouldLookLikeThis(DataTable arg1) throws Throwable {
        // Write code here that turns the phrase above into concrete actions
        // For automatic transformation, change DataTable to one of
        // List<YourType>, List<List<E>>, List<Map<K,V>> or Map<K,V>.
        // E,K,V must be a scalar (String, Integer, Date, enum etc)
        throw new PendingException();
    }
}
```

Notice that the snippets for the two step definitions where we're going to receive a table are a little different. There's a comment telling you about *automatic conversion* of the DataTable argument you're being passed, but we'll ignore that for now (don't worry—we'll talk a lot about automatic conversion later). The cucumber.api.DataTable is a really rich object with lots of methods for interacting with its data. We'll show you some of the most useful ones now.

Let's start fleshing out those step definitions.

### Turning the Table into a List of Lists

Under the hood, the table is just a List of Lists of Strings: List<List<String>>. Often we'll want to work with it in that raw form, so we can call the raw method on it to do just that. Let's get the raw data from the table and store it in an instance variable board, which we can manipulate in our second step when we want to make a move.

As an experiment, add an implementation for the second step definition that just prints the raw board out so we can see what it looks like:

expressive_scenarios/02/src/test/java/tic_tac_toe/BoardSteps.java
```java
package tic_tac_toe;

import cucumber.api.java.en.*;
import cucumber.api.PendingException;
import cucumber.api.DataTable;

import java.util.List;

public class BoardSteps {
    private List<List<String>> board;

    @Given("^a board like this:$")
    public void aBoardLikeThis(DataTable table) throws Throwable {
        this.board = table.raw();
    }

    @When("^player x plays in row (\\d+), column (\\d+)$")
    public void playerXPlaysInRowColumn(int arg1, int arg2) throws Throwable {
        System.out.println(board.toString());

        throw new PendingException();
    }

    @Then("^the board should look like this:$")
    public void theBoardShouldLookLikeThis(DataTable arg1) throws Throwable {
        // Write code here that turns the phrase above into concrete actions
        // For automatic transformation, change DataTable to one of
        // List<YourType>, List<List<E>>, List<Map<K,V>> or Map<K,V>.
        // E,K,V must be a scalar (String, Integer, Date, enum etc)
        throw new PendingException();
    }
}
```

When you run ./cucumber, you should see the two-dimensional array printed.

```
$ ./cucumber

-------------------------------------------------------
 T E S T S
-------------------------------------------------------
Running RunCukesTest
Feature:
[[, 1, 2, 3], [1, , , ], [2, , , ], [3, , , ]]

  Scenario:                                # tic_tac_toe/tic_tac_toe.feature:2
    Given a board like this:
    When player x plays in row 2, column 1
```

```
cucumber.api.PendingException: TODO: implement me
  at tic_tac_toe.BoardSteps.playerXPlaysInRowColumn(BoardSteps.java:21)
  at *.When player x plays in row 2, column 1(tic_tac_toe.feature:8)
Then the board should look like this:
```

```
1 Scenarios (1 pending)
3 Steps (1 skipped, 1 pending, 1 passed)
```

Notice that the raw table includes the column and row headings.

### Comparing Tables with Diff

So that we can start out with a failing test, we'll skip doing any manipulation of the board in this step for now. So, remove the body of the second step definition and make the following implementation in the last step definition:

```
expressive_scenarios/03/src/test/java/tic_tac_toe/BoardSteps.java
@When("^player x plays in row (\\d+), column (\\d+)$")
public void playerXPlaysInRowColumn(int arg1, int arg2) throws Throwable {
}

@Then("^the board should look like this:$")
public void theBoardShouldLookLikeThis(DataTable expectedTable) throws Throwable {
    expectedTable.diff(board);
}
```

We've used the diff method on the table that describes how things should look, passing it the actual board as we see it in our application. When you run mvn clean test again, you should see that the step has failed because the tables were not identical:

```
$ mvn clean test

-------------------------------------------------------
 T E S T S
-------------------------------------------------------
Running RunCukesTest
Feature:

  Scenario:                                # tic_tac_toe/tic_tac_toe.feature:2
    Given a board like this:
    When player x plays in row 2, column 1
    Then the board should look like this:
      cucumber.runtime.table.TableDiffException: Tables were not identical:
          |   | 1 | 2 | 3 |
          | 1 |   |   |   |
        - | 2 | x |   |   |
        + | 2 |   |   |   |
          | 3 |   |   |   |

      at cucumber.runtime.table.TableDiffer.calculateDiffs(TableDiffer.java:37)
```

```
        at cucumber.api.DataTable.diff(DataTable.java:169)
        at cucumber.api.DataTable.diff(DataTable.java:159)
        at tic_tac_toe.BoardSteps.theBoardShouldLookLikeThis(BoardSteps.java:24)
        at *.Then the board should look like this:(tic_tac_toe.feature:9)
```

```
1 Scenarios (1 failed)
3 Steps (1 failed, 2 passed)
```

Rows that differ from what was expected will be printed twice—the first (preceded by a "-") is what was expected, followed by another (preceded by a "+") which is what was actually returned.

Let's fix the @When step to make the scenario pass. Add this implementation to the second step definition:

**expressive_scenarios/04/src/test/java/tic_tac_toe/BoardSteps.java**
```
@When("^player x plays in row (\\d+), column (\\d+)$")
public void playerXPlaysInRowColumn(int row, int col) throws Throwable {
    board.get(row).set(col, "x");
}
```

Run the scenario, and unfortunately you will now see a runtime error:

```
java.lang.UnsupportedOperationException
        at java.util.Collections$UnmodifiableList.set(Collections.java:1311)
        at tic_tac_toe.BoardSteps.playerXPlaysInRowColumn(BoardSteps.java:20)
        at *.When player x plays in row 2, column 1(tic_tac_toe.feature:8)
```

The error happens because the DataTable is unmodifiable. We'll explain why Cucumber works this way later, but for now, let's make a modifiable copy of the raw data by modifying the first step definition:

**expressive_scenarios/05/src/test/java/tic_tac_toe/BoardSteps.java**
```
@Given("^a board like this:$")
public void aBoardLikeThis(DataTable table) throws Throwable {
    this.board = new ArrayList<List<String>>();
    for (List<String> row : table.raw()) {
        this.board.add(new ArrayList<String>(row));
    }
}
```

Run the scenario, and now you should see it pass.

This is just a taste of what you can do with data tables in Cucumber. We encourage you to read the documentation[1] for cucumber.api.DataTable and play around with it yourself.

---

1.  http://cukes.info/api/cucumber/jvm/javadoc/cucumber/api/DataTable.html

Data tables are a great feature of Gherkin. They're really versatile, and they help you express data concisely, as you'd want to in a normal specification document. With backgrounds and data tables, you can do a lot to reduce the noise and clutter in your scenarios. Even when you use these tools, you'll still sometimes see a pattern where one scenario looks a lot like the one that came before it and the one after it. This is where a *scenario outline* can help.

## Scenario Outline

Sometimes you have several scenarios that follow exactly the same pattern of steps, just with different input values or expected outcomes. For example, suppose we're testing each of the fixed amount withdrawal buttons on the ATM:

```
Feature: Withdraw Fixed Amount

  The "Withdraw Cash" menu contains several fixed amounts to
  speed up transactions for users.

  Scenario: Withdraw fixed amount of $50
    Given I have $500 in my account
    When I choose to withdraw the fixed amount of $50
    Then I should receive $50 cash
    And the balance of my account should be $450

  Scenario: Withdraw fixed amount of $100
    Given I have $500 in my account
    When I choose to withdraw the fixed amount of $100
    Then I should receive $100 cash
    And the balance of my account should be $400

  Scenario: Withdraw fixed amount of $200
    Given I have $500 in my account
    When I choose to withdraw the fixed amount of $200
    Then I should receive $200 cash
    And the balance of my account should be $300
```

Once again, all the repetition in this feature makes it boring to read. It's hard to see the essence of each scenario, which is the amount of money involved in each transaction. We can use a scenario outline to specify the steps once and then play multiple sets of values through them. Here's that scenario again, refactored to use a scenario outline:

```
Feature: Withdraw Fixed Amount

  The "Withdraw Cash" menu contains several fixed amounts to
  speed up transactions for users.

  Scenario Outline: Withdraw fixed amount
    Given I have <Balance> in my account
    When I choose to withdraw the fixed amount of <Withdrawal>
    Then I should receive <Received> cash
    And the balance of my account should be <Remaining>

    Examples:
      | Balance | Withdrawal | Received | Remaining |
      | $500    | $50        | $50      | $450      |
      | $500    | $100       | $100     | $400      |
      | $500    | $200       | $200     | $300      |
```

We indicate *placeholders* within the scenario outline using angle brackets
(<..>) where we want real values to be substituted. The scenario outline itself
is useless without an Examples table, which lists rows of values to be substituted
for each placeholder.

You can have any number of Scenario Outline elements in a feature and any
number of Examples tables under each scenario outline. Behind the scenes,
Cucumber converts each row in the Examples table into a scenario before executing it.

One of the advantages of using a scenario outline is that you can clearly see
gaps in your examples. In our example, we haven't tested any edge cases,
such as when you try to withdraw more money than you have available. This
becomes much more obvious when you can see all the values lined up
together in a table.

Remember that although the syntax for writing them in Gherkin is the same,
these tables are totally different from the data tables we described earlier in
this chapter. Data tables just describe a lump of data to attach to a single
step of a single scenario. In a scenario outline, each row of an Examples table
represents a whole scenario to be executed by Cucumber. In fact, you might
want to use the keyword Scenarios (note the extra *s*) in place of Examples if you
find that more readable.

## Bigger Placeholders

It's easy to imagine that you can use scenario outline placeholders only where
there's a piece of data in the step. In fact, when Cucumber compiles a scenario
outline's table of examples down into scenarios ready to execute, it doesn't

care where the placeholders are. So, you can substitute as much or as little as you like from any step's text.

Let's illustrate this by testing the edge case where we try to withdraw more money than we have. What should we do in this case? Give users as much as we can, given their remaining balance, or just show them an error message? We ask our stakeholders for clarification, and they're happy for us to show them an error message. Here's how we write the scenario first:

```
Scenario: Try to withdraw too much
  Given I have $100 in my account
  When I choose to withdraw the fixed amount of $200
  Then I should see an error message
  And the balance of my account should be $100
```

There's still a good deal of duplication here with the flow of the scenarios above it, but because the Then step is so different, we can't put this one into the scenario outline. Or can we?

Let's change the scenario outline, replacing the <Received> placeholder with a more abstract <Outcome>:

```
Scenario Outline: Withdraw fixed amount
  Given I have <Balance> in my account
  When I choose to withdraw the fixed amount of <Withdrawal>
  Then I should <Outcome>
  And the balance of my account should be <Remaining>

  Examples:
    | Balance | Withdrawal | Remaining | Outcome          |
    | $500    | $50        | $450      | receive $50 cash |
    | $500    | $100       | $400      | receive $100 cash |
    | $500    | $200       | $300      | receive $200 cash |
```

Now we can simply add our failure case to the bottom of that table:

```
Scenario Outline: Withdraw fixed amount
  Given I have <Balance> in my account
  When I choose to withdraw the fixed amount of <Withdrawal>
  Then I should <Outcome>
  And the balance of my account should be <Remaining>

  Examples:
    | Balance | Withdrawal | Remaining | Outcome               |
    | $500    | $50        | $450      | receive $50 cash      |
    | $500    | $100       | $400      | receive $100 cash     |
    | $500    | $200       | $300      | receive $200 cash     |
    | $100    | $200       | $100      | see an error message  |
```

We can use a placeholder to replace any of the text we like in a step. Notice that it doesn't matter what order the placeholders appear in the table; what counts is that the column header matches the text in the placeholder in the scenario outline.

 **Joe asks:**
## How Many Examples Should I Use?

Once you have a scenario outline with a few examples, it's very easy to think of more examples, and even easier to add them. Before you know it, you have a huge, very comprehensive table of examples—and a problem.

Why?

On a system of any serious complexity, you can quite quickly start to experience what mathematicians call *combinatorial explosion*, where the number of different combinations of inputs and expected outputs becomes unmanageable. In trying to cover every possible eventuality, you end up with rows and rows of example data for Cucumber to execute. Remember that each of those little rows represents a whole scenario that might take several seconds to execute, and that can quickly start to add up. When your tests take longer to run, you slow down your feedback loop, making the whole team less productive as a result.

A really long table is also very hard to read. It's better to aim to make your examples *illustrative* or *representative* than *exhaustive*. Try to stick to what Gojko Adzic calls the *key examples*.[a] If you study the code you're testing, you'll often find that some rows of your examples table cover the same logic as another row in the table. You might also find that the test cases in your table are already covered by unit tests of the underlying code. If they're not, consider whether they should be.

Remember that readability is what's most important. If your stakeholders feel comforted by exhaustive tests, perhaps because your software operates in a safety-critical environment, then by all means put them in. Just remember that you'll never be able to prove there are no bugs. As logicians say, absence of proof is not proof of absence.

a.   *Specification by Example [Ad 11]*

Although this is a useful technique, be careful that your programmer's instinct to reduce duplication at all costs doesn't take over here.[2] If you move too much of the text of a step into the examples table, it can be very hard to read the flow of the scenario. Remember your goal is readability, so don't take this too far, and always test your features by getting other people to regularly read them and give you feedback.

---

2.   See this point explained in detail by David Chelimsky: http://confreaks.net/videos/434.

## Multiple Tables of Examples

Cucumber will happily handle any number of Examples elements beneath a Scenario Outline, meaning you can group different kinds of examples together, if you want. For example:

```
Scenario Outline: Withdraw fixed amount
  Given I have <Balance> in my account
  When I choose to withdraw the fixed amount of <Withdrawal>
  Then I should <Outcome>
  And the balance of my account should be <Remaining>

  Examples: Successful withdrawal
    | Balance | Withdrawal | Outcome           | Remaining |
    | $500    | $50        | receive $50 cash  | $450      |
    | $500    | $100       | receive $100 cash | $400      |

  Examples: Attempt to withdraw too much
    | Balance | Withdrawal | Outcome               | Remaining |
    | $100    | $200       | see an error message  | $100      |
    | $0      | $50        | see an error message  | $0        |
```

As usual, you have the option of a name and description for each Examples table. When you have a large set of examples, splitting it into multiple tables can make it easier for a reader to understand.

## Explain Yourself

You'll normally be using a scenario outline and examples table to help specify the implementation of a business rule. Remember to include a plain-language description of the underlying rule that the examples are supposed to illustrate! It's amazing how often people forget to do this.

For example, look at this feature:

```
Feature: Account Creation

  Scenario Outline: Password validation
    Given I try to create an account with password "<Password>"
    Then I should see that the password is <Valid or Invalid>

    Examples:
      | Password | Valid or Invalid |
      | abc      | invalid          |
      | ab1      | invalid          |
      | abc1     | valid            |
      | abcd     | invalid          |
      | abcd1    | valid            |
```

If you have to implement the code to make this feature pass, can you tell what the underlying rule is?

Not very easily. So, let's modify the feature to make it more self-explanatory, like this:

```
Feature: Account Creation

  Scenario Outline: Password validation
    Given I try to create an account with password "<Password>"
    Then I should see that the password is <Valid or Invalid>

  Examples: Too Short
    Passwords are invalid if less than 4 characters

    | Password | Valid or Invalid |
    | abc      | invalid          |
    | ab1      | invalid          |

  Examples: Letters and Numbers
    Passwords need both letters and numbers to be valid

    | Password | Valid or Invalid |
    | abc1     | valid            |
    | abcd     | invalid          |
    | abcd1    | valid            |
```

By separating the examples into two sets and giving each one a name and description, we've explained the rule *and* given examples of the rule at the same time.

## Too Much Information

Finding the right level of detail, or *abstraction*, to use in your scenarios is a skill that takes some time to master. What many people don't realize is that different levels of detail are appropriate for different scenarios in the same system—sometimes in the same feature—depending on what it is they're describing.

As an example, here's a scenario for the user of our ATM authenticating with their PIN:

```
Scenario: Successful login with PIN
  Given I have pushed my card in the slot
  When I enter my PIN
  And I press "OK"
  Then I should see the main menu
```

It's entirely appropriate to go into this much detail about the authentication process in this scenario, because that's where our focus is. Now consider our cash withdrawal scenario from earlier, which has a different focus but still needs to be authenticated. Does it make sense to express the PIN authentication steps of this scenario at the same level of detail? Let's try it:

```
Scenario: Withdraw fixed amount of $50
  Given I have $500 in my account
  And I have pushed my card into the slot
  And I enter my PIN
  And I press "OK"
  When I choose to withdraw the fixed amount of $50
  Then I should receive $50 cash
  And the balance of my account should be $450
```

That's awful! There's so much noise about authentication that we hardly notice the important part: the part about withdrawing cash. That detail was useful in the PIN scenario where it was relevant, but now it's just distracting. We'll talk more about the dangers of overly detailed or *imperative* scenarios in Chapter 6, *Keeping Your Cucumbers Sweet*, on page 91; right now we want to encourage you to extract these details into a separate step definition so our scenario stays easy to read.

## Extract the Details

Let's take the three authentication steps and summarize what they do with a single high-level step:

```
Given I have authenticated with the correct PIN
```

Delete those three lines from the scenario, and replace them with that single step. Now run ./cucumber to generate the step definition snippet for your new high-level step. It should look like this:

```
@Given("^I have authenticated with the correct PIN$")
public void iHaveAuthenticatedWithTheCorrectPIN() throws Throwable {
  // Express the Regexp above with the code you wish you had
  throw new PendingException();
}
```

Now, create a method in your step definition file called authenticateWithPIN that does whatever is necessary to authenticate with a PIN, and modify your step definition to look like this:

```
@Given("^I have authenticated with the correct PIN$")
public void iHaveAuthenticatedWithTheCorrectPIN() throws Throwable {
  authenticateWithPIN();
}
```

Your authenticateWithPIN may make exactly the same calls as the three step definitions it is replacing, or there may be another way to get the ATM into an authenticated state. Either way, the scenario is now much more readable:

```
Scenario: Withdraw fixed amount of $50
  Given I have $500 in my account
  And I have authenticated with the correct PIN
  When I choose to withdraw the fixed amount of $50
  Then I should receive $50 cash
  And the balance of my account should be $450
```

## Doc Strings

Doc strings allow you to specify a larger piece of text than you could fit on a single line. For example, if you need to describe the precise content of an email message, you could do it like this:

```
Scenario: Ban Unscrupulous Users
  When I behave unscrupulously
  Then I should receive an email containing:
    """
    Dear Sir,

    Your account privileges have been revoked due to your unscrupulous behavior.

    Sincerely,
    The Management
    """
  And my account should be locked
```

Just like a data table, the entire string between the """ triple quotes is attached to the step above it. The indentation of the opening """ is not important, although common practice is to indent two spaces from the enclosing step, as we've shown. The indentation inside the triple quotes, however, is significant: imagine the left margin running down from the start of the first """. If you want to include indentation within your string, you need to indent it within this margin.

Doc strings open up all kinds of possibilities for specifying data in your steps. We've seen teams use these arguments to specify snippets of JSON or XML data when writing features for an API, for example. There's an example of how to do this in Chapter 15, *Working with a REST Web Service*, on page 273. You do need to be cautious when including this much detail in a scenario. It's easy to create a lot of clutter with a large piece of data, making it hard to read the scenario as a whole. You can also easily create brittle scenarios, where the slightest change to the system causes the scenario to fail because it's behaving slightly differently than the way it was described in the doc string.

OK, we've covered the more advanced features of Gherkin you can use to express your business requirements. The last thing we want to talk about in this chapter is keeping things organized.

## Staying Organized with Tags and Subfolders

It's easy to be organized when you have only a couple of features, but as your test suite starts to grow, you'll want to keep things tidy so that the documentation is easy to read and navigate. One simple way to do this is to start using subfolders to categorize your features. This gives you only one axis for organization, though, so you can also use tags to attach a label to any scenario, allowing you to have as many different ways of slicing your features as you like.

### Subfolders

This is the easiest way to organize your features. You may find yourself torn as to how to choose a category, though: do you organize by user type, with a features/admins folder, a features/logged_in_users folder, and a features/visitors folder, for example? Or do you organize them by domain entity or something else?

Of course, this is a decision for you and your team to make, but we can offer a bit of advice. We've had most success using subfolders to represent different high-level tasks that a user might try to do. So, if we were building an intranet reporting system, we might organize it like this:

```
features/
  reading_reports/
  report_building/
  user_administration/
```

Don't get too hung up about getting your folder structure right the first time. Make a decision to try a structure, reorganize all the existing feature files, and then stick to it for a while as you add new features. Put a note in the calendar to take some time out in a couple of weeks and reflect on whether the new structure is working.

If you think about your features as a book that describes what your system does, then the subfolders are like the chapters in that book. So, as you tell the story of your system, what do you want the reader to see when they scan the table of contents?

**Aslak says:**
## Features Are Not User Stories

Long ago, Cucumber started life as a tool called the RSpec Story Runner. In those days, the plain-language tests used a .story extension. When I created Cucumber, I made a deliberate decision to name the files features rather than stories. Why did I do that?

User stories are a great tool for planning. Each story contains a little bit of functionality that you can prioritize, build, test, and release. Once a story has been released, we don't want it to leave a trace in the code. We use refactoring to clean up the design so that the code absorbs the new behavior specified by the user story, leaving it looking as though that behavior had always been there.

We want the same thing to happen with our Cucumber features. The features should describe how the system behaves today, but they don't need to document the history of how it was built; that's what a version control system is for!

We've seen teams whose features directory looks like this:

```
features/
  story_38971_generate_new_report.feature
  story_38986_run_report.feature
  story_39004_log_in.feature
  ...
```

We strongly encourage you *not* to do this. You'll end up with fragmented features that just don't work as documentation for your system. One user story might map to one feature, but another user story might cause you to go and add or modify scenarios in several existing features—if the story changes the way users have to authenticate, for example. It's unlikely that there will always be a one-to-one mapping from each user story to each feature, so don't try to force it. If you need to keep a story identifier for a scenario, use a tag instead.

## Tags

If subfolders are the chapters in your book of features, then tags are the sticky notes you've put on pages you want to be able to find easily. You tag a scenario by putting a word prefixed with the @ character on the line before the Scenario keyword, like this:

```
@widgets
Scenario: Generate report
  Given I am logged in
  And there is a report "Best selling widgets"
  ...
```

In fact, you can attach multiple tags to the same scenario, separated with spaces:

```
@slow @widgets @nightly
Scenario: Generate overnight report
  Given I am logged in
  And there is a report "Total widget sales history"
  ...
```

If you want to tag all the scenarios in a feature at once, just tag the Feature element at the top, and all the scenarios will inherit the tag. You can still tag individual scenarios as well.

```
@nightly @slow
Feature: Nightly Reports

  @widgets
  Scenario: Generate overnight widgets report
    ...

  @doofers
  Scenario: Generate overnight doofers report
    ...
```

In the previous example, the scenario called Generate overnight widgets report will have three tags: @nightly, @slow, and @widgets, whereas the scenario called Generate overnight doofers report will have the tags @nightly, @slow, and @doofers. You can also tag Scenario Outline elements and the individual Examples tables under them.

There are three main reasons for tagging scenarios:

- *Documentation*: You want to use a tag to attach a label to certain scenarios, for example to label them with an ID from a project management tool.

- *Filtering*: Cucumber allows you to use tags as a filter to pick out specific scenarios to run or report on. You can even have Cucumber fail your test run if a certain tag appears too many times.

- *Hooks*: Run a block of code whenever a scenario with a particular tag is about to start or has just finished.

We'll cover hooks later in *Tagged Hooks*, on page 157, and we'll explain how to filter based on tags in *Filtering with Tag Expressions*, on page 261. In case you can't wait until then, here's a quick example of how to run Cucumber, selecting just scenarios with a certain tag:

```
$ ./cucumber --tags @nightly
```

That will select and run only the scenarios tagged with @nightly.

## What We Just Learned

Congratulations, you've graduated from Gherkin school! Let's look back over what we've learned in this chapter.

- Readability should be your number-one goal when writing Gherkin features. Always try to sit together with a stakeholder when you write your scenarios, or at the very least pass them over for feedback once you've written them. Keep fine-tuning the language in your scenarios to make them more readable.

- Use a Background to factor out repeated steps from a feature and to help tell a story.

- Repetitive scenarios can be collapsed into a Scenario Outline.

- Steps can be extended with multiline strings or data tables.

- You can organize features into subfolders, like chapters in a book.

- Tags allow you to mark up scenarios and features so you select particular sets to run or report on.

Have you noticed that we're going outside-in as we work through this part of the book? We started with an overview, then looked at the most useful bits of Gherkin, and then did the same for step definitions. Now that you've learned about the more advanced features of Gherkin, you're almost ready to dive deep into step definition code. In the next part of the book, that's exactly what we'll do, with a worked example that will give you a chance to practice everything you've learned, and more. First, though, we're going to take a step back and examine some of the common problems you and your team might encounter as you start to use Cucumber and what to do about them.

### Try This

Review the scenarios that you've written for your system, and see whether you can find an opportunity to use a Background, a Scenario Outline, or a data table. Refactor the feature to make use of the new keyword and compare the new version of the feature with the old one. Which one do you think is more readable? Show it to someone else on your team; what does that person think?

# CHAPTER 6

# Keeping Your Cucumbers Sweet

When your team first starts to use Cucumber, it won't be long before you begin to notice that you seem to be creating code with fewer bugs than you did before. You might find yourself bravely refactoring code that previously you would have been too scared to touch. You might continue adding feature after feature, inspired by the delight you felt on seeing your first passing scenario.

After a while, however, things start to turn sour. Suddenly it dawns on you that the tests take a really long time to run. Or perhaps you've started to notice a couple of scenarios that seem to fail at random, usually just when you're up against a tight deadline. Perhaps the nontechnical stakeholders have lost interest in the process, and only developers are reading the features anymore. People might even start to ask this:

*Is Cucumber holding us back?*

The good news is, you don't have to live with these problems. In our coaching and consulting work, we've seen all kinds of problems experienced by all kinds of teams as they learn to use Cucumber. In this chapter, we'll describe the most common problems we've seen. We'll help you understand their root causes, and we'll make suggestions for tackling them or, ideally, avoiding them in the first place. There won't be much code in this chapter, but you'll find lots of useful advice.

We'll start where it hurts, by describing four different symptoms your team might be experiencing. Then we'll dig down into the underlying causes of these before finally looking at solutions. By the end of the chapter, you should feel much more confident about how to help your team stay successful with Cucumber in the long run.

# Feeling the Pain

We've identified four main types of pain that your team might start to feel if their Cucumber goes bad. Take a look and see whether you recognize any:

| Symptom | Problem |
|---|---|
| Some of our tests fail randomly. | *Flickering scenarios* |
| We keep breaking tests unintentionally. | *Brittle features* |
| Our features take too long to run. | *Slow features* |
| Our stakeholders don't read our features. | *Bored stakeholders* |

Let's take a closer look at each of these symptoms.

## Flickering Scenarios

When a scenario that was passing yesterday is failing today, with the same source code running in the same environment, you have what we call a *flickering scenario*—one that fails occasionally and at random. The same scenario, run on the same codebase in the same environment, will mostly pass but sometimes fail. These apparently uncontrollable failures cause the team to lose confidence in their tests, in their code, and in themselves.

The worst thing about a flickering scenario is that as soon as you try to reproduce it so that you can fix it, it refuses to fail. Fixing a flickering scenario is one of the hardest tasks you can take on, yet it's also one of the most important. For a suite of automated tests to be useful, the team must have absolute trust in it. When even just a single test is compromising that trust, it has a corrosive effect on how everyone feels about the whole test suite.

To fix a flickering scenario, you have to study the code and try to understand why it might be happening. This is a scientific process of making a hypothesis about the cause of the failure, creating an experiment to prove or disprove that hypothesis, and then running the experiment to see whether you were right. You might need to go around this loop several times before you crack the problem, and it might take several days to run an experiment if the flickering scenario fails only intermittently. If you run out of ideas, consider simply deleting the test altogether rather than have it come back and fail on you at a time of its own choosing.

Flickering scenarios are normally caused by one of the following problems:

- *Shared Environments*, on page 105
- *Leaky Scenarios*, on page 103
- *Race Conditions and Sleepy Steps*, on page 104

## Brittle Features

When you feel like you can hardly move in the test suite without making an apparently unrelated test fail for no good reason, you have what we call *brittle features*. A brittle feature is easy to break. When features are brittle, a necessary change in one part of the test suite or main codebase causes apparently unrelated scenarios to break.

When you encounter a brittle scenario, it's usually when you're in the middle of doing something else. You're interrupted by the unexpected failure and waste time dashing over to fix the unexpected broken test. On a bad day, this can happen several times before you emerge from the rabbit warren. Brittle features are self-fulfilling: when developers perceive their tests to be brittle, they tend to be less courageous about refactoring and cleaning up test code and instead try to get in and out as quickly as they can, leaving the tests and production codebase in an increasingly hard-to-maintain state.

Brittle features are normally caused by one of the following:

- *Fixture Data*, on page 107
- *Duplication*, on page 98
- *Leaky Scenarios*, on page 103
- *Tester Apartheid*, on page 106

## Slow Features

Each time you add a new scenario to your test suite, you're adding a few seconds to the total test runtime. For a successful application whose users continue to demand new features, that test runtime is only going to get longer. A long test run creeps up on you: first five minutes seems like an eternity to wait, then fifteen minutes seems bad, but you get used to going to grab a coffee while it runs. Pretty soon, you come back from your coffee and it still hasn't finished, and fifteen minutes becomes twenty-five minutes. Before you know it, your features are taking more than an hour or even longer.

Once a new scenario is passing, the main reason to keep running it is for feedback: you want that scenario to warn you if you somehow accidentally break the functionality that it checks for. The value of that feedback diminishes as your test run starts taking longer and longer. When the build is slow, developers don't run all the tests before committing code and will rely on the continuous integration server to give them feedback instead. If a few developers do this at the same time, the chances of all of their changes integrating successfully are slim, and a broken build becomes the norm.

Long test runs also mean people are scared to refactor and do other general maintenance on the Cucumber tests themselves. Refactoring the code in a step definition that's used in 340 scenarios is scary, because you'll need to run all 340 scenarios to tell you for certain whether your change broke anything.

A slow feature run is normally caused by a combination of the following:

- *Race Conditions and Sleepy Steps*, on page 104
- *Lots of Scenarios*, on page 108
- *Big Ball of Mud*, on page 109

---

### Running Cucumber Tests in Parallel

If you're stuck with a slow set of features, a pragmatic option can be to run them in parallel. The simplest approach to this is to partition your features using tags or folders and then run each of those partitioned sets at the same time. Many continuous integration tools like Jenkins[a] allow you to delegate builds to slave machines so you can ensure that each partitioned set of features gets its own dedicated environment.

---

a.    http://jenkins-ci.org/

---

## Bored Stakeholders

"Our stakeholders don't read our features." This is a common complaint from teams that have tried Cucumber but failed to make it stick as anything other than a tool for automating their test scripts. Yet many other teams attest to the transformative effect Cucumber has had, helping development teams to collaborate much more effectively with their business stakeholders. What could be the difference between these two experiences?

The answer lies partly in starting with the right kind of collaborative relationship with those business stakeholders. If they think they're too busy to help you understand exactly what they want, then you have a deeper team problem that Cucumber can't help you solve. On the other hand, many teams who start out with keen and interested stakeholders waste the opportunity Cucumber gives them to build that collaborative relationship. When features are written by testers or developers working alone, they inevitably use technical terms that make the stakeholders feel marginalized when they read them. This becomes a vicious circle: as stakeholders lose interest, they spend less time helping write the features in a language that makes sense to them. Before you know it, the features have become nothing more than a testing tool.

This painful symptom is normally caused by a combination of the following underlying problems:

- *Incidental Details*, on page 95
- *Imperative Steps*, on page 97
- *Duplication*, on page 98
- *Ubiquitous What?*, on page 100
- *Siloed Features*, on page 101

Once you've spotted any of these symptoms in your team, you need to know what to do. It's time to look at the underlying problems that are at work and what you can do about them.

## Working Together

Cucumber features are what Gojko Adzic[1] calls *living documentation*. That term neatly sums up the two main benefits of using Cucumber:

- *Living:* It tests the system automatically so you can work on it safely.

- *Documentation:* It facilitates good communication about the current or planned behavior of the system.

When your team is struggling with Cucumber, the problems you're having will hit you in one of these two places. Either they'll result in Cucumber scenarios that provide poor feedback for the developers or they'll mean Cucumber fails to help your team communicate. We'll start by looking at what might be holding you back from making the features work as a communication tool.

### Incidental Details

Consider the following scenario for an online email client:

```
Scenario: Check inbox
  Given a User "Dave" with password "password"
  And a User "Sue" with password "secret"
  And an email to "Dave" from "Sue"
  When I sign in as "Dave" with password "password"
  Then I should see 1 email from "Sue" in my inbox
```

There is a lot of detail in this scenario: we have the username and password of the main actor, Dave, and we also have the username and password of another user, Sue. The usernames are quite useful, because they help tell the story of the scenario, but the passwords are just noise; the passwords of the users have nothing to do with what's being tested and in fact are making

---

1. *Specification by Example [Ad 11]*

it harder to read. For example, Sue has a different password than Dave. As you read the scenario, wondering whether this is relevant, you're distracted from the main point of the scenario: to check that Dave can see Sue's email.

We call details like the passwords *incidental details*,[2] which are details that are mentioned in the scenario but that actually have no relevance to the purpose of the scenario. This kind of irrelevant detail makes the scenario harder to read, which in turn can cause your stakeholders to lose interest in reading them. Let's rewrite the scenario without the passwords:

```
Scenario: Check inbox
  Given a User "Dave"
  And a User "Sue"
  And an email to "Dave" from "Sue"
  When I sign in as "Dave"
  Then I should see 1 email from "Sue" in my inbox
```

This is definitely an improvement, making it easier to read and understand the essence of the scenario. Let's try stripping away some more of the noise:

```
Scenario: Check inbox
  Given I have received an email from "Sue"
  When I sign in
  Then I should see 1 email from "Sue" in my inbox
```

Now we have a simple three-step scenario that's clear and concise. It's also more maintainable: if our product owner wants us to change the authentication mechanism, we can just rewrite the underlying step definition code without having to touch the features.

### Avoiding Incidental Details

If you're a programmer, you're probably practiced at filtering out irrelevant details as you read code each day. Bear that in mind when you write scenarios, because you may not even notice these incidental details slipping in.

Try to avoid being guided by existing step definitions when you write your scenarios and just write down exactly what you want to happen, in plain English. In fact, try to avoid programmers or testers writing scenarios on their own. Instead, get nontechnical stakeholders or analysts to write the first draft of each scenario from a purely business-focused perspective or ideally in a pair with a programmer to help them share their mental model. With a well-engineered support layer, you can confidently and quickly write new step definitions to match the way the scenario has been expressed.

---

2. This term comes from the excellent paper "Writing Maintainable Acceptance Tests" by Dale Emery: http://dhemery.com/pdf/writing_maintainable_automated_acceptance_tests.pdf.

## Imperative Steps

In computer programming, there are two contrasting styles for expressing the instructions you give to a computer to make it do something for you. These styles are called *imperative programming* and *declarative programming*.

Imperative programming means using a sequence of commands for the computer to perform in a particular order. Java is an example of an imperative language: you write a program as a series of statements that Java runs one at a time, in order. A declarative program tells the computer *what* it should do without prescribing precisely *how* to do it. CSS is an example of a declarative language: you tell the computer what you want the various elements on a web page to look like, and you leave it to take care of the rest.

Gherkin is, of course, an imperative language. Cucumber executes each of the steps in a scenario, one at a time, in the sequence you've written them in. However, that doesn't mean those steps need to be read like the instructions for assembling a piece of flat-pack furniture. Let's take a look at a typical example written in an imperative style:

```
Scenario: Redirect user to originally requested page after logging in
  Given a User "dave" exists with password "secret"
  And I am not logged in
  When I navigate to the home page
  Then I am redirected to the login form
  When I fill in "Username" with "dave"
  And I fill in "Password" with "secret"
  And I press "Login"
  Then I should be on the home page
```

What's good about this scenario? Well, it uses very generic step definitions, like `"^I fill in \"(.*)\" with \"(.*)\"$"`, which means you can write lots of scenarios like this without having to create much step definition code. You could also probably just about make the argument that it acts as a guide to what the user interface will look like, since it names the fields and buttons that will be used in the login form.

However, when a team uses such an imperative style for their step definitions, it won't be long before they're experiencing the pain of brittle tests *and* bored stakeholders. Scenarios written in this style are not only noisy, long, and boring to read, but they're easy to break: if the user-experience people decided to change the wording on the submit button from `Login` to `Log in`, the scenario will fail, for no good reason at all.

Worst of all, scenarios that use generic step definitions like this are failing to create their own domain language. The language of this scenario, using words and phrases like *fill in* and *press*, is expressed in the domain of user interface widgets, a generic and relatively low-level domain.

### Use a Declarative Style Instead

Let's raise the level of abstraction in this scenario and rewrite it using a more declarative style:

```
Scenario: Redirect user to originally requested page after logging in
  Given I am an unauthenticated User
  When I attempt to view some restricted content
  Then I am shown a login form
  When I authenticate with valid credentials
  Then I should be shown the restricted content
```

The beauty of this style is that it is not coupled to any specific implementation of the user interface. This same scenario could apply to a thick-client or mobile application. The words it uses aren't technical and are instead written in a language (*unauthenticated*, *restricted*, *credentials*) that any stakeholder interested in security should be able to clearly understand. It's by expressing every scenario at this level of abstraction that you discover your team's ubiquitous language.

It's true that using declarative style will mean you have to write more step definitions, but you can keep the code in those step definitions short and easy to maintain by pushing the actual work off into helper methods in your support code. We'll show you how to do this in Chapter 8, *Support Code*, on page 141.

## Duplication

All good computer programmers understand how destructive duplication is to the maintainability of their code. Yet we often see duplication rife in teams' Cucumber features. Duplication obviously makes your scenarios brittle, but it also makes them boring.

Gherkin has the Background and Scenario Outline keywords you can use to reduce duplication, as we showed you in Chapter 5, *Expressive Scenarios*, on page 69, but stay vigilant for where the duplication is a sign that your steps are written at too low a level of abstraction. If you have steps that are too imperative, any amount of moving them into Backgrounds or Scenario Outlines won't help you. Work with nontechnical members of your team to get their feedback about the kind of duplication they can accept and the kinds that make their eyes glaze over.

## The Spectrum from Imperative to Declarative

In Gherkin features, there isn't a clear line between imperative and declarative styles. Instead, there's a spectrum, and the right place on that spectrum for each step in each scenario depends on lots of things: the area of the system you're describing, the kind of application you're building, the domain expertise of the programmers, and the level of trust that the nontechnical stakeholders have in the programmers. If your stakeholders want to see a lot of detail in the features, it may indicate that you need to work on that trust, but it may just mean you're working on the kind of system that needs to be specified in lots of detail.

You can take declarative style too far, removing so much of the detail from a scenario that it loses its ability to tell a story:

```
Scenario: The whole system
  Given the system exists
  When I use it
  Then it should work, perfectly
```

This scenario is ridiculous, of course, but it illustrates what can happen when you raise the level of abstraction so high that your scenario doesn't tell the reader anything interesting at all. A team that used this scenario would need an incredibly high level of trust in their programmers. We're encouraging you to push your team toward the more abstract, declarative end of the spectrum, but as always, the most important thing is to work with your nontechnical stakeholders to get the level right for them.

### Let Your Examples Flow
by: Dan North

The DRY principle[3] (Don't Repeat Yourself) says that the definition of any concept should appear once and only once in your code. This is an admirable aim in that if you have to change the behavior of the system, you want to be able to change it in one place and be confident that your change will apply consistently across the codebase. If there are multiple definitions of that behavior scattered around the code, the chances are that not only will you not catch them all but someone before you didn't catch them all and the multiple definitions are already inconsistent, and who wants that?

However, when you are using examples to drive your code, there is another principle in play that I believe trumps the DRY principle: *the examples should tell a good story*. They are the documentation narrative that will guide future programmers (including you when you come back to change this code in three months time and you've forgotten what it does). In this case, clarity of intent is found in the quality of the narrative, not necessarily in minimizing duplication.

Some years ago I had my first experience of pair programming with Martin Fowler. That is, I had done quite a bit of pair programming, just not with Martin before. We were looking at some Ruby code I had written test-first, and Martin asked to see the tests "to find out what the code does." Then he did a rather odd thing. He started *moving the tests around*. I had a few helper

---

3.   *The Pragmatic Programmer: From Journeyman to Master [HT00]*

classes and utility methods in the source file, neatly at the end out of the way. He moved them up and dropped them inline just ahead of the first test that used them.

Madness! I thought—now the supporting code is all over the place! It really offended my sense of tidiness. But then I saw a pattern beginning to emerge: the test code was starting to read like a story. He would introduce these little methods and classes just before their one walk-on line in the narrative. It was quite an eye-opener for me. The test code flowed and unfolded the story of the class under test.

The a-ha! moment for me was when I imagined reading a book where the plot and characters had been DRYed out. Everything would be in footnotes or appendixes. All the character descriptions, plot elements, subtexts, and so on, would be carefully extracted into fully cross-referenced paragraphs. That is great if you are reading an encyclopedia but not so appropriate if you want to get into the flow and find out what happens. You would be forever flicking back and forth in the book, and you would very quickly forget where you even were in the story. In the words of the old joke, dictionaries have lousy plots, but at least they explain all the words as they go.

Some people refer to this as the DAMP principle: Descriptive and Meaningful Phrases. When you're writing examples, readability is paramount, and DAMP trumps DRY.

## Ubiquitous What?

The ubiquitous language your team uses will be driven by the domain you're working in. If you're building a system for live-music fans, your ubiquitous language will include words like *concert*, *performance*, *artist*, and *venue*. If you're building a catalog of TV shows, you'll have words like *broadcaster*, *genre*, *duration*, and *transmission date* in your ubiquitous language.

The point is for *everyone* on the team to use the same words, everywhere. It's not OK to have a database table called tbl_Performer if the rows in that table represent things that most of the team refers to as *artists*. Wherever you see schism like this, stop, decide which is the right word to use, make the appropriate correction, and then stick with it.

We talk about *developing* a ubiquitous language because it's an ongoing process. That development takes work. It takes effort to really listen to one another and agree on the words you'll use, and it takes discipline to stick to those commitments.

The rewards are great. Teams that use a ubiquitous language make fewer mistakes and *enjoy* their work more because they can communicate effectively about the work. When a team doesn't appreciate the value of a ubiquitous language, they'll be careless with the wording of their scenarios, missing a valuable opportunity to build strong bridges between the technical and business-focused sides of the team. When you try to correct people or clarify terminology, you might end up feeling like you're just being picky.

Take time to explain the concept of a ubiquitous language to your team and what its benefits are. Once everyone understands why it's important, you'll find they're much more willing to help make the effort to discuss and decide on the right words to use.

Used correctly, Cucumber helps a team to develop their ubiquitous language. When programmers and businesspeople work together to write scenarios, you'll find all kinds of arguments breaking out about how precisely to word things. Great! Each of those disagreements has exposed a potential misunderstanding between the two groups—in other words, a bug magnet. For a new team, these sessions can be hard at first, but as the language develops, they get easier and easier. *Three Amigos*, on page 101 is a good way to structure these meetings.

### Three Amigos

The best Gherkin scenarios are created when the three amigos come together, bringing three very different perspectives:

- The first amigo is a tester, who thinks about how to break things. The tester will typically come up with lots of scenarios, sometimes covering obscure edge cases and sometimes covering very important ones that no one else had thought of.

- The second amigo is a programmer, who thinks about how to make things. The programmer will typically add steps to scenarios, as he asks clarifying questions about what exactly should happen.

- The third amigo is the product owner, who cares about scope. When the tester thinks of scenarios that hit edge cases the product owner doesn't care about, she can tell the team to drop that scenario out of scope altogether, or the group can decide to test it with unit tests only. When the programmer explains that implementing a particular scenario will be complicated, the product owner has the authority to help decide on alternatives or to drop it altogether.

Many teams practicing BDD have found the three amigos make a great partnership for thrashing out Gherkin scenarios that the whole team believes in. You don't have to stop at three amigos, though: invite your team's user experience specialists or operations staff, for example, if the feature being discussed will affect them.

## Siloed Features

Cucumber can feel like a very technical tool. It's run from the command line, and the feature files are designed to be checked into source control along with the code that they test. Yet it's supposed to help the business stakeholders on your team feel more in control of the development process. When testers and developers tuck their features away in source control, the rest of the team can feel as though their documentation has been locked away in a cupboard to which they don't have the keys.

Your features act as a design tool for specifying new features, but they also act as a great reference document for what the system already does today. For a system of any significant size, no one person will remember exactly what it will do in every situation, so when you get a bug report from a user or are considering adding new functionality to some part of the system, you want this reference right at your side.

Cucumber itself has only limited support for sharing features in a way that's accessible for nontechnical audiences, but there are plenty of plug-ins and tools springing up around it that do. For example, if you use GitHub for source control, the pages for your project will have syntax-highlighted features that people can even comment on.

Relish[4] is a service that was created by members of the Cucumber and RSpec teams to provide an easy way to publish Cucumber features as documentation. The RSpec project now uses its Relish documentation as its home page, and your team can use it too.

You can achieve well over half of the benefit of Cucumber just by having the discipline to sit down with your business stakeholders and write scenarios collaboratively. The conversations sparked by that process will uncover so many potential bugs or schedule overruns that you'll already have made a huge win, even if you choose to never automate your features.

Assuming you do want to automate them, however, read on to find out how to do it well.

## Caring for Your Tests

The benefit of automating your features is that you'll be able to trust them as living documentation in the long run, because you'll be checking each scenario against the production code to make sure it's still valid. For the programmers working on the code, there's another benefit too: those tests act as a safety net when they're working on the system, alerting them to any mistakes they make that break existing behavior.

---

4.   http://relishapp.com

So, your features work as a feedback mechanism to the whole team about the behavior of the system and to the programmers about whether they've broken anything. For these feedback loops to be useful, the tests need to be fast and they need to be reliable. Let's start by looking at problems that affect the reliability of your tests.

## Leaky Scenarios

Cucumber scenarios are basically state-transition tests: you put the system into a Given state A, you perform action X (When), and Then you check that it has moved into expected state B. So, each scenario needs the system to be in a certain state before it begins, and yet each scenario also leaves the system in a new, dirty state when it's finished.

When the state of the system is not reset between tests, we say that they allow state to *leak* between them. This is a major cause of brittle tests.

When one scenario depends upon state left behind by another earlier scenario in order for it to pass, you've created a dependency between the two scenarios. When you have a chain of several scenarios depending on each other like this, it's only a matter of time before you end up with a train wreck.

If that first scenario—the one that happens to leave the system in just the right state for the next one to pick it up—is ever changed, the next scenario will suddenly start to fail. Even if you don't change that earlier scenario, what happens if you want to run only the second scenario on its own? Without the state leaked out by the earlier scenario, it will fail.

The opposite of this, *independent scenarios*, ensures they put the system into a clean state and then add their own data on top of it. This makes them able to stand on their own, rather than being coupled to the data left behind by other tests or shared fixture data. Investing in building up a good reliable library of *Test Data Builders*, on page 104 makes this much easier to achieve.

We can't stress enough how fundamental independent scenarios are to successful automated testing. Apart from the added reliability of scenarios that independently set up their own data, they're also clearer to read and debug. When you can see precisely what data is used by a scenario just by reading it, rather than having to root around in a fixture data script or, worse, in the database itself, you'll be able to understand and diagnose a failure much more easily.

> ## Test Data Builders
>
> You may already know the Test Data Builder[a] pattern (a specialization of the Builder pattern—see *Design Patterns: Elements of Reusable Object-Oriented Software [GHJV95]*). For the uninitiated, here's a quick summary of its benefits.
>
> Suppose you're testing a payroll system and you need to create a PayCheck record as part of a scenario. The way your domain model is structured, a PayCheck needs an Employee, and the Employee in turn needs an Address. Each of them also has a few mandatory fields. Instead of having to create all these objects individually in your step definition code or having a big fat set of fixture data, you can simply say this:
>
> ```
> @Given("^I have been paid$")
> public void i_have_been_paid() {
>   PayCheck paycheck = new PayCheckBuilder().build();
> }
> ```
>
> Once you've created a PayCheckBuilder, all you need to do is ask it for a PayCheck, and it'll create not only the PayCheck object but all the dependent objects as well, setting the mandatory fields with reasonable default values. If you care about a field having a specific value, you provide a method to override the default:
>
> ```
> @Given("^I have been paid 50 dollars$")
> public void i_have_been_paid_50_dollars() {
>   PayCheck paycheck = new PayCheckBuilder()
>     .dollarAmount(50)
>     .build();
> }
> ```
>
> When it's this easy to create data, you no longer need to carry around the baggage of big fixture data sets. There's a small amount of up-front investment in creating these builders, of course, but it quickly pays off in reliable, readable scenarios and step definition code.
>
> ---
>
> a.    http://www.natpryce.com/articles/000714.html

## Race Conditions and Sleepy Steps

If you write *full-stack* integration tests for a reasonably complex system, you'll eventually encounter this problem. Race conditions occur when two or more parts of the system are running in parallel, but success depends on a particular one of them finishing first. In the case of a Cucumber test, your When step might cause the system to start some work that it runs in the background, such as generating a PDF or updating a search index. If this background task happens to finish before Cucumber runs your Then step, the scenario will pass. If Cucumber wins the race and the Then step executes before the background task is finished, the scenario will fail.

When it's a close race, you'll have a flickering scenario, where the scenario will pass and fail intermittently. If there's a clear winner, a race condition can go unnoticed for a long time, until a new change to the system evens up the stakes and the scenario starts to fail at random.

A crude solution to this problem is to introduce a fixed-length pause, or *sleep*, into the scenario to give the system time to finish processing the background task. Although this is definitely a useful technique in the very short term to diagnose a race condition, you should resist the temptation to leave a sleep in your tests once you understand the cause of the problem. Introducing sleepy steps won't solve the flickering problem but just make it less likely to happen. In the meantime, you've added a few extra seconds to your total test runtime, swapping one set of problems for another.

If we really had to choose, we'd choose slow, reliable tests over faster unreliable ones, but there's no need to make this compromise. When testers and programmers pair up to automate scenarios, they can craft tests that are built with knowledge of how the system works. This means they can make use of cues from the system to let the tests know when it's safe to proceed, so instead of using crude fixed-length sleeps, the tests can proceed as quickly as possible. For an example of working with asynchronous code and further detail, see Chapter 9, *Message Queues and Asynchronous Components*, on page 169.

### Shared Environments

This is a problem that we've often found in teams that are transitioning from a manual acceptance testing regime to using automated acceptance tests. Traditionally, the manual testers on the team would have a special environment, often called *system test*, where a recent build of the system would be deployed. They'd run their manual tests in that environment, reporting bugs back to the development team. If more than one team member needed to run tests in that same environment, they'd communicate between each other to make sure they didn't tread on each other's toes.

If it's even slightly awkward to install the system in a new environment, the likelihood is that when the team starts to automate their tests, they'll follow the path of least resistance and point their test scripts at this existing system test environment. Now the environment is shared between not only the human members of the team but the test scripts too. Suppose a developer gets a bug report and wants to reproduce it for himself. He logs in to the system test environment and clicks a few buttons, but he doesn't realize the automated tests are running at the same time. As part of the steps to reproduce the bug, the developer unwittingly deletes a database record that the automated test

**Matt says:**
## Fixture Is an Overloaded Term

The word *fixture* has at least three meanings in the domain of automated testing, which can cause confusion. We've used the term *fixture data* in this chapter to mean data that's used to set up the context for a scenario or test case. This is the common meaning of the term as used in various xUnit testing tools.[a]

There is a long tradition (coming from the hardware world, where test fixtures originated) of calling the link between the test system and the system under test a fixture. This is the "glue code" role that we've referred to in this book as *automation code*. The FIT testing framework[b] uses this meaning of the term.

Some unit testing tools (such as NUnit) have further confused the issue by referring to the test case class itself as a fixture. So much for a ubiquitous language!

---

a.  *xUnit Test Patterns [Mes07]*
b.  http://fit.c2.com/

relied on, and the automated test fails. This kind of situation is a classic cause of flickering scenarios.

The shared use of a single environment can also contribute to unreliable tests by causing heavy and inconsistent load on in-demand resources like databases. When the shared database is under excessive load, normally reliable tests will time out and fail.

To deal with this problem, it needs to be so easy to spin up the system in a new environment that you can do it for fun. You need a *One-Click System Setup*, on page 107.

## Tester Apartheid

Testers are too often unfairly regarded as second-class citizens on a software team. As we'll explain in Chapter 8, *Support Code*, on page 141, developing a healthy suite of Cucumber features requires not only testing skill but programming skill too. When testers are left alone to build their own Cucumber tests, they may lack the software engineering skill to keep their step definition and support code well organized. Before you know it, the tests are a brittle muddle that people are scared to change.

Combat this problem by encouraging programmers and testers to work together when writing step definition and support code. The programmers can show the tester how to keep the code organized and factor out reusable components or libraries that other teams can use. By pairing with testers like

## One-Click System Setup

To avoid flickering scenarios that result from using shared environments, the team needs a setup script that will create a new instance of the system from scratch, at the click of a button.

If the system has a database, the database generated by the script should contain the latest schema, as well as any stored procedures, views, functions, and so on. It should contain just the very minimum baseline data necessary for the system to be able to function, such as configuration data. Any more should be left for the independent scenarios to create for themselves.

If there are message queues, or memcache daemons, the setup script should start them too, with the minimal configuration that you'd expect to be there on the running system.

this, programmers also develop a better understanding of what it takes to make their code *testable*.

When Cucumber is being used to good effect on a team, testers should be able to delegate the work of running basic checks to Cucumber. This frees them up to do the much more interesting, creative work of *exploratory testing*, as explained in *Agile Testing: A Practical Guide for Testers and Agile Teams* [CG08].

### Fixture Data

When manually testing a system, it's useful to populate it with realistic data so that you can wander around the system just like you would in the live application. When your team transitions from manual to automated tests, you can often be tempted to just port over a subset of production data so that the automated tests have a functioning system to work with right away.

The alternative, having each test set up its own data, might seem like it's just too hard. In a legacy system—especially one where the design has evolved organically—where creating the single object actually needed for the test you're working on means you need to create a huge tree of other dependent objects, you'll feel like the easiest option is just to create this tree once in the fixture data and then share it with all the other tests.

This approach has a couple of significant problems. A set of fixture data, even if it starts out relatively lean, will only tend to grow in size over time. As more and more scenarios come to rely on the data, each needing their own specific little tweaks, the size and complexity of the fixture data grows and grows. You'll start to feel the pain of brittle features when you make a change to the data for one scenario, but that change causes other scenarios to fail. Because you have so many different scenarios depending on the fixture data, you'll tend to plaster on more data because it's safer than changing the existing data. When a scenario does fail, it's hard to know which of the masses of data in the system could be relevant to the failure, making diagnosis much more difficult.

When you have a large set of fixture data, it can be slow to set it up between each test. This puts pressure on you to write leaky scenarios that don't reset the state of the system between each scenario, because it's quicker not to do so. We've already explained where this can lead.

We consider fixture data to be an antipattern. We much prefer using *Test Data Builders*, on page 104, where the relevant data is created within the test itself, rather than being buried away in a big tangled set of fixture data.

## Lots of Scenarios

It might seem like stating the obvious, but having a lot of scenarios is by far the easiest way to give yourself a slow overall feature run. We're not trying to suggest you give up on BDD and go back to cowboy coding, but we do suggest you treat a slow feature run as a red flag. Having lots of tests has other disadvantages than just waiting a long time for feedback. It's hard to keep a large set of features organized, making them awkward for readers to navigate around. Maintenance is also harder on the underlying step definitions and support code.

We find that teams that have a single humongous build also tend to have an architecture that could best be described as a big ball of mud. Because all of the behavior in the system is implemented in one place, all the tests have to live in one place, too, and have to all be run together as one big lump. This is a classic ailment of long-lived applications, which have grown organically without obvious interfaces between their subsystems.

We'll talk more about what to do with big balls of mud in the next section. It's really important to face up to this problem and tackle it once you realize it's happening, but it isn't a problem you'll be able to solve overnight.

In the meantime, you can keep your features organized using subfolders and tags (see Chapter 5, *Expressive Scenarios*, on page 69). Tagging is especially helpful, because you can use tags to partition your tests. You can choose to run partitioned sets of tests in parallel or even demote some of them to run in a *Nightly Build*, on page 109.

> ### Nightly Build
>
> When you have *Slow Features*, on page 93, caused by *Lots of Scenarios*, on page 108, it's worth considering splitting your build in two. Use tags to annotate the scenarios that should be run on every check-in, and demote the rest to a nightly build.
>
> Use of this pattern depends on your team's appetite for risk, as well as their tendency to make mistakes. The scenarios that should be demoted to a nightly build are the ones that rarely, if ever, fail. They're the scenarios for functionality that hasn't changed for months, and they cover stable code that isn't being worked on. They're the scenarios that if you had to, you'd be prepared to delete altogether.
>
> There's a maintenance overhead in keeping the tags for the check-in build on the right scenarios. Over time, some of those scenarios will stabilize and should be demoted to the nightly build, to be replaced by newer scenarios.
>
> Although a nightly build can be a good way to get you out of a hole, usually the right long-term solution is to break up your *Big Ball of Mud*, on page 109.

It's also worth thinking about whether some of the behavior you've specified in Cucumber scenarios could be pushed down and expressed in fast unit tests instead. Teams that enthusiastically embrace Cucumber sometimes forget to write unit tests as well and rely too much on slow integration tests for feedback. Try to think of your Cucumber scenarios as broad brush strokes that communicate the general behavior of the code to the business but still try to get as good a coverage as you can from fast unit tests. Help make this happen by having testers and programmers work in pairs when implementing Cucumber scenarios. This pair can make good decisions about whether a piece of behavior necessarily needs to be implemented in a slow, full-stack Cucumber scenario and drive out the behavior using a fast unit test instead.

## Big Ball of Mud

The "Big Ball of Mud"[5] is an ironic name given to the type of software design you see when nobody has made much effort to do any software design. In other words, it's a big, tangled mess.

We've explained where a big ball of mud will manifest itself as problems in your Cucumber tests: slow features, fixture data, and shared environments are all examples of the trouble it can cause. Look out for these signals and be brave about making changes to your system's design to make it easier to test.

---

5.   http://www.laputan.org/mud/

We suggest Alistair Cockburn's *ports and adapters* architecture[6] as a way of designing your system to be testable. Michael Feathers's *Working Effectively with Legacy Code [Fea04]* gives many practical examples of breaking up large systems that weren't designed to be tested.

Hold regular sessions with your team to talk about your architecture: what you like, what you don't like, and where you'd like to take it. It's easy to get carried away with ambitious ideas that evaporate into thin air soon after you get back to your desks, so make sure you try to leave these sessions with realistic, practical steps that will move you in the right direction.

That covers the most common problems you're likely to hit as you adopt Cucumber into your team. However, it's one thing to understand these problems, but it's quite another to get the time to do anything about them. Next we'll talk about an important technique for making that time.

## Stop the Line and Defect Prevention

Of all the activities that your team does, which do you think is the most important? Writing code for new features? Fixing bugs found in testing? Fixing bugs found in production? Speeding up your features?

Sadly, test maintenance does not come near the top of most software teams' list of priorities. If the elevators are broken in your office building, you can be sure that someone will be on the phone to the facilities team right away. When your tests are slow or brittle, the problem is invisible to everyone but the programmers and testers who rely on them. If you do test maintenance at all, you generally do it when things have gotten so bad that you can't stand it any longer, or you simply can't get a release out because the tests are so broken. There just always seems to be something more important to do.

Team members who think in this way about their tests have got it all wrong. The automated tests are the heartbeat of the team that relies on them, and they need meticulous care and attention to keep them healthy.

### Stop the Line at Toyota

In Toyota's manufacturing plants, every shop-floor worker has the authority and the responsibility to stop an entire production line whenever a problem arises. The problem is then given immediate and focused attention by experienced staff, and the line is restarted only once the problem has been resolved. Once the line has restarted, a team is tasked with performing a *root-cause analysis* on the problem to understand why it happened so that the source of the problem can be resolved.

---

6.  http://alistair.cockburn.us/Hexagonal+architecture

When Taiichi Ohno[7] first introduced this idea, his managers thought he was crazy. At the time, it was taken for granted within the manufacturing industry that the most important thing you could do was keep your assembly lines running, day and night if necessary.

When Ohno first told his managers to implement this new system, some of them listened and some of them didn't. At first, the managers who had implemented the policy saw their productivity drop. Stopping to deal with each problem immediately was slowing them down, and when they compared their output numbers with the managers who had ignored their boss, it looked like the boss had got it wrong.

Gradually, however, those managers who allowed their lines to stop and deal with every problem started to see their lines stopping less frequently. Because each problem was being dealt with using defect prevention, those lines had been investing in continuously improving the quality of the machines and processes that ran the line. That investment started to pay off, and their lines started to get faster and faster. Soon their output was much greater than that of the lines controlled by the managers who had ignored their apparently crazy boss. Their production lines were still clunking along at the same old rate, suffering the same old problems.

## Defect Prevention

Toyota's counterintuitive but hugely successful policy of stopping the line works because it's part of a wider process, known as *defect prevention*, that focuses on continuously improving the manufacturing system. Without this wider process, stop the line itself would have very little effect. There are four steps to this process:

1. Detect the abnormality.
2. Stop what you're doing.
3. Fix or correct the immediate problem.
4. Investigate the root cause and install a countermeasure.

This fourth step is crucial because it seizes the opportunity offered by the problem at hand to understand something more fundamental about your process. It also means that fixing things becomes a habit, rather than something you put off to do someday later when you're not in such a hurry.

For example, suppose the build has broken with a failing test. It turns out that the guy who pushed the commit with the failing test didn't run all the tests before he pushed. Why not? Well, it turns out that he thinks the tests take too long to run, so he ran just what he thought were the ones covering the change he made and then crossed his fingers and pushed his commit anyway. So, the underlying cause is that the features are slow. Now that we understand the root cause, we can work to fix it.

---

7. *Toyota Production System: Beyond Large Scale Production [Ohn88]*

Some teams keep a log of build failures, recording the root cause each time. When they have sufficient evidence that a particular root cause is worth tackling, they can put some concentrated effort into tackling it properly.

Imagine your team as a production line, cranking out valuable features for your users. If you spot a problem that's slowing the production line down, *stop the line* and fix the problem for good. Implementing stop the line means you've decided to make a fast, high-quality, reliable test run your whole team's top priority, second only to dealing with production issues that are affecting your customers. When there's a problem with the tests—whether that's an urgent problem like a failing test or a nagging annoyance like a flickering scenario—put your best people on it, and fix it forever.

## What We Just Learned

Cucumber features are a valuable asset to your company. We've seen teams that have ripped out and rewritten big parts of their systems, safe in the knowledge that they had a set of accurate, executable specifications to ensure the new solution worked just as well as the original. To those teams, the features were more valuable than the production code itself. If you're going to invest in writing Cucumber features, you need to protect that investment by caring for them so that they're as useful as possible to the whole team. Don't settle for features that are slow, that fail intermittently, or that are read by only half the team: iron out problems as they happen, and use each problem as a reason to make the tests even better than they were before.

Cucumber might just seem like a testing tool, but at its heart it's really a *collaboration* tool. If you make a genuine effort to write features that work as documentation for the nontechnical stakeholders on your team, you'll find you are forced to talk with them about details that you might never have otherwise made the time to talk about. Those conversations reveal insights about their understanding of the problem, insights that will help you build a much better solution than you would have otherwise. This is Cucumber's big secret: the tests and documentation are just a happy side effect; the real value lies in the knowledge you discover during those conversations.

### Try This

Here are some exercises for you to try for yourself.

### Defect Prevention on Your Team

Think of three things that are slowing down your team's production line. What is the root cause of each of them? What could you do to change them for the better?

### Incidental Details Practice

Here is a scenario, written in a hideously imperative style, riddled with incidental details:

```
Scenario: Create an invoice
  Given I am a signed-in user with role: admin
  And a client "Test Client" exists with name: "Test Client"
  And a project "Test Project" exists with:
    | name   | "Test Project"       |
    | client | client "Test Client" |
  And an issue "Test Issue" exists with:
    | project | project "Test Project" |
    | name    | "Test Issue"           |
  And a work_unit "Test Work Unit" exists with:
    | issue        | issue "Test Issue" |
    | completed_on | "2011-08-24"       |
    | hours        | "7.5"              |
  And I am on the admin invoices page
  Then I should see "Test Client"
  And I follow "Test Client"
  And I fill in "invoice_id" with "abc"
  And I press "Submit"
  Then I am on the admin invoices page
  And I should not see "Test Client"
```

Start by just trying to work out what's going on: what do you think this system does? What is the purpose of the scenario? What behavior is it trying to test? Notice how the incidental details are like overgrown weeds, getting in the way of you figuring out what the test is actually trying to do.

Now that you understand the *essence* of the scenario, rewrite it in your own words. You should need much fewer steps, but you might want to consider using more than one scenario.

Now that you've rewritten the scenario in a more declarative style, can you spot the crucial Then step that was missing from the original scenario?

# Part II

# A Worked Example

*The next few chapters are going to take you through a worked example. Although it will probably be smaller and simpler than the applications you normally work on, it uses real-world tools and solves real-world problems. Not only will you quickly learn how to turn your specifications into automated acceptance tests using Cucumber, but you'll soon be finding out how to deal with complex problems, such as asynchronous processes and database transactions.*

*And because we know that you're dealing with real-world problems we'll also show you powerful techniques for keeping your automated acceptance tests easy to maintain and fast to run.*

# CHAPTER 7

# Step Definitions: On the Inside

It's time to pull together everything that you've learned in the first part of the book and use it in practice. There are a few advanced concepts left about Cucumber that we want to explain to you, and they'll be much easier to demonstrate with an example. A lot of what we'll do in this part of the book will blur the line between testing and development. If you're more of a tester than a developer, don't let that worry you: the Java code we'll build is just about as simple as it gets. By following along, you'll get a good sense of how we like to work, as well as pick up some new knowledge about working with Cucumber.

At the end of *Returning Results*, on page 58, we'd just started work on a greenfield project to build the software for an ATM. We had a single scenario for the most important behavior of the system: letting someone walk up to the machine and withdraw cash.

step_definitions_inside/01/src/test/resources/cash_withdrawal.feature
```
Feature: Cash Withdrawal
  Scenario: Successful withdrawal from an account in credit
    Given I have deposited $100 in my account
    When I request $20
    Then $20 should be dispensed
```

Now we're going to pick up this scenario and work outside-in, designing the system as we go, just as we would on a real project. In this chapter, we'll get the scenario to pass by driving out a simple domain model for our ATM. Then, in the next chapter, we'll get a nasty surprise when we discover that there's a missing step in our scenario. Finally, we'll demonstrate the benefits of well-engineered test code by introducing a user interface around the domain model.

By the end of this chapter, you'll have learned about how you can manage state that's shared between step definitions. We'll write some custom helper methods that will introduce a layer of decoupling between our step definitions and the application we're building. We'll show you how to use *transforms* to reduce duplication in your step definitions and make it easier to work with meaningful datatypes. Finally, we'll show you how we like to organize the files in our projects so that they're easy to work with and maintain.

## Sketching Out the Domain Model

The heart of any object-oriented program is the domain model. When we start to build a new system, we like to work directly with the domain model. This allows us to iterate and learn quickly about the problem we're working on without getting distracted by user interface gizmos. Once we have a domain model that really reflects our understanding of the system, it's easy to wrap it in a pretty skin.

We're going to let Cucumber drive our work, building the domain model classes directly in the step definitions. As usual, we start by running mvn clean test on our scenario to remind us what to do next:

```
-------------------------------------------------------
 T E S T S
-------------------------------------------------------
Running RunCukesTest
Feature: Cash Withdrawal

  Scenario: Successful withdrawal from an account in credit
    Given I have deposited $100 in my account
    When I request $20
      cucumber.api.PendingException: TODO: implement me
        at nicebank.Steps.iRequest$(Steps.java:22)
        at *.When I request $20(cash_withdrawal.feature:4)
    Then $20 should be dispensed

1 Scenarios (1 pending)
3 Steps (1 skipped, 1 pending, 1 passed)
0m0.090s

cucumber.api.PendingException: TODO: implement me
        at nicebank.Steps.iRequest$(Steps.java:22)
        at *.When I request $20(cash_withdrawal.feature:4)
```

When we last worked on this scenario, we'd just reached the point where we had written the regular expressions for each of our step definitions and implemented the first one. Here's how our steps file looks:

`step_definitions_inside/01/src/test/java/nicebank/Steps.java`

```java
package nicebank;

import cucumber.api.java.en.*;
import cucumber.api.PendingException;

public class Steps {

  class Account {
    public Account(int openingBalance) {
    }
  }

  @Given("^I have deposited \\$(\\d+) in my account$")
  public void iHaveDeposited$InMyAccount(int amount) throws Throwable {
      new Account(amount);
  }

  @When("^I request \\$(\\d+)$")
  public void iRequest$(int arg1) throws Throwable {
      // Write code here that turns the phrase above into concrete actions
      throw new PendingException();
  }

  @Then("^\\$(\\d+) should be dispensed$")
  public void $ShouldBeDispensed(int arg1) throws Throwable {
      // Write code here that turns the phrase above into concrete actions
      throw new PendingException();
  }
}
```

In that first step definition, we create an instance of our new Account class. Cucumber then tells us that we need to work on our second step definition, which is still marked as Pending. Before we do that, let's review the code in our step definition and see what we think. There are a few things we're not happy about:

- Some inconsistent language is creeping in; the step talks about *depositing* funds, but the code passes funds to the Account constructor.

- The step is lying to us! It says Given I have deposited $100 in my account, and it's passed. Yet we know from our implementation that nothing has been deposited anywhere.

- Bank balances don't always contain whole numbers of dollars, but our step definition uses an int. We should be able to deposit dollars and cents.

We'll work through each of these points before we move on to the next step in the scenario.

## Getting the Words Right

We want to clarify the wording before we do anything else, so let's think about how we could make the code in the step definition read more like the text in the step. We could go back and reword the step to say something like Given an Account with a balance of $100. In reality, though, the only way that an account would have a balance is if someone deposited funds into it. So, let's change the way we talk to the domain model inside our step definition to reflect that:

step_definitions_inside/02/src/test/java/nicebank/Steps.java
```
class Account {
  public void deposit(int amount) {

  }
}
```

step_definitions_inside/02/src/test/java/nicebank/Steps.java
```
@Given("^I have deposited \\$(\\d+) in my account$")
public void iHaveDeposited$InMyAccount(int amount) throws Throwable {
    Account myAccount = new Account();
    myAccount.deposit(amount);
}
```

That seems better.

There's something else in the wording that bothers us. In the step, we talk about *my account*, which implies the existence of a protagonist in the scenario who has a relationship to the account, perhaps a Customer. This is a sign that we're probably missing a domain concept. However, until we get to a scenario where we have to deal with more than one customer, we'd prefer to keep things simple and focus on designing the fewest classes we need to get this scenario running. So, we'll park this concern for now.

## Telling the Truth

Now that we're happier with the interface to our Account class, we can resolve the next issue from our code review. After we've deposited the funds in the account, we can check its balance with an assertion:

step_definitions_inside/03/src/test/java/nicebank/Steps.java
```
@Given("^I have deposited \\$(\\d+) in my account$")
public void iHaveDeposited$InMyAccount(int amount) throws Throwable {
    Account myAccount = new Account();
    myAccount.deposit(amount);

    Assert.assertEquals("Incorrect account balance -",
                        amount, myAccount.getBalance());
}
```

We've used a JUnit assertion here, but if you prefer another assertion library, feel free to use that. It might seem odd to put an assertion in a Given step, but it communicates to future readers of this code what state we expect the system to be in once the step has run. We'll need to add a balance method to the Account so that we can run this code:

```
step_definitions_inside/03/src/test/java/nicebank/Steps.java
class Account {
    public void deposit(int amount) {
    }

    public int getBalance() {
      return 0;
    }
}
```

Notice that we're just sketching out the interface to the class, rather than adding any implementation to it. This way of working is fundamental to outside-in development. We try not to think about *how* the Account is going to work yet but concentrate on *what* it should be able to do.

Now when we run the test, we get a nice helpful failure message:

```
  Scenario: Successful withdrawal from an account in credit
    Given I have deposited $100 in my account
      java.lang.AssertionError: Incorrect account balance
                                          - expected:<100> but was:<0>
        at org.junit.Assert.fail(Assert.java:88)
        at org.junit.Assert.failNotEquals(Assert.java:743)
        at org.junit.Assert.assertEquals(Assert.java:118)
        at org.junit.Assert.assertEquals(Assert.java:555)
        at nicebank.Steps.iHaveDeposited$InMyAccount(Steps.java:29)
        at *.Given I have deposited $100 in my account(cash_withdrawal.feature:3)
    When I request $20
    Then $20 should be dispensed

1 Scenarios (1 failed)
3 Steps (1 failed, 2 skipped)
0m0.076s

java.lang.AssertionError: Incorrect account balance
                                    - expected:<100> but was:<0>
```

Now our step definition is much more robust, because we know it will sound an alarm bell if it isn't able to deposit the funds into the account as we've asked it to do. Adding assertions to Given and When steps like this means that if there's ever a regression later in the project, it's much easier to diagnose because the scenario will fail right where the problem occurs. This technique is most useful when you're sketching things out; eventually, we'll probably move this check further down the testing stack into a *unit test* for the Account class and take it out of the step definition.

## Doing the Simplest Thing

We're at a decision point here. We've effectively finished implementing our first step definition, but we can't move on to the next one until we've made some changes to the implementation of the Account class so that the step passes.

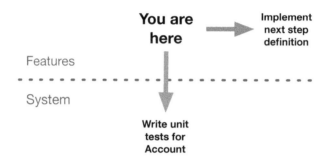

It's tempting to pause here, move the Account class into a separate file, and start driving out the behavior we want using unit tests. We're going to try to resist that temptation for now and stay on the outside of the Account class. If we can get a full tour through the scenario from this perspective, we'll be more confident in the design of the class's interface once we do step inside and start implementing it.

So, we'll keep working on our very simple implementation of the Account class that's obviously incomplete but just right enough to make this first step pass. Think of this like putting up scaffolding on a construction site: we're going to take it down eventually, but it will help things to stand up in the meantime.

Change Account to look like this, and now the first step should pass:

```
step_definitions_inside/04/src/test/java/nicebank/Steps.java
class Account {
    private int balance;

    public void deposit(int amount) {
        balance += amount;
    }

    public int getBalance() {
      return balance;
    }
}
```

Good. We still have one issue left on our list, which is our use of int as our balance. Now that our step is passing, we can do that refactoring with confidence.

## Staying Honest with Transforms

Another issue we have with the first step definition is that our regular expression is capturing an integer, but we would expect to be able to deposit dollars and cents into the account. So let's change the feature to demonstrate this:

**step_definitions_inside/05/src/test/resources/cash_withdrawal.feature**
```
Feature: Cash Withdrawal
  Scenario: Successful withdrawal from an account in credit
    Given I have deposited $100.00 in my account
    When I request $20
    Then $20 should be dispensed
```

Now when we run mvn clean test it reports that we have an undefined step definition and tells us what regular expression we now need to use to match our feature:

```
Feature: Cash Withdrawal

  Scenario: Successful withdrawal from an account in credit
    Given I have deposited $100.00 in my account
    When I request $20
    Then $20 should be dispensed


1 Scenarios (1 undefined)
3 Steps (2 skipped, 1 undefined)
0m0.000s


You can implement missing steps with the snippets below:

@Given("^I have deposited \\$(\\d+)\\.(\\d+) in my account$")
public void iHaveDeposited$InMyAccount(int arg1, int arg2) throws Throwable {
    // Write code here that turns the phrase above into concrete actions
    throw new PendingException();
}


Tests run: 5, Failures: 0, Errors: 0, Skipped: 4, Time elapsed: 0.458 sec
```

Cucumber has recognized two numbers in the step and has generated a regular expression that is capturing each separately and passing them as two integers to our step definition. Rather than pass two integers around, we're going to use a Money class written specially for this example, which you can find in src/main/java/nicebank.

**Seb says:**
**Do We Really Have to Reinvent Money?**

You might think that a language like Java would have its own money class, but as of this writing it doesn't. There are a number of classes available, such as Joda Money, but we're still waiting for JSR 354 (which will define a Java Money class) to be released.

In our step definition we can now create an instance of the Money class:

step_definitions_inside/06/src/test/java/nicebank/Steps.java
```java
@Given("^I have deposited \\$(\\d+)\\.(\\d+) in my account$")
public void iHaveDeposited$InMyAccount(int dollars, int cents) throws Throwable {
    Account myAccount = new Account();
    Money amount = new Money(dollars, cents);
    myAccount.deposit(amount);

    Assert.assertEquals("Incorrect account balance -",
                        amount, myAccount.getBalance());
}
```

And we change our implementation of Account to handle deposits of Money:

step_definitions_inside/06/src/test/java/nicebank/Steps.java
```java
class Account {
    private Money balance = new Money();

    public void deposit(Money amount) {
        balance = balance.add(amount);
    }

    public Money getBalance() {
      return balance;
    }
}
```

This is fine, but it still means that we have to create an instance of Money in every step definition that works with dollars and cents. It would be much nicer if Cucumber could just pass a Money object directly to the step definition.

The first thing we need to do to make this happen is to change the step definition so that:

- the regular expression captures the whole amount in a single capture group

- its signature expects a Money parameter

## Auto-Conversion Magic

Have you wondered how Cucumber knows what arguments to use in the step definition snippets it generates? First, it generates one argument per capture group in the regular expression. Then, for each capture group, if it matches only numbers it creates an int parameter; otherwise it creates a String parameter. For example:

```
@Given("^a (\\w+) amount \\$(\\d+)$")
public void aDollarAmount$(String arg1, int arg2) throws Throwable {
}
```

What if you wanted to manipulate digits as a String? No problem—these snippets are just a hint from Cucumber to you. If you'd like to work with a different type, then just change the signature of the step definition, like so:

```
@Given("^a (\\w+) amount \\$(\\d+)$")
public void aDollarAmount$(String arg1, String arg2) throws Throwable {
}
```

Under the hood, Cucumber represents each capture group in the regular expression as a String. Then, when calling the step definition it converts the String into the type expected. If it can't perform the conversion, it throws a cucumber.runtime.CucumberException, but otherwise the conversion happens automatically—as if by magic.

step_definitions_inside/07/src/test/java/nicebank/Steps.java
```
@Given("^I have deposited \\$(\\d+\\.\\d+) in my account$")
public void iHaveDeposited$InMyAccount(Money amount) throws Throwable {
    Account myAccount = new Account();
    myAccount.deposit(amount);

    Assert.assertEquals("Incorrect account balance -",
                        amount, myAccount.getBalance());
}
```

Now all we need to do is tell Cucumber how to convert a String object into a Money object. One approach would be to give our Money class a single argument constructor that takes a String. Cucumber would then automatically invoke this constructor when calling the step definition, passing in the original String that matched the regular expression in our capture group.

step_definitions_inside/07/src/main/java/nicebank/Money.java
```
public Money(String amount) {
    Pattern pattern = Pattern.compile("^[^\\d]*([\\d]+)\\.([\\d][\\d])$");
    Matcher matcher = pattern.matcher(amount);

    matcher.find();
    this.dollars = Integer.parseInt(matcher.group(1));
    this.cents = Integer.parseInt(matcher.group(2));
}
```

But what if the Money didn't have a String constructor and wasn't ours to modify? In that case, we're going to need to learn about another Cucumber feature, the Transformer class, which allows us to create the instances of Money that we want without giving it a new constructor.

Transformers work on captured arguments. Each transform is responsible for converting a captured String into something more meaningful. For example, we can use a Transformer to take a String argument that contains a monetary amount and turn it into an instance of our Money class. Let's create a MoneyConverter transformer and put it in a new folder, test/transforms:

```
step_definitions_inside/08/src/test/java/transforms/MoneyConverter.java
package transforms;

import cucumber.api.Transformer;

import nicebank.Money;

public class MoneyConverter extends Transformer<Money> {
    public Money transform(String amount) {
        String[] numbers = amount.split("\\.");

        int dollars = Integer.parseInt(numbers[0]);
        int cents = Integer.parseInt(numbers[1]);

        return new Money(dollars, cents);
    }
}
```

Then we annotate the parameter in the step definition to tell Cucumber which Transformer to use:

```
step_definitions_inside/08/src/test/java/nicebank/Steps.java
@Given("^I have deposited \\$(\\d+\\.\\d+) in my account$")
public void iHaveDeposited$InMyAccount(
                        @Transform(MoneyConverter.class) Money amount)
                                                    throws Throwable {
    Account myAccount = new Account();
    myAccount.deposit(amount);

    Assert.assertEquals("Incorrect account balance -",
                    amount, myAccount.getBalance());
}
```

Great! That code looks much cleaner and easier to read.

We can tidy this up a little further by moving the dollar sign into the capture group. This makes the code more cohesive, because we're bringing together the whole regular expression statement for capturing the amount of funds deposited. It also gives us the option to capture other currencies in the future.

step_definitions_inside/09/src/test/java/nicebank/Steps.java
```
@Given("^I have deposited (\\$\\d+\\.\\d+) in my account$")
public void iHaveDeposited$InMyAccount(
                          @Transform(MoneyConverter.class) Money amount)
                                                    throws Throwable {

    Account myAccount = new Account();
    myAccount.deposit(amount);

    Assert.assertEquals("Incorrect account balance -",
                        amount, myAccount.getBalance());
}
```

Of course we have to make a corresponding change to MoneyConverter to ensure it handles the currency sign correctly. For the time being (since we're not handling multiple currencies) we'll just discard the dollar sign:

step_definitions_inside/09/src/test/java/transforms/MoneyConverter.java
```
String[] numbers = amount.substring(1).split("\\.");
```

Let's take another look at our to-do list. Using the transform has cleared up the final point from the initial code review. As we went along, we collected a new to-do list item: that we need to implement the Account properly, with unit tests. Let's leave that one on the list for now and move on to the next step of the scenario.

## Adding Custom Helper Methods

We've implemented the first step of our scenario to set up an account with a sufficient balance that the withdrawal should work. After all that talking about transforms, it's hard to remember exactly what we need to do next, but we can always rely on cucumber to remind us where we are:

```
Feature: Cash Withdrawal

  Scenario: Successful withdrawal from an account in credit
    Given I have deposited $100.00 in my account
    When I request $20
      cucumber.api.PendingException: TODO: implement me
        at nicebank.Steps.iRequest$(Steps.java:44)
        at *.When I request $20(cash_withdrawal.feature:4)
    Then $20 should be dispensed

1 Scenarios (1 pending)
3 Steps (1 skipped, 1 pending, 1 passed)
0m0.099s
```

```
cucumber.api.PendingException: TODO: implement me
        at nicebank.Steps.iRequest$(Steps.java:44)
        at *.When I request $20(cash_withdrawal.feature:4)
```

```
Tests run: 5, Failures: 0, Errors: 0, Skipped: 3, Time elapsed: 0.509 sec
```

The first step is passing as we'd expect, and the second one is failing with a
pending message. So, our next task is to implement the step to simulate a
customer withdrawing cash from the ATM. Here's the empty step definition:

**step_definitions_inside/09/src/test/java/nicebank/Steps.java**
```java
@When("^I request \\$(\\d+)$")
public void iRequest$(int arg1) throws Throwable {
  // Write code here that turns the phrase above into concrete actions
  throw new PendingException();
}
```

We need somewhere to withdraw the cash from, which means we need to
bring a new actor into this scenario. This new class is going to handle our
request to withdraw cash from our account. If we walked into a bank in real
life, that role would be played by a *teller*. Thinking outside-in again, let's
sketch out the code we'd like:

```java
@When("^I request \\$(\\d+)$")
public void iRequest$(int amount) throws Throwable {
  Teller teller = new Teller();
  teller.withdrawFrom(myAccount, amount);
}
```

That looks pretty good. The teller will need to know which account to take
the cash from and how much to take. There's a little inconsistency creeping
into the language again, though: the step definition talks about *requesting*
the cash, but in the code we're *withdrawing* it. *Withdraw* is the term we use
most often, so let's change the text in the scenario to match.

**step_definitions_inside/10/src/test/resources/cash_withdrawal.feature**
```
Feature: Cash Withdrawal
  Scenario: Successful withdrawal from an account in credit
    Given I have deposited $100.00 in my account
    When I withdraw $20
    Then $20 should be dispensed
```

**step_definitions_inside/10/src/test/java/nicebank/Steps.java**
```java
@When("^I withdraw \\$(\\d+)$")
public void iWithdraw$(int arg1) throws Throwable {
    Teller teller = new Teller();
    teller.withdrawFrom(myAccount, amount);
}
```

That's better. Now the language in the scenario more closely reflects what's going on in the code beneath it. Run mvn clean test again, and you should be prompted to create a Teller class. Let's create one:

step_definitions_inside/11/src/test/java/nicebank/Steps.java
```
class Teller {
    public void withdrawFrom(Account account, int dollars) {

    }
}
```

Again, we've just sketched out the interface for now, without adding any implementation. With that in place, try running mvn clean test again:

```
[INFO] ------------------------------------------------------------
[ERROR] COMPILATION ERROR :
[INFO] ------------------------------------------------------------
[ERROR] src/test/java/nicebank/Steps.java:[52,28] error: cannot find symbol
[INFO] 1 error
```

A-ha. We defined myAccount in the first step definition, but when we try to use it in the second step definition, Java can't see it. How can we make myAccount available to both step definitions? The answer lies in understanding something fundamental about how Cucumber executes step definitions.

## Sharing State Between Steps

Before Cucumber can execute a step definition, it creates an instance of the class that defines the step definition. Only one instance of each step definition class is created while executing a scenario. And once the scenario has finished, Cucumber throws away all those step definition instances to ensure that each scenario runs in isolation from all the others.

Just like methods on a regular Java class, we can use *instance variables* to pass state between step definitions that are defined in the same class. Here's how the code looks with myAccount stored as an instance variable in the step definition:

```
private Account myAccount;

@Given("^I have deposited (\\$\\d+\\.\\d\\d) in my account$")
public void iHaveDeposited$InMyAccount(
                        @Transform(MoneyConverter.class) Money amount)
                                              throws Throwable {
    myAccount = new Account();
    myAccount.deposit(amount);

    Assert.assertEquals("Incorrect account balance -", amount, myAccount.balance());
}
```

```java
@When("^I withdraw \\$(\\d+)$")
public void iWithdraw$(int dollars) throws Throwable {
    Teller teller = new Teller();
    teller.withdrawFrom(helper.getMyAccount(), dollars);
}
```

Try it. It works!

This solution is OK, but we don't like leaving instance variables in step definitions. The problem with instance variables is that if you don't set them they just stay null. We hate nulls, because they creep around your system, causing weird bugs that are hard to track down. For example, if someone were to later come along and use the second step definition in another scenario that hadn't already set myAccount, a null would get passed into Teller.withdrawFrom.

Cucumber uses *dependency injection* to facilitate sharing state between steps. (We talk about this later in the chapter, in *Dependency Injection*, on page 137.) For now we'll create a helper class to share our state between steps.

## Creating a Custom Helper Class

In a regular class we might avoid nulls by putting the instance variables behind an accessor method, like this:

```java
private Account myAccount;

public Account getMyAccount() {
  if (myAccount == null){
    myAccount = new Account();
  }
  return myAccount;
}
```

We can do the same in Cucumber. Let's define a new helper class and then use it in our step definitions. Here's what we could do:

```java
step_definitions_inside/12/src/test/java/nicebank/Steps.java
class KnowsMyAccount {
    private Account myAccount;

    public Account getMyAccount() {
      if (myAccount == null){
        myAccount = new Account();
      }

      return myAccount;
    }
}
```

We've defined getMyAccount on a class KnowsMyAccount. We then create a step definition constructor where we create an instance of this helper class:

step_definitions_inside/12/src/test/java/nicebank/Steps.java
```
KnowsMyAccount helper;

public Steps() {
  helper = new KnowsMyAccount();
}
```

This means we can get rid of the code that initializes the Account from the first step definition, and we can get rid of the Account instance variable, so the step definitions can use the getMyAccount method instead:

step_definitions_inside/12/src/test/java/nicebank/Steps.java
```
@Given("^I have deposited (\\$\\d+\\.\\d+) in my account$")
public void iHaveDeposited$InMyAccount(
                            @Transform(MoneyConverter.class) Money amount)
                                                    throws Throwable {

    helper.getMyAccount().deposit(amount);

    Assert.assertEquals("Incorrect account balance -",
                        amount, helper.getMyAccount().getBalance());
}

@When("^I withdraw \\$(\\d+)$")
public void iWithdraw$(int dollars) throws Throwable {
    Teller teller = new Teller();
    teller.withdrawFrom(helper.getMyAccount(), dollars);
}
```

With this change in place, run mvn clean test, and the first two steps should now be passing.

## Designing Our Way to the Finish Line

Now let's try to get our final step to pass. We can see that the first two steps are passing and the final one is pending. Almost there! Let's take a look at that last step definition:

step_definitions_inside/12/src/test/java/nicebank/Steps.java
```
@Then("^\\$(\\d+) should be dispensed$")
public void $ShouldBeDispensed(int arg1) throws Throwable {
  // Write code here that turns the phrase above into concrete actions
  throw new PendingException();
}
```

The big question here is: where will the cash be dispensed? Which part of the system can we examine for evidence of whether it doled out the money? It seems as if we're missing a domain concept. In the physical ATM, the cash will end up poking out of a slot on the ATM, something like this:

step_definitions_inside/13/src/test/java/nicebank/Steps.java
```
@Then("^\\$(\\d+) should be dispensed$")
public void $ShouldBeDispensed(int dollars) throws Throwable {
    Assert.assertEquals("Incorrect amount dispensed -",
                                    dollars, helper.getCashSlot().contents());
}
```

That looks good. When we hook our code up to the real hardware, we're going to need some way of talking to it, and this object will work fine as a *test double* in the meantime. Let's start running mvn clean test to drive this out. First it tells us that we need to define the getCashSlot method, of course. Let's add another method to our helper class and rename it to reflect its new role.

step_definitions_inside/13/src/test/java/nicebank/Steps.java
```
class KnowsTheDomain {
    private Account myAccount;
    private CashSlot cashSlot;

    public Account getMyAccount() {
      if (myAccount == null){
        myAccount = new Account();
      }

      return myAccount;
    }

    public CashSlot getCashSlot() {
      if (cashSlot == null){
        cashSlot = new CashSlot();
      }

      return cashSlot;
    }
}
```

We run mvn clean test again, and this time it wants us to define the CashSlot class, so let's go ahead and do as we're told. Again, we just build a sketch of the interface we want to use, with minimal implementation:

step_definitions_inside/14/src/test/java/nicebank/Steps.java
```
class CashSlot {
    public int getContents() {
        return 0;
    }
}
```

Now when you run `mvn clean test`, you'll see we've moved closer to our goal: all the classes and methods are wired up, and our final step is failing just because there's no cash coming out of the CashSlot:

```
java.lang.AssertionError: Incorrect amount dispensed
                             - expected:<20> but was:<0>
      at org.junit.Assert.fail(Assert.java:88)
      at org.junit.Assert.failNotEquals(Assert.java:743)
      at org.junit.Assert.assertEquals(Assert.java:118)
      at org.junit.Assert.assertEquals(Assert.java:555)
      at nicebank.Steps.$ShouldBeDispensed(Steps.java:95)
      at *.Then $20 should be dispensed(cash_withdrawal.feature:5)
```

To get this last step to pass, someone needs to tell the CashSlot to dispense the cash when the customer makes a withdrawal. It's the Teller who's in charge of the transaction, but at the moment it doesn't know anything about the CashSlot. We'll use *dependency injection* to pass the CashSlot in to Teller's constructor. Now we can imagine a new CashSlot method that the Teller can use to tell it to dispense the cash:

**step_definitions_inside/15/src/test/java/nicebank/Steps.java**
```
class Teller {
    private CashSlot cashSlot;

    public Teller(CashSlot cashSlot) {
        this.cashSlot = cashSlot;
    }

    public void withdrawFrom(Account account, int dollars) {
        cashSlot.dispense(dollars);
    }
}
```

This seems like the simplest implementation of Teller that we need to get the scenario to pass. It's odd that when we designed this method from the outside we thought we'd need the account parameter, but now we don't seem to need it. Let's stay focused, though; we'll make a note on our to-do list to look into this later and carry on getting this step to pass.

There are two changes we need to make now. We need to add the new dispense method to CashSlot, and we have to change the second step definition to create the Teller correctly:

```
@When("^I withdraw $(\\d+)$")
public void iWithdraw$(int dollars) {
  Teller teller = new Teller(helper.getCashSlot());
  teller.withdrawFrom(helper.getMyAccount(), dollars);
}
```

This call to new Teller() seems out of place in a step definition now. All our other classes are created inside our helper class, so let's do the same with Teller. This means our step definition becomes a lot less cluttered:

step_definitions_inside/15/src/test/java/nicebank/Steps.java
```
@When("^I withdraw \\$(\\d+)$")
public void iWithdraw$(int dollars) throws Throwable {
    helper.getTeller().withdrawFrom(helper.getMyAccount(), dollars);
}
```

The step definition code all reads very nicely now. Pushing some of the details down into our helper class means the step definition code is at a *higher level of abstraction*. This makes it less of a mental leap when you come into the step definitions from a business-facing scenario, because the code doesn't contain too much detail.

This scenario isn't going to pass until we do some work on our CashSlot, though. Our new class is still missing the dispense method. A simple implementation should get this working:

step_definitions_inside/15/src/test/java/nicebank/Steps.java
```
class CashSlot {
    private int contents;

    public int getContents() {
        return contents;
    }

    public void dispense(int dollars){
        contents = dollars;
    }
}
```

Run mvn clean test one last time, and you should see the scenario pass.

Excellent! Go and grab a drink—then we can sit down, review the code, and do some refactoring.

## Organizing the Code

Before we finish this session, let's be kind to our future selves and tidy up a little. As we worked, we just created everything we needed inline in our src/test/java/nicebank/Steps.java file. We'll move most of that stuff out of there, and put it into a more conventional place. Here's a list of what we'd like to fix:

- The application's domain model classes should move into the src/main/java tree.

- The KnowsTheDomain class can move into its own file.

- The Steps file can be split to organize the step definitions better. This is arguably unnecessary for a project with only three step definitions, but we'll do it anyway to illustrate how we'd do this on a bigger project.

## Separating the Application Code

It's conventional in Java projects to store the system's code in an src folder in the root of the project. Normally your production code would be created in a relevantly named package. Our company is trying to stand out from the crowd with the brand name NiceBank, so we'll put our production code into the folder src/main/java/nicebank alongside the Money class that has already been written.

Let's move the three classes, Account, Teller, and CashSlot, into the files Account.java, Teller.java, and CashSlot.java in the src/main/java/nicebank folder. As we do this, we'll need to specify that the classes are in the nicebank package and make them public.

Since Steps is also in the nicebank package, no imports are needed.

Save the files and run mvn clean test.

## Dry Run

As we start to move files around, it's useful to test that everything still matches using Cucumber's "dry run" feature. A dry run aims to parse your features and step definitions but not actually run any of them.

step_definitions_inside/16/src/test/java/RunCukesTest.java
```
import cucumber.api.junit.Cucumber;
import cucumber.api.CucumberOptions;
import cucumber.api.SnippetType;
import org.junit.runner.RunWith;

@RunWith(Cucumber.class)
@CucumberOptions(plugin="pretty", snippets=SnippetType.CAMELCASE, dryRun=true)
public class RunCukesTest {
}
```

This is much faster than a real test run if you just want to check for undefined steps and to make sure that all your paths are set up correctly. Get used to using dryRun to help refactor your scenarios and step definitions, but remember that since no calls are actually made to your step definitions this doesn't test your conversions or transforms.

## Separating the Support Code

We should also tidy away the helper class. This is what we call *support* code, so we'll put it in a new folder, src/test/java/support. Take the KnowsTheDomain class and move it into a new file, called src/test/java/support/KnowsTheDomain.java. As we add more methods to our KnowsTheDomain, we will split it into multiple classes; however, this is fine for now.

Since KnowsTheDomain is in the support package, we'll need import statements for the domain classes Account, CashSlot, and Teller.

```
step_definitions_inside/17/src/test/java/support/KnowsTheDomain.java
import nicebank.Account;
import nicebank.CashSlot;
import nicebank.Teller;
```

## Organizing Our Step Definitions

We've managed to get this far with a single file of step definitions called Steps.java, and for a project of this size, we might as well stick with a single file for a while longer. As the number of step definitions starts to grow, we'll want to split up the files so that the code is more cohesive. We've found that our favorite way to organize step definition files is to organize them with one file per domain entity. So, in our example, we'd have three files:

```
src/test/nicebank/AccountSteps.java
src/test/nicebank/TellerSteps.java
src/test/nicebank/CashSlotSteps.java
```

In our first attempt at doing this refactor, we give each of the step classes its own constructor that creates an instance of KnowsTheDomain:

```
step_definitions_inside/18/src/test/java/nicebank/AccountSteps.java
KnowsTheDomain helper;

public AccountSteps() {
  helper = new KnowsTheDomain();
}
```

Let's run mvn clean test and see what happens:

```
java.lang.AssertionError: Incorrect amount dispensed
                                - expected:<20> but was:<0>
        at org.junit.Assert.fail(Assert.java:88)
        at org.junit.Assert.failNotEquals(Assert.java:743)
        at org.junit.Assert.assertEquals(Assert.java:118)
        at org.junit.Assert.assertEquals(Assert.java:555)
        at nicebank.Steps.$ShouldBeDispensed(Steps.java:95)
        at *.Then $20 should be dispensed(cash_withdrawal.feature:5)
```

Our final step is failing again. Can you see why?

Previously, we were sharing state by using a local instance of the KnowsTheDomain class created in the Steps constructor, but now we have three separate step definition classes and three separate instances of KnowsTheDomain. We only want a single instance of KnowsTheDomain and this is where Cucumber's dependency injection functionality comes to the rescue.

## Dependency Injection

Dependency injection (DI) is a technique that allows us to isolate a class from its concrete dependencies until runtime.[1] Often this is used to defer the decision about which actual implementation of an interface we're going to use. On this occasion, however, Cucumber uses a dependency injection framework to create a single instance of a class and share that instance between all the step definition classes that need to use it. (We'll talk about Cucumber's use of DI much more in Chapter 11, *Simplifying Design with Dependency Injection*, on page 205.)

Cucumber ships with integrations to several popular DI frameworks to choose from. We'll use PicoContainer[2] which is probably the most lightweight and is also available under the BSD license. Let's modify our pom.xml to add PicoContainer as a dependency:

```
step_definitions_inside/19/pom.xml
<dependency>
    <groupId>info.cukes</groupId>
    <artifactId>cucumber-picocontainer</artifactId>
    <version>${cucumber.version}</version>
    <scope>test</scope>
</dependency>
<dependency>
    <groupId>org.picocontainer</groupId>
    <artifactId>picocontainer</artifactId>
    <version>${picocontainer.version}</version>
    <scope>test</scope>
</dependency>
```

Now all we need to do is change the constructor in each of our step definitions. The following is an example:

---

1. http://www.martinfowler.com/articles/injection.html
2. http://picocontainer.codehaus.org

```
step_definitions_inside/19/src/test/java/nicebank/AccountSteps.java
KnowsTheDomain helper;

public AccountSteps(KnowsTheDomain helper) {
  this.helper = helper;
}
```

Now when we run mvn clean test all the steps pass again. Try it!

## What We Just Learned

It might seem like the system we've been building here is just a toy. There aren't any concrete components that a user could interact with yet: our CashSlot is just a plain old Java class, and there aren't any buttons for the user to push. What we do have, though, are the beginnings of a domain model and a greater understanding of the problem. Outside-in doesn't always mean starting with the user interface; it means starting with the outside of whatever you want to discover.

We know it isn't always possible to work like this. You'll often be adding tests to a legacy system or working on a project where the user interface is already well defined by the time you're asked to develop the code. Even in these situations, modeling your domain in Java classes will help your own understanding and also make the test code more maintainable in the long term.

Here are some of the more concrete subjects we've covered in this chapter:

- Transforms help with maintainability by removing annoying duplicate code to process captured arguments from steps.

- Java code that supports the step definitions can be factored out into separate classes.

- It's good practice to organize step definition files with one file per domain entity.

- You can pass state between steps using helper classes that are instantiated and managed by Cucumber's integration with one of several dependency injection frameworks.

By adding our own KnowsTheDomain class, we've made the step definition code easier to read, and we've started to decouple the step definitions from the system. The benefit of this decoupling will come later as the system itself evolves. In fact, in the next chapter, we'll show you how we can introduce a web user interface for withdrawing the cash without having to change a line in the step definitions.

## Try This

There are lots of places you could take this example now that we have it up and running. Let's look at one idea for you to try.

### The Big Rewrite

Now that we've discovered the domain model together, why not see whether you can do it again, for practice? Delete everything except the feature, the transform, and the step definitions. Then delete the body of each step definition, and change it back to pending. Close the book, run mvn clean test, and off you go!

Try to forget about what we did and enjoy the process of discovering a domain model for yourself.

### Bug Hunt

There's one remaining item on our to-do list, reminding us that we need to investigate why we originally designed the Teller.withdrawFrom() method to take two parameters, but we're using only one of them.

See whether you can figure out what this inconsistency means, and think about what changes you'd like to make in order to resolve it. Play with the code and try some solutions. We'll work on this issue at the beginning of the next chapter, so you won't have long to wait if you're not sure of the answer.

### Edge Cases

We have a single scenario here for the *happy path* through the process of withdrawing cash. Can you think of some simple variations on the scenario that would cause a different outcome? For example, what would happen if your account had a lower balance?

Write your new scenarios out in the same cash_withdrawal.feature file, and if you're up for the challenge, have a go at automating them.

# CHAPTER 8

# Support Code

In the previous chapter, we started working through an example of how to use Cucumber to build a real application, outside-in. The system we're building is an automated teller machine (ATM) for a bank, and we used Cucumber to help us design a simple domain model that satisfied this scenario:

```
support_code/01/src/test/resources/cash_withdrawal.feature
Feature: Cash Withdrawal
  Scenario: Successful withdrawal from an account in credit
    Given I have deposited $100.00 in my account
    When I withdraw $20
    Then $20 should be dispensed
```

The code we've written makes the scenario pass, but the system isn't really of any use yet: there's no external interface for a user to interact with, just a handful of Java classes. Now we're going to fix that by wrapping the domain model with a user interface where the user can request the amount of cash they want to withdraw.

In this chapter, we're going to focus mostly on the code in the src/test/java/support folder. This is the lowest level of your test code, where it connects, or *couples*, to your actual application. If this coupling is well engineered, your tests will be a pleasure to modify as your project grows. If the coupling is too tight, your tests will be brittle and break any time anything moves. That's why we created a separation layer between the step definitions and the system using helper classes like KnowsTheDomain. This separation layer provides just the decoupling we'll need as we start to introduce a user interface.

Before we get started with the user interface, we have one item left on our to-do list we need to check off first.

## Fixing the Bug

Sometimes the signals you'll get from the code that something is wrong are pretty faint. We always try to keep a to-do list handy and write down everything that concerns us as we go. That way, we can stay focused on the task at hand but know that we'll get a chance to check over and clean up any inconsistencies before we move on to the next task.

As we were finishing off the last scenario, we noticed that Teller.withdraw_from() takes two arguments, but only one of them was used in the method to make the scenario pass. This inconsistency means that something is wrong, but we need to investigate further to know what we need to do about it. Let's take a look at the code that uses the method:

support_code/01/src/test/java/nicebank/TellerSteps.java
```
package nicebank;

import cucumber.api.java.en.*;

import support.KnowsTheDomain;

public class TellerSteps {

  KnowsTheDomain helper;

  public TellerSteps(KnowsTheDomain helper) {
      this.helper = helper;
  }

  @When("^I withdraw \\$(\\d+)$")
  public void iWithdraw$(int amount) throws Throwable {
      helper.getTeller().withdrawFrom(helper.getMyAccount(), amount);
  }
}
```

It seems pretty obvious what we intended to happen here. The Teller should take the specified amount of money out of the account and hand it to the CashSlot. So, how did we manage to make the scenario pass without having to do anything to the account when we implemented that method? Let's take another look at the scenario:

support_code/01/src/test/resources/cash_withdrawal.feature
```
Feature: Cash Withdrawal
  Scenario: Successful withdrawal from an account in credit
    Given I have deposited $100.00 in my account
    When I withdraw $20
    Then $20 should be dispensed
```

A-ha! There's nothing here that actually checks that the balance of the account has been reduced to $80. It's a good thing we caught this now—our code would have been handing out cash to customers for free!

Let's tack on this extra outcome as another Then step:

support_code/02/src/test/resources/cash_withdrawal.feature
```
Feature: Cash Withdrawal
  Scenario: Successful withdrawal from an account in credit
    Given I have deposited $100.00 in my account
    When I withdraw $20
    Then $20 should be dispensed
    And the balance of my account should be $80.00
```

Run mvn clean test and paste the snippet for the new step definition into the file AccountSteps.java:

support_code/02/src/test/java/nicebank/AccountSteps.java
```
@Then("^the balance of my account should be \\$(\\d+)\\.(\\d+)$")
public void theBalanceOfMyAccountShouldBe$(int arg1, int arg2) throws Throwable {
    // Write code here that turns the phrase above into concrete actions
    throw new PendingException();
}
```

We can write the new snippet using the transform we created in the previous chapter and duplicating the assertion from the previous step definition:

support_code/03/src/test/java/nicebank/AccountSteps.java
```
@Then("^the balance of my account should be (\\$\\d+\\.\\d+)$")
public void theBalanceOfMyAccountShouldBe$(
                              @Transform(MoneyConverter.class) Money amount)
                                                        throws Throwable {
    Assert.assertEquals("Incorrect account balance -",
                              amount, helper.getMyAccount().getBalance());
}
```

We want to carry on and fix the bug, so we'll make a note on our to-do list to tidy up the duplication that we have just introduced. Run mvn clean test now to see whether we have it trapped:

```
And the balance of my account should be $80.00
      java.lang.AssertionError: Incorrect account balance
                                        - expected:<$80.00> but was:<$100.00>
        at org.junit.Assert.fail(Assert.java:88)
        . . .
        at nicebank.AccountSteps.theBalanceOfMyAccountShouldBe$
                                                (AccountSteps.java:36)
        at *.And the balance of my account should be $80.00

1 Scenarios (1 failed)
4 Steps (1 failed, 3 passed)
```

**Matt says:**
# That's Not a Bug; It's Just a Missing Scenario

One of the wonderful things I discovered when I first used Cucumber to build a complete application from the outside-in was when we started manual exploratory testing and discovered some bugs. Almost without exception, every one of those bugs could be traced back to a gap in the Cucumber scenarios we'd written for that part of the system. Because we'd written the scenarios collaboratively, with businesspeople and developers working together to get them right, it wasn't anybody's fault that there was a bug. It was just an edge case we hadn't originally anticipated.

In my experience, bugs are a big source of friction and unhappiness in software teams. Businesspeople blame them on careless developers, and developers blame them on inadequate requirements from the businesspeople. Actually they're just a natural consequence of software development being a complex endeavor. Using Cucumber helped the team see that closing these gaps is everyone's job. The blaming just didn't happen, and we were a much happier team as a result.

Great—the bug has been caught by our scenario. Just as we suspected, the account's balance remains untouched by the withdrawal. But not for long! Crack open Teller.java, and take a look at our Teller class:

```
support_code/03/src/main/java/nicebank/Teller.java
public void withdrawFrom(Account account, int dollars) {
    cashSlot.dispense(dollars);
}
```

Change the withdrawFrom method to tell the account what to do:

```
support_code/04/src/main/java/nicebank/Teller.java
public void withdrawFrom(Account account, int dollars) {
    account.debit(dollars);
    cashSlot.dispense(dollars);
}
```

Now when we run mvn clean test, we have a compilation failure, which tells us that we need to create this new debit method on the Account. On a real project, we'd drop down a gear at this point and start writing unit tests for the Account class to drive out that method. We don't mind sketching out interfaces to classes with a few basic method stubs with only Cucumber to back us up, but as soon as we start adding interesting behavior to a class, we like to make sure that behavior has been specified in a unit test. *The RSpec Book [CADH09]* and *Growing Object-Oriented Software, Guided by Tests [FP09]* both do a great job of explaining this balance with plenty of examples, but since this book is focused on Cucumber, we're going to gloss over this step and carry on.

Add the debit to the Account class:

```
support_code/05/src/main/java/nicebank/Account.java
public void debit(int dollars) {
  balance = balance.minus(new Money(dollars, 0));
}
```

We've implemented a new method called debit that decrements the balance by the given amount. Let's run mvn clean test and see whether we've managed to fix the bug:

```
Running RunCukesTest
Feature: Cash Withdrawal

  Scenario: Successful withdrawal from an account in credit
    Given I have deposited $100.00 in my account
    When I withdraw $20
    Then $20 should be dispensed
    And the balance of my account should be $80.00

1 Scenarios (1 passed)
4 Steps (4 passed)
0m0.079s

Tests run: 5, Failures: 0, Errors: 0, Skipped: 0, Time elapsed: 0.513 sec
```

Hooray, we did it! Now it's time for some refactoring before we move on.

## Reviewing and Refactoring

In *Extreme Programming Explained [Bec00]*, Kent Beck gives four criteria for a simple design. In order, with the most important first, they are as follows:

1. Passes all the tests
2. Reveals all the intention
3. Contains no duplication
4. Uses the fewest number of classes or methods

Let's review our current code against those four criteria. It's been driven from a single test made from a single Cucumber scenario that is passing, so that's rule 1 taken care of. How about rule 2? Revealing intention is essentially about how things are named, which matters to us a great deal. Let's take a look at the methods on our Account class:

```
support_code/05/src/main/java/nicebank/Account.java
package nicebank;

public class Account {
    private Money balance = new Money();
```

```
    public void deposit(Money amount) {
        balance = balance.add(amount);
    }

    public void debit(int dollars) {
      balance = balance.minus(new Money(dollars, 0));
    }

    public Money getBalance() {
      return balance;
    }
}
```

Reflecting on it, it's confusing that we've used the two method names deposit and debit. Really, we'd like to see either deposit and withdraw or credit and debit, but not a combination of the two. Which pair is more appropriate for our Account class?

We spend a bit of time chatting with one of our domain experts, and it becomes clear that credit and debit are the right names for the methods on Account. In fact, deposit is something you'd more likely ask a Teller to do for you. These conversations happen all the time as you start to establish a *ubiquitous language*, and you'll find they become easier and easier as your knowledge of the domain, and the ubiquitous language you all use to discuss it, grows.

We're going to rename the Account.deposit method to Account.credit. Since our test is nice and fast, we can just rename the method and see what breaks. (Of course you could invoke the Rename refactoring in your favorite IDE, but we want to show how you could do this with only a text editor and a compiler):

```
test/step_definitions/AccountSteps.java:26: error: cannot find symbol
    helper.getMyAccount().deposit(amount);
                          ^
  symbol:   method deposit(Money)
  location: class Account
1 error
```

In *Refactoring: Improving the Design of Existing Code [FBBO99]*, this technique (make the change, see what breaks) is called *leaning on the compiler*. From the compilation failure, it looks like we need to change line 26 of AccountSteps.java. Go ahead and change that, and run mvn clean test again.

Our scenario is passing, but we're not quite done yet! The language in the step is now inconsistent with the code inside the step definition we've just changed:

support_code/07/src/test/java/nicebank/AccountSteps.java
```
@Given("^I have deposited (\\$\\d+\\.\\d+) in my account$")
public void iHaveDeposited$InMyAccount(
                            @Transform(MoneyConverter.class) Money amount)
                                                    throws Throwable {

    helper.getMyAccount().credit(amount);

    Assert.assertEquals("Incorrect account balance -",
                        amount, helper.getMyAccount().getBalance());
}
```

In the step, we're still using the term *deposited*, but now we're *crediting* the account in the Java code underneath. How much does this matter? Perhaps not much, but we'd prefer our test code to be as transparent as possible. After another discussion with our domain expert, we decide to reword the step to read Given my account has been credited with $100.00. We'll change the feature and the underlying step definition:

support_code/08/src/test/resources/cash_withdrawal.feature
```
Feature: Cash Withdrawal
  Scenario: Successful withdrawal from an account in credit
    Given my account has been credited with $100.00
    When I withdraw $20
    Then $20 should be dispensed
    And the balance of my account should be $80.00
```

support_code/08/src/test/java/nicebank/AccountSteps.java
```
@Given("^my account has been credited with (\\$\\d+\\.\\d+)$")
public void myAccountHasBeenCreditedWith$(
                            @Transform(MoneyConverter.class) Money amount)
                                                    throws Throwable {

    helper.getMyAccount().credit(amount);

    Assert.assertEquals("Incorrect account balance -",
                        amount, helper.getMyAccount().getBalance());
}
```

Looking at this step definition now, it doesn't make sense to check that the balance is the same as the amount credited. If this step definition were used in another scenario that involved other credit or debit transactions before this one, the balance might not be the same as the amount credited, and that would be quite all right. So, we don't want this assertion here any more.

That gives us an easy way to cross off the last item on our to-do list: removing the duplication of the balance assertion in the two-step definitions for the account. We can simply delete the first one, because it's no longer relevant:

## Test Automation Is Software Development

You'll have noticed the painstaking care with which we've moved back and forth between the features, the step definitions, and the system itself, keeping everything as clean and consistent as we can. You might be wondering whether we honestly work this way in our everyday practice. We certainly try to do so. We've alluded to this earlier in the book, but we feel like it's time to make the point clearly: if you're writing automated tests, you're developing software. If you value those tests enough to have written them in the first place, you'll want to be able to come back and change them in the future. That means that all the same good habits we normally use to write maintainable software apply to the test code we write too.

This important point is often missed, especially in a company where testing has traditionally been done manually. People who specialize in testing sometimes aren't the best people to be automating tests if they lack the necessary experience in software design. Without support from people who do understand how to write maintainable code, the team can end up with messy test code that's hard to change. It's around this point that people start to realize their automated tests are actually making it harder to change the software, not easier, and consider giving up on Cucumber altogether. The following diagram shows how software development skill becomes increasingly important as you move down the stack from Gherkin features to support code.

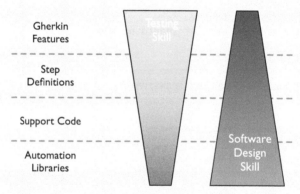

Testing and software design are complementary skills, and a strong team needs a mix of both specialties. Different people will sit at different points on this spectrum: some people will be great testers but not at all interested in automation or programming, and some will just want to write code without thinking about how to break it. That's fine, but the team needs to recognize that there isn't a clear division of responsibility when you're working with automated tests. Everyone needs to work together to create and maintain high-quality tests.

```
support_code/09/src/test/java/nicebank/AccountSteps.java
@Given("^my account has been credited with (\\$\\d+\\.\\d+)$")
public void myAccountHasBeenCreditedWith$(
                        @Transform(MoneyConverter.class) Money amount)
                                                throws Throwable {
    helper.getMyAccount().credit(amount);
}

@Then("^the balance of my account should be (\\$\\d+\\.\\d+)$")
public void theBalanceOfMyAccountShouldBe$(
                        @Transform(MoneyConverter.class) Money amount)
                                                throws Throwable {
    Assert.assertEquals("Incorrect account balance -",
                        amount, helper.getMyAccount().getBalance());
}
```

That completes our refactoring. The code is now as clear and communicative and free of duplication as we can imagine at this stage. We're ready to add some new functionality.

## Bootstrapping the User Interface

Now that we have a model we're happy with, we're going to wrap it in a simple user interface that allows users to specify how much cash they want to withdraw. Even though it might not be a typical choice for a real ATM, we're going to use a web form. We'll use the Jetty[1] web server to serve our user interface, and we'll use Selenium WebDriver[2] to automate it. We won't go into much detail about how Selenium works here, but you'll learn much more in Chapter 12, *Working with Web Applications*, on page 225.

We'll start by bringing the necessary dependencies into our project to get the web server up and running.

### Creating a Website with Jetty

We're going to use Jetty to build a very simple UI for our ATM. We'll start by adding a dependency on Embedded Jetty to our pom.xml:

```
support_code/10/pom.xml
<dependency>
  <groupId>org.eclipse.jetty</groupId>
  <artifactId>jetty-webapp</artifactId>
  <version>${jetty.version}</version>
</dependency>
```

---

1. http://www.eclipse.org/jetty/
2. http://www.seleniumhq.org/projects/webdriver/

Now we'll create a simple servlet to render a static page:

support_code/10/src/main/java/nicebank/AtmServlet.java

```java
package nicebank;

import java.io.IOException;
import javax.servlet.ServletException;
import javax.servlet.http.HttpServlet;
import javax.servlet.http.HttpServletRequest;
import javax.servlet.http.HttpServletResponse;

public class AtmServlet extends HttpServlet
{
    protected void doGet(HttpServletRequest request, HttpServletResponse response)
                                        throws ServletException, IOException
    {
        response.setContentType("text/html");
        response.setStatus(HttpServletResponse.SC_OK);
        response.getWriter().println(
            "<html><head><title>Nice Bank ATM</title></head>"
                + "<body><h1>Welcome to our nice bank!</h1></body></html>");
    }
}
```

Finally, we'll create AtmServer to wire our web app together:

support_code/10/src/main/java/nicebank/AtmServer.java

```java
package nicebank;


import org.eclipse.jetty.server.Server;
import org.eclipse.jetty.servlet.ServletContextHandler;
import org.eclipse.jetty.servlet.ServletHolder;

public class AtmServer
{
    private final Server server;

    public AtmServer(int port) {
        server = new Server(9988);

        ServletContextHandler context =
            new ServletContextHandler(ServletContextHandler.SESSIONS);
        context.setContextPath("/");
        server.setHandler(context);

        context.addServlet(new ServletHolder(new AtmServlet()),"/*");
    }

    public void start() throws Exception {
        server.start();
```

```
        System.out.println("Listening on " + server.getURI());
    }

    public void stop() throws Exception {
        server.stop();
    }

    public static void main(String[] args) throws Exception {
        new AtmServer(9988).start();
    }
}
```

### Starting Our Server

To start the server by starting AtmServer, type mvn exec:java -Dexec.mainClass="nice-bank.AtmServer". Once you see the message "Listening on http://127.0.0.1:9988/", open your favorite browser and navigate to http://localhost:9988, where you should see the message "Welcome to our nice bank."

## Making the Switch

Our goal is to introduce a user interface for requesting the cash withdrawal. We want Cucumber to cover us as we make these changes, so we need to change how our test code interacts with the application. Up until now, all our step definitions were talking directly to the domain model. We're going to change that so that some of them hit the new user interface instead. This is shown in the adjacent figure.

But, which steps need to change?

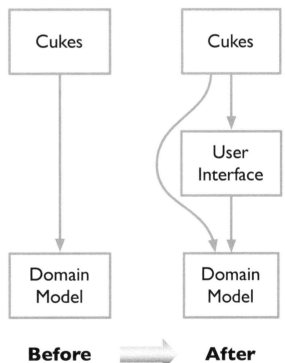

Let's take a look at our scenario again:

support_code/10/src/test/resources/cash_withdrawal.feature
```
Feature: Cash Withdrawal
  Scenario: Successful withdrawal from an account in credit
    Given my account has been credited with $100.00
    When I withdraw $20
    Then $20 should be dispensed
    And the balance of my account should be $80.00
```

We haven't specified anything about *how* we do the cash withdrawal, so there's nothing we need to change about the scenario at all. Great! Let's jump down into the step definition for withdrawing cash and see what needs to change there:

support_code/10/src/test/java/nicebank/TellerSteps.java
```java
package nicebank;

import cucumber.api.java.en.*;

import support.KnowsTheDomain;

public class TellerSteps {

  KnowsTheDomain helper;

  public TellerSteps(KnowsTheDomain helper) {
      this.helper = helper;
  }

  @When("^I withdraw \\$(\\d+)$")
  public void iWithdraw$(int amount) throws Throwable {
      helper.getTeller().withdrawFrom(helper.getMyAccount(), amount);
  }
}
```

All we're doing here is calling withdrawFrom on something. Right now that something is an instance of the Teller class in our domain model. But what if we made getTeller return something else, like an interface that offers the behaviors we need to interact with a teller? That's the beauty of object-oriented programming—as long as the object understands the withdrawFrom method, this step definition is going to be happy. What we need to do is create an interface that describes the responsibilities of a teller, and make our existing Teller implement it.

We now have one of the hardest problems in programming to solve:[3] what should we call the interface? The best name for the interface is Teller, so we need to rename our existing class to give it a properly descriptive name, like AutomatedTeller:

support_code/11/src/main/java/nicebank/Teller.java
```java
package nicebank;

public interface Teller {
    void withdrawFrom(Account account, int dollars);
}
```

support_code/11/src/main/java/nicebank/AutomatedTeller.java
```java
package nicebank;

public class AutomatedTeller  implements Teller {
    private CashSlot cashSlot;

    public AutomatedTeller(CashSlot cashSlot) {
        this.cashSlot = cashSlot;
    }

    public void withdrawFrom(Account account, int dollars) {
        account.debit(dollars);
        cashSlot.dispense(dollars);
    }
}
```

Now let's drop down into our KnowsTheDomain class. We need to reimplement the getTeller method to return a class that implements the Teller interface but that knows how to interact with the user interface. For now, just build an empty class that implements the Teller interface and change getTeller to return an instance of the new class:

support_code/11/src/test/java/support/AtmUserInterface.java
```java
package support;

import nicebank.Account;
import nicebank.Teller;

class AtmUserInterface implements Teller {

    public void withdrawFrom(Account account, int dollars) {
    }
}
```

---

3.  http://martinfowler.com/bliki/TwoHardThings.html

```
support_code/11/src/test/java/support/KnowsTheDomain.java
public Teller getTeller() {
  if (teller == null){
    teller = new AtmUserInterface();
  }

  return teller;
}
```

Now we've disconnected the action-invoking When step in our scenario from the domain model and connected it to this new AtmUserInterface class. If you run mvn clean test now, you should see the scenario fail:

```
Then $20 should be dispensed
    java.lang.AssertionError: Incorrect amount dispensed
                                      - expected:<20> but was:<0>
      at org.junit.Assert.fail(Assert.java:88)
      at org.junit.Assert.failNotEquals(Assert.java:743)
      at org.junit.Assert.assertEquals(Assert.java:118)
      at org.junit.Assert.assertEquals(Assert.java:555)
      at nicebank.CashSlotSteps.$ShouldBeDispensed(CashSlotSteps.java:21)
      at *.Then $20 should be dispensed(cash_withdrawal.feature:5)
  And the balance of my account should be $80.00


1 Scenarios (1 failed)
4 Steps (1 failed, 1 skipped, 2 passed)
```

The scenario failed because our new support module hasn't been wired up to the system yet, so nothing was found in the cash slot. Now we have a goal: get that scenario to pass again, but this time, through the user interface.

## Designing the User Interface

So, what should this shiny new user interface look like? We gathered around the whiteboard with our user experience team and sketched out a wireframe for the first iteration of the cash withdrawal form. The plan is for it to look roughly like this.

Amount:

```
┌────────────────────────┐
│ 500                    │
└────────────────────────┘
```

Let's flesh out our AtmUserInterface class to talk to that form:

```
support_code/12/src/test/java/support/AtmUserInterface.java
class AtmUserInterface implements Teller {

    private final EventFiringWebDriver webDriver;

    public AtmUserInterface(){
        this.webDriver = new EventFiringWebDriver(new FirefoxDriver());
    }
```

```
    public void withdrawFrom(Account account, int dollars) {
        try {
            webDriver.get("http://localhost:9988");
            webDriver.findElement(By.id("Amount"))
                    .sendKeys(String.valueOf(dollars));
            webDriver.findElement(By.id("Withdraw")).click();
        }
        finally {
            webDriver.close();
        }
    }
}
```

We're using Selenium WebDriver in the AtmUserInterface class to interact with the web user interface. First we get the home page, then we find the text field labeled Amount and fill it with the amount to withdraw, and finally we click the Withdraw button. This is the design we just looked at on the wireframe, formalized in code.

Since we're using Selenium, we'll add the necessary dependencies in our pom.xml:

```
support_code/12/pom.xml
<dependency>
    <groupId>org.seleniumhq.selenium</groupId>
    <artifactId>selenium-server</artifactId>
    <version>${selenium.version}</version>
</dependency>
```

When we run mvn clean test against this, it's going to fail of course, for these reasons:

1.  We haven't started the server yet. (If you've been following along, your server may still be running from when we tested it earlier in *Starting Our Server*, on page 151. If it is running, then stop it by pressing Ctrl-C.)

2.  We haven't built the form yet.

Let's run mvn clean test anyway just to check we're on track:

```
When I withdraw $20
  org.openqa.selenium.NoSuchElementException:
                  Unable to locate element: {"method":"id","selector":"Amount"}
  Command duration or timeout: 14 milliseconds
```

OK, so Selenium is telling us that it hasn't found an Amount field to fill in. First, we need to ensure that the server is up and running. To do this, we need to take some time out to learn about a new feature of Cucumber.

**Seb says:**
## Selenium Web Drivers

If you start seeing strange errors when using your Selenium web driver, it may be caused by incompatibilities between their versions. New versions of browsers are released regularly and this often means that you'll need to update your Selenium version too.

This book was prepared using Firefox 28.0 and Selenium 2.41.0.

## Using Hooks

Cucumber supports hooks, which are methods that run before or after each scenario. You can define them anywhere in your support or step definition layers, using the annotations @Before and @After.

To test them, add a file src/test/java/hooks/SomeTestHooks.java that looks like this:

support_code/13/src/test/java/hooks/SomeTestHooks.java
```
package hooks;

import cucumber.api.java.After;
import cucumber.api.java.Before;
import cucumber.api.Scenario;

public class SomeTestHooks {
    @Before
    public void beforeCallingScenario() {
        System.out.println("*********** About to start the scenario.");
    }

    @After
    public void afterRunningScenario(Scenario scenario) {
        System.out.println("*********** Just finished running scenario: "
                            + scenario.getStatus());
    }
}
```

If you run mvn clean test, you'll see the two messages printed in the output at the beginning and end of the scenario. Cucumber's @Before and @After hooks are a lot like the SetUp and TearDown methods in the xUnit family of testing tools.

The most common use of @Before and @After hooks is to clear up any residual state left in external systems like databases so that each scenario starts with the system in a known state. We'll explain this in detail in Chapter 10, *Databases*, on page 185.

Hooks are global by default, meaning they run for every scenario in your features. If you want them to run for just certain scenarios, you need to tag those scenarios and then use a tagged hook.

## Tagged Hooks

Both @Before and @After accept a tag expression, which you can use to selectively add the hook to only certain scenarios. For example, suppose you're writing features for the administrative area of a website. Each of the administrator features starts with the following background:

```
Feature: Delete Widgets

  Background:
    Given I am logged in as an administrator

  ...
```

An alternative is to tag the feature and then use a @Before hook to run this same code to log in as an administrator.

```
@admin
Feature: Delete Widgets

  ...

@Before("@admin")
public void logInAsAdmin() {
  // Log in as admin user
}
```

Now, to run a scenario logged in as an administrator, you just have to tag the scenario with @admin, and this code will automatically run before the steps of the scenario. In *Filtering with Tag Expressions*, on page 261, we will explain more complex tag expressions using logical operations, but a simple tag will do for now.

Tagged hooks can be useful for ensuring technical things like external services are started, without making too much fuss about them in the text of the scenario itself.

## Examining the Scenario

If we want it to, our hook can accept a single argument that represents the scenario. For example, we can ask a scenario for its status:

### Aslak says:
## Step Definitions Are Global

When you define a step definition, it is defined globally. There is no way to reduce the scope of a step definition to certain scenarios like you can do with tagged hooks.

People occasionally ask for a way to scope step definitions in a similar way to tagged hooks, such as making *When I turn it off* invoke one step definition for some scenarios and another one for others.

This is a feature that would be easy to add to Cucumber, and one day I actually implemented it to get some feedback from the nice people on the Cukes mailing list. My question was, *Can anyone think of how people might misuse this?* Richard Lawrence, an old-timer on the list, answered:

*Feature-coupled steps is the extreme. The more subtle issue is that the beneficial pressure to grow a ubiquitous language goes away when it becomes too easy to say, "Oh, that's just another context, I'll use the same words to mean something different here." Thinking about some of the conversations I've had coaching teams to learn ubiquitous language, I would expect this to happen a lot.*

The term "feature-coupled steps" is a term I came up with in the early days of Cucumber when I was documenting good and bad Cucumber practices in the wiki. I consider feature-coupled steps to be a code smell since they quickly cause a lot of duplication and do nothing to promote a ubiquitous language.

When Dan North—the originator of BDD—wrote his first BDD framework, step definitions were coupled to features. He told me the ability to have global step definitions shared across features was one of the *improvements* Cucumber brought on.

In retrospect, it's rather amusing to observe the clones and spinoffs of Cucumber reintroducing mechanisms that we deliberately got rid of.

In Cucumber, the same sentence can mean only one thing.

```
@After
public void afterCallingScenario(Scenario scenario) {
  System.out.println("The scenario completed with a status of "
                     + scenario.getStatus());
}
```

For more details on the Scenario object, look at the documentation for cucumber.api.Scenario.[4]

---

## Hooks That Run at Other Times

If you want to run code before all of your features start, the way to do that is to use Java language features, such as static fields.

If you want to run code after all of your features have finished, you can use Java's built-in addShutdownHook, which will be run just before the Cucumber process exits. You'll typically use this mechanism to tear down some external system that you've started from your support code.

Sometimes people also ask about running specific setup and cleanup code once for a particular feature, not for each scenario within the feature. There are a number of ways to achieve this without needing Cucumber to provide any additional functionality, one of which was described in detail by Paolo Ambrosio.[5]

Armed with this new knowledge about hooks, let's get back to work on our ATM.

---

**Joe asks:**
# What Order Do My Hooks Run In?

Sometimes it's important to be able to specify the exact order that your hooks run in. The @Before and @After annotations have an order parameter that you can set. The default value is 10000 for any hook that doesn't have a specific order set.

```
@Before( order=5 )
public void oneHook() {
   // ....
}

@After( order = 200 )
public void anotherHook() {
   // ...
}
```

Cucumber runs @Before hooks from low to high. A @Before hook with an order of 10 will run before one with an order of 20. @After hooks run in the opposite direction—from high to low—so an @After hook with an order of 20 will run before one with an order of 10.

If you need to use order on a tagged hook, you have to use the value parameter:

```
@Before( value="myTag", order=5 )
public void oneHook() {
   // ....
}
```

---

5.    https://groups.google.com/d/msg/cukes/Z2mWgk0rSgs/4F2H85PcmRsJ

## Getting to Green

Where were we? We were just trying to get our scenario to talk to the UI when we realized that we needed to learn about how to get Cucumber to start and stop the web server. Once we get that working, we'll need to design and build a UI. And finally we'll have to wire our shiny new UI up to our existing domain model.

Let's get started!

### Starting the Server

We want to start our server before each scenario runs and stop the server after each scenario completes. This is exactly what the @Before and @After hooks are intended for. Let's create a new file, src/test/java/hooks/ServerHooks.java, where we'll create our hooks.

```
support_code/14/src/test/java/hooks/ServerHooks.java
package hooks;

import cucumber.api.java.After;
import cucumber.api.java.Before;
import cucumber.api.Scenario;

import nicebank.AtmServer;

public class ServerHooks {
    public static final int PORT = 8887;

    private AtmServer server;

    @Before
    public void startServer() throws Exception {
        server = new AtmServer(PORT);
        server.start();
    }

    @After
    public void stopServer() throws Exception {
        server.stop();
    }
}
```

We'll also want to use the constant PORT that we've just introduced in our class that drives the Teller through the user interface:

```
support_code/14/src/test/java/support/AtmUserInterface.java
public void withdrawFrom(Account account, int dollars) {
    try {
        webDriver.get("http://localhost:" + ServerHooks.PORT);
        webDriver.findElement(By.id("Amount"))
                .sendKeys(String.valueOf(dollars));
        webDriver.findElement(By.id("Withdraw")).click();
    }
    finally {
        webDriver.close();
    }
}
```

Now when we run mvn clean test we see the browser fire up and display our web page with the message "Welcome to our nice bank." The scenario still fails, because the UI that our step expects hasn't been implemented yet.

## Building the User Interface

Even though we can see the page that's failing in the browser, it would be useful to learn how to save exactly what's visible in the browser when a test fails. That way, when our feature file contains lots of scenarios we'll still be able to find out what went wrong. Let's add a debugging hook to show us what's going on in our failing scenario. Let's start by creating WebDriverHooks and fleshing out what we want to do:

```
support_code/15/src/test/java/hooks/WebDriverHooks.java
@After
public void finish(Scenario scenario) {
    try {
        byte[] screenshot =
                    helper.getWebDriver().getScreenshotAs(OutputType.BYTES);
        scenario.embed(screenshot, "image/png");
    } catch (WebDriverException somePlatformsDontSupportScreenshots) {
        System.err.println(somePlatformsDontSupportScreenshots.getMessage());
    }
    finally {
        helper.getWebDriver().close();
    }
}
```

The method embed is provided by Cucumber's Scenario class. It only saves an image when we use Cucumber's HTML formatter, so we'll need to make a change to the Options in RunCukesTest.java to request HTML output:

support_code/15/src/test/java/RunCukesTest.java

```
@RunWith(Cucumber.class)
@CucumberOptions(plugin={"pretty", "html:out"}, snippets=SnippetType.CAMELCASE)
public class RunCukesTest {
}
```

We have to share the same instance of the Selenium web driver between WebDriverHooks and AtmUserInterface. So, we use KnowsTheDomain to manage the shared web driver in just the same way we use it to manage the shared account, cash slot, and teller:

support_code/15/src/test/java/support/KnowsTheDomain.java

```
public EventFiringWebDriver getWebDriver() {
    if (webDriver == null){
      webDriver = new EventFiringWebDriver(new FirefoxDriver());
    }

    return webDriver;
}
```

Now, after you have run mvn clean test, the web page that Cucumber can see should be saved to disk. Open up out/index.html in your browser and take a look. This can be a very helpful debugging tool. What it's shown us is the simple greeting message we added earlier when we created our Jetty servlet AtmServlet.java.

Now let's hard-code the HTML for the ATM withdrawal form we want right into the Jetty servlet AtmServlet.java so that you can easily see what's going on. The form contains a single field with a label and a submit button that posts back to the server.

support_code/16/src/main/java/nicebank/AtmServlet.java

```
package nicebank;

import java.io.IOException;
import javax.servlet.ServletException;
import javax.servlet.http.HttpServlet;
import javax.servlet.http.HttpServletRequest;
import javax.servlet.http.HttpServletResponse;

public class AtmServlet extends HttpServlet
{
    protected void doGet(HttpServletRequest request, HttpServletResponse response)
                                                throws ServletException, IOException
    {
        response.setContentType("text/html");
        response.setStatus(HttpServletResponse.SC_OK);
        response.getWriter().println(
            "<html><head><title>ATM</title></head>" +
```

```
        "<body><form action=\"/withdraw\" method=\"post\">" +
        "<label for=\"amount\">Amount</label>" +
        "<input type=\"text\" id=\"amount\" name=\"amount\">" +
        "<button type=\"submit\" id=\"withdraw\">Withdraw</button>" +
        "</form></body></html>");
    }
}
```

We'll also create a new post request handler so that the form has somewhere to post back to, although it's just a stub that will raise an error if it's called:

support_code/16/src/main/java/nicebank/WithdrawalServlet.java
```
package nicebank;

import java.io.IOException;
import javax.servlet.ServletException;
import javax.servlet.http.HttpServlet;
import javax.servlet.http.HttpServletRequest;
import javax.servlet.http.HttpServletResponse;

public class WithdrawalServlet extends HttpServlet
{
    protected void doPost(HttpServletRequest request, HttpServletResponse response)
                                        throws ServletException, IOException
    {
        response.setContentType("text/html");
        response.setStatus(HttpServletResponse.SC_OK);
        response.getWriter().println(
            "<html><head><title>Nice Bank ATM</title></head>" +
            "<body>I don't know how to withdraw money yet, sorry</body>" +
            "</html>");
    }
}
```

Finally we add the WithdrawalServlet to the AtmServer:

support_code/16/src/main/java/nicebank/AtmServer.java
```
package nicebank;


import org.eclipse.jetty.server.Server;
import org.eclipse.jetty.servlet.ServletContextHandler;
import org.eclipse.jetty.servlet.ServletHolder;

public class AtmServer
{
    private final Server server;

    public AtmServer(int port) {
        server = new Server(port);
```

```
    ServletContextHandler context =
        new ServletContextHandler(ServletContextHandler.SESSIONS);
    context.setContextPath("/");
    server.setHandler(context);

    context.addServlet(new ServletHolder(new WithdrawalServlet()),"/withdraw");
    context.addServlet(new ServletHolder(new AtmServlet()),"/");
}

public void start() throws Exception {
    server.start();
    System.out.println("Listening on " + server.getURI());
}

public void stop() throws Exception {
    server.stop();
    System.out.println("Server shutdown");
}

public static void main(String[] args) throws Exception
{
    new AtmServer(9988).start();
}
}
```

Try running mvn clean test now. If everything has gone according to plan, you'll see the error I don't know how to withdraw yet, sorry displayed in Cucumber's output. Our next step is to implement the right code in the WithdrawalServlet request handler to actually withdraw the cash.

## Dispensing the Cash

We've already built a domain model, so we have a significant head start. The class that knows how to carry out the withdrawal is Teller, so we'll need to create an instance of that class when we receive the posted form data on the web server. To create an instance of the Teller, we need a CashSlot to pass to the constructor. The slightly tricky thing about this is that we need to make sure that the step definitions are also looking at the same instance of CashSlot; otherwise, they won't be able to see the cash we've dispensed.

And if we want to call withdrawFrom on the teller, we'll also need an Account. As our project progresses, we'll probably end up determining the Account by reading the user's card, but at the moment our domain model doesn't go that far. For the time being, we need a way for the step definitions to be able to say to the web application *look, just trust me and use this account.*

The simplest way to do this is to pass shared instances of CashSlot and Account into the server when we create it. It simply passes them on to the Withdrawal-Handler:

support_code/17/src/main/java/nicebank/AtmServer.java
```
public AtmServer(int port, CashSlot cashSlot, Account account) {
    server = new Server(port);

    ServletContextHandler context =
        new ServletContextHandler(ServletContextHandler.SESSIONS);
    context.setContextPath("/");
    server.setHandler(context);

    context.addServlet(new ServletHolder(
            new WithdrawalServlet(cashSlot, account)),"/withdraw");
    context.addServlet(new ServletHolder(new AtmServlet()),"/");
}
```

We now need to update our server hook so that it makes use of these two touchpoints for sharing the CashSlot and Account when we start the server:

support_code/17/src/test/java/hooks/ServerHooks.java
```
@Before
public void startServer() throws Exception {
    server = new AtmServer(PORT, helper.getCashSlot(), helper.getMyAccount());
    server.start();
}
```

Supplying the account like this is a temporary shortcut around the process of authenticating the user with their physical card and PIN, because we don't want to worry about that part of the process yet.

Then the last thing to do is modify the WithdrawalServlet to actually request the withdrawal and inform the user that the money has been dispensed:

support_code/17/src/main/java/nicebank/WithdrawalServlet.java
```
protected void doPost(HttpServletRequest request, HttpServletResponse response)
                                          throws ServletException, IOException
{
    Teller teller = new AutomatedTeller(cashSlot);
    int amount = Integer.parseInt(request.getParameter("amount"));
    teller.withdrawFrom(account, amount);

    response.setContentType("text/html");
    response.setStatus(HttpServletResponse.SC_OK);
    response.getWriter().println(
        "<html><head><title>ATM</title></head>" +
                "<body>Please take your $" + amount + "</body></html>");
}
```

Run mvn clean test now, and the scenario should be passing:

```
-------------------------------------------------------
 T E S T S
-------------------------------------------------------
Running RunCukesTest
Feature: Cash Withdrawal
Listening on http://192.168.1.11:8887/
Server shutdown

  Scenario: Successful withdrawal from an account in credit
    Given my account has been credited with $100.00
    When I withdraw $20
    Then $20 should be dispensed
    And the balance of my account should be $80.00

1 Scenarios (1 passed)
4 Steps (4 passed)
```

Phew! We've managed to convert our tests to run against a web interface, without changing the Cucumber scenario or the production domain code. If we wanted, we could set up our tests to switch between the two, giving us fast tests that go directly to the domain model and slower, more thorough tests that go right through the user interface.

## What We Just Learned

Working outside-in with Cucumber blurs the lines between testing and development. Always be ready to learn something new about the problem domain, whether you're deciding on the wording in a Cucumber scenario or choosing the parameters for a method. By taking care to craft a clean interface between your tests and the system underneath, you'll end up with tests that can easily evolve with the system's changing requirements.

In this chapter, we showed you how to use Cucumber to trap a bug. In Chapter 16, *Working with Legacy Applications*, on page 285, we'll talk much more about this.

We covered the basics of creating Jetty applications and testing them using Selenium. Jetty is a lightweight, well-used, standards-compliant servlet engine and HTTP server. Our usage barely scratched the surface of its functionality.

We also showed you how to use Cucumber's hooks to invoke Java code before and after each scenario or to run them before specific scenarios using tags.

Next we'll introduce a new problem by changing the architecture to make the system asynchronous.

## Try This

Here are some exercises for you to try for yourself.

### Redesign

Our user experience aficionados have reconsidered. Early reports from user testing are that most users don't want to have to type in a precise amount of money; they want to click a button with a fixed amount. Without changing the Cucumber scenario, can you change the support code and then the user interface itself so that users have to click only a single button to get their $20?

Can you add some more scenarios (and some more buttons) for other fixed amounts?

### Preventing Overdraws

We need to help our customers not to overdraw. Add a new scenario that looks like this:

```
Feature: Prevent users from going overdrawn

  Scenario: User tries to withdraw more than their balance
    Given my account has been credited with $100
    When I withdraw $200
    Then nothing should be dispensed
    And I should be told that I have insufficient funds in my account
```

Can you implement it?

### Balancing Act

Our users would like to be able to check their balance from the ATM. Decide how you'd like the user interface to be—perhaps you'll show a menu from which they can choose to make a withdrawal or check their balance—and then implement this scenario:

```
Feature: Display balance

  Scenario: User checks the balance of an account in credit
    Given my account has been credited with $100
    When I check my balance
    Then I should see that my balance is $100
```

# CHAPTER 9

# Message Queues and Asynchronous Components

Our worked example has been pretty simplistic so far. We're testing a single web server process that doesn't even have a database, and we've used only a single scenario to test it. The real systems you have to work on when you put this book down are probably much more complicated than that, with several services interacting to deliver the behavior you've described in your Cucumber features.

In this chapter, we're going to make our system more enterprisey, splitting the architecture into a front-end and back-end so that we can show you how to test these kinds of systems. On the way, we'll get the chance to explain some fundamental concepts about testing asynchronous systems.

## Our New Asynchronous Architecture

In a real banking system, the ATM isn't the only thing making debits on your account. You might use your debit card in a restaurant or supermarket, or you might walk into a bank and withdraw cash over the counter. You might have written a check that gets cashed a few days later. You'll also get credits into your account, like when you deposit checks at the bank. The bank treats each of these events as a *transaction*, which it processes some time after the actual event has happened. Note that this kind of transaction is completely different from a *database transaction*, which we'll talk about in the next chapter.

We're going to change our architecture so that when the customer makes a withdrawal from the ATM, it posts a message about the debit transaction into a message queue. We'll move the responsibility for processing this queue into a separate back-end service. As the back-end service works through the queue of transactions, it will store the updated account balance in a database so that the ATM (and our tests) can access it.

The following figure shows how the new architecture looks.

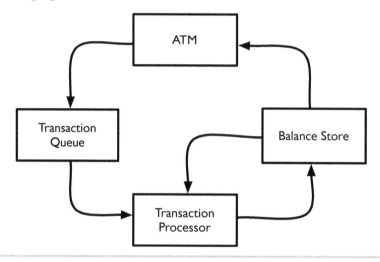

**Figure 3—Enterprise messaging architecture**

The ATM posts messages about transactions into the Transaction Queue. The Transaction Processor reads messages off that queue, reads the existing balance from the Balance Store, and then stores the updated balance back in the Balance Store. The ATM reads the account balance from the Balance Store.

Let's look at the implications this new architecture will have on how we test the system.

## How to Synchronize

In our current implementation, the debit and credit transactions are processed synchronously by our simplistic Account class:

support_code/17/src/main/java/nicebank/Account.java
```
package nicebank;

public class Account {
    private Money balance = new Money();

    public void credit(Money amount) {
        balance = balance.add(amount);
    }
}
```

```
    public void debit(int dollars) {
      balance = balance.minus(new Money(dollars, 0));
    }

    public Money getBalance() {
      return balance;
    }
}
```

This implementation, where the balance is updated *during* the method call to credit or debit, means that we can be certain the balance will have been updated by the time Cucumber checks the account balance in the final Then step of our scenario.

support_code/17/src/test/resources/cash_withdrawal.feature
```
Feature: Cash Withdrawal
  Scenario: Successful withdrawal from an account in credit
    Given my account has been credited with $100.00
    When I withdraw $20
    Then $20 should be dispensed
    And the balance of my account should be $80.00
```

When we change to our new architecture, however, the transactions will be processed by a separate back-end service. Because the tests and back-end service are running in separate processes, it's quite possible that Cucumber will run the Then step before the transaction processor has finished its work. If that happened, the test would fail even though the system is actually working as expected: if only Cucumber had waited a few more moments, it would have seen the right balance. This is what we call a flickering scenario, as described in Chapter 6, *Keeping Your Cucumbers Sweet*, on page 91. How can we tell when it's safe to check the account balance?

Adding asynchronous components into a system introduces a degree of randomness, but for our tests to be reliable, we need to ensure that the behavior is completely deterministic. To do that, we need to understand how we can *synchronize* our tests with the system so that we make our checks only when the system is ready. In *Growing Object-Oriented Software, Guided by Tests [FP09]*, Steve Freeman and Nat Pryce identify two ways to synchronize your tests with an asynchronous system: sampling and listening.

## Synchronizing by Listening

Listening for events is the fastest and most reliable way to synchronize your tests with an asynchronous system. For this technique to work, the system under test has to be designed to fire events when certain things happen. The tests subscribe to these events and can use them to create *synchronization points* in the scenario.

For example, if the Transaction Processor were emitting BalanceUpdated events into a publish-subscribe message channel, we could wait at the top of our Then step until we heard that event. Once we'd received that event, we'd know it was safe to proceed and check the balance. We would use a timeout to ensure the tests didn't wait forever if something was wrong with the system.

Using events like this involves a sophisticated coordination of your testing and development efforts, but it results in fast tests because they don't waste any time waiting for the system: as soon as they're notified of the right event, they spring back into action and carry on.

### Synchronization by Sampling

When it isn't possible to listen to events from the system, the next best option is to repeatedly poll the system for the state change you're expecting. If it doesn't appear within a certain timeout, you give up and fail the test.

Sampling can result in tests that are a little bit slower than listening, because of the polling interval. The more often you poll the system for changes, the quicker the tests can react and carry on when the system is working as expected. If you poll too frequently, however, you could put excessive load on the system.

Sampling is usually the pragmatic choice when you don't have the option to receive events from the system under test. In the rest of this chapter, we'll show you how to use sampling to make our tests work reliably with the new architecture.

## Implementing the New Architecture

So that we can show you what it's like to have a flickering scenario, we'll start by changing the architecture underneath the same test code. We'll demonstrate the flickering scenario and, in a final flourish, fix it by changing the tests to use sampling to synchronize with the system.

### Driving Out the Interfaces

The Account class is where the ATM is going to interface with our new back-end services. As shown in Figure 3, *Enterprise messaging architecture*, on page 170, the two touch points are the TransactionQueue and the BalanceStore. Let's design the interfaces to those objects by changing our Account class to use two imaginary objects that can talk to these services:

message_queues/01/src/main/java/nicebank/Account.java

```
package nicebank;

public class Account {
    private TransactionQueue queue = new TransactionQueue();

    public void credit(Money amount) {
        queue.write("+" + amount.toString());
    }

    public void debit(int dollars) {
        Money amount = new Money(dollars, 0);
        queue.write("-" + amount.toString());
    }

    public Money getBalance() {
      return BalanceStore.getBalance();
    }
}
```

Getting the balance is a simple matter of delegating to the BalanceStore. In a more realistic system, we'd need to tell the BalanceStore which account we wanted the balance for, but in our simple example we're dealing only with a single account, so we don't need to worry about that.

For debits and credits, we're serializing the transaction as a string, using a + or - to indicate whether the amount is a credit or a debit, and then writing it to the queue.

## Building the TransactionQueue

Let's build our transaction queue. We want to keep the technology simple for this example, so we're going to use the file system as our message store, with each message stored as a file in a messages directory. As a message is read from the queue, we'll delete the file. Here's the code:

message_queues/01/src/main/java/nicebank/TransactionQueue.java

```
Line 1  package nicebank;
     -
     -  import org.apache.commons.io.FileUtils;
     -
     5  import java.io.*;
     -  import java.util.Arrays;
     -  import java.util.Comparator;
     -  import java.util.Scanner;
     -
    10  public class TransactionQueue {
     -      private static String MESSAGES_FOLDER = "./messages";
     -      private static String MESSAGE_FILE_PATH = "%s/%03d";
```

```
-        private int nextId = 1;
-
15       public static void clear() {
-            try {
-                FileUtils.deleteDirectory(new File(MESSAGES_FOLDER));
-            } catch (IOException e) {
-                e.printStackTrace();
20           }
-            new File(MESSAGES_FOLDER).mkdirs();
-        }
-
-        public void write(String transaction){
25           String messageFilePath
-                    = String.format(MESSAGE_FILE_PATH, MESSAGES_FOLDER, nextId);
-
-            PrintWriter writer = null;
-            try {
30               writer = new PrintWriter(messageFilePath, "UTF-8");
-            } catch (FileNotFoundException e) {
-                e.printStackTrace();
-            } catch (UnsupportedEncodingException e) {
-                e.printStackTrace();
35           }
-
-            writer.println(transaction);
-            writer.close();
-
40           nextId++;
-        }
-
-        public String read() {
-            // Get files in 'messages'
45           File messagesFolder = new File(MESSAGES_FOLDER);
-            File[] messages = messagesFolder.listFiles();
-
-            String message = "";
-
50           // If message file found
-            if (messages != null && messages.length > 0){
-                Arrays.sort(messages, new Comparator<File>() {
-                    @Override
-                    public int compare(File f1, File f2) {
55                   return Integer.parseInt(f1.getName())
-                            - Integer.parseInt(f2.getName());
-                    }
-                });
-
60               // Open it
-                Scanner scanner = null;
-                try {
```

```
   -                scanner = new Scanner(messages[0]);
   -
  65                if (scanner.hasNextLine()) {
   -                    message = scanner.nextLine();
   -                    scanner.close();
   -
   -                    // Delete it
  70                    messages[0].delete();
   -                }
   -                else {
   -                    scanner.close();
   -                }
  75
   -            } catch (FileNotFoundException e) {
   -                // File has gone away!
   -            }
   -        }
  80
   -        return message;
   -    }
   - }
```

This is fairly simple Java code, but it's the most complicated we've had in the book so far, so let's run through how it works. First we have a static method, TransactionQueue.clear starting on line 15, which we'll use to ensure the queue is cleaned up between scenarios. When we initialize the TransactionQueue, we create an instance variable nextId on line 13, which will be used to give each new message a unique filename. When we're asked to write a message (line 24), we create a new file in the messages directory (line 30), write the contents of the message into the file (line 37), and then increment nextId (line 40) ready for naming the next message's file.

When we're asked to read a message (line 43), we get a listing of all the files in the messages directory (line 46). If the directory is empty, we just return an empty message from the method (line 81). If the directory is not empty, then we sort the list of messages by message ID (line 52). We open the first message (line 63), read the message (line 66), delete the message from the queue (line 70), and return the contents to the caller (line 81).

## Building the BalanceStore

The BalanceStore is a database where the latest account balance is stored. Again, we want to keep the technology simple for this example, so we'll use a very simple kind of database: a text file on disk. Here's the code:

**message_queues/01/src/main/java/nicebank/BalanceStore.java**

```
Line 1  package nicebank;

     -  import java.io.File;
     -  import java.io.FileNotFoundException;
     5  import java.io.PrintWriter;
     -  import java.io.UnsupportedEncodingException;
     -  import java.util.Scanner;

     -  public class BalanceStore {
    10      private static String BALANCE_FILE_PATH = "./balance";

     -      public static void clear() {
     -          new File(BALANCE_FILE_PATH).delete();

    15          setBalance(new Money(0,0));
     -      }

     -      public static Money getBalance() {
     -          File balanceFile = new File(BALANCE_FILE_PATH);
    20          Scanner scanner = null;
     -          try {
     -              scanner = new Scanner(balanceFile);
     -          } catch (FileNotFoundException e) {
     -              e.printStackTrace();
    25          }
     -          // Probably need regex here
     -          Money balance = new Money(scanner.nextLine());
     -          scanner.close();

    30          return balance;
     -      }

     -      public static void setBalance(Money newBalance){

    35          PrintWriter writer = null;
     -          try {
     -              writer = new PrintWriter(BALANCE_FILE_PATH, "UTF-8");
     -          } catch (FileNotFoundException e) {
     -              e.printStackTrace();
    40          } catch (UnsupportedEncodingException e) {
     -              e.printStackTrace();
     -          }
     -          writer.println(newBalance.toString());
     -          writer.close();
    45      }
     -  }
```

We have two methods, one that reads the balance (line 18) and another that sets it (line 33). They both work with a file in the root of our project called balance (line 10). When asked for the balance, the BalanceStore opens the balance file (line 19), reads the contents (line 22), and converts them to a number (line 27). When it's asked to set the balance, the BalanceStore opens the balance file (line 37) and writes the new balance into it (line 43). Simple!

Now that we're persisting state to disk in our TransactionQueue and BalanceStore, we need to be careful that we don't leak any state out of our scenario. Even though we have only a single scenario in our features at the moment, we need to clean up each time it runs so that balances and messages don't leak from one test run into the next.

## Adding Hooks to Reset State

We have two places where state will need to be cleaned up before our scenario runs. We need to set the user's account balance to zero, and we need to remove any messages that have been left in the transaction queue. Add a file src/test/java/hooks/ResetHooks.java with the following code in it:

message_queues/01/src/test/java/hooks/ResetHooks.java
```
package hooks;

import cucumber.api.java.Before;

import nicebank.TransactionQueue;
import nicebank.BalanceStore;

public class ResetHooks {
    @Before
    public void reset() {
        TransactionQueue.clear();
        BalanceStore.clear();
    }
}
```

We've created a new instance of the BalanceStore directly so that we can tell it to set the balance to zero. Then we use the TransactionQueue.clear method we created earlier to empty any messages out of the transaction queue.

Let's put the last piece in the puzzle by writing our TransactionProcessor.

## Building the TransactionProcessor

The TransactionProcessor is some code that will run in the background, deep in the bowels of our bank's server room. Here's the code:

message_queues/01/src/main/java/nicebank/TransactionProcessor.java

```java
package nicebank;

public class TransactionProcessor {
    private TransactionQueue queue = new TransactionQueue();

    public void process() {
        do {
            String message = queue.read();

            try {
                Thread.sleep(1000);
            } catch (InterruptedException e) {

            }

            if (message.length() > 0) {
                Money balance = BalanceStore.getBalance();
                Money transactionAmount = new Money(message);

                if (isCreditTransaction(message)){
                    BalanceStore.setBalance(balance.add(transactionAmount));
                } else {
                    BalanceStore.setBalance(balance.minus(transactionAmount));
                }
            }
        } while (true);
    }

    private boolean isCreditTransaction(String message) {
        return !message.startsWith("-");
    }
}
```

The transaction processor starts by creating an instance of the TransactionQueue and BalanceStore classes. Once it's started up, it then enters a loop that tries to read a message off the transaction queue. If it finds one, it pauses for a second, calculates the new balance, and then stores it on the BalanceStore. We've introduced the pause to demonstrate the effects of working with an asynchronous component in our system; this delay should mean the test will fail consistently because the back-end will take so long to update the balance that Cucumber will have already finished the scenario.

That should complete the implementation of our new architecture. Now it's time to test it.

# Fixing the Flickering Scenario

We're almost ready to run our scenario again, but before we do, there's one thing we need to change in our tests. Right now, when we run mvn clean test, we rely on Selenium to control the web server part of our architecture, but we need a way to start up the back-end transaction processor too. To do that, we'll use another hook.

## Starting and Stopping the Transaction Processor

Let's create a new file src/test/java/hooks/BackgroundProcessHooks.java, which contains the following code:

```
message_queues/01/src/test/java/hooks/BackgroundProcessHooks.java
package hooks;

import cucumber.api.java.After;
import cucumber.api.java.Before;

import nicebank.TransactionProcessor;

public class BackgroundProcessHooks {
    private Thread transactionProcessorThread;

    @Before
    public void startBackgroundThread() {
        transactionProcessorThread = new Thread() {
            public void run() {
                TransactionProcessor processor = new TransactionProcessor();
                processor.process();
            }
        };

        transactionProcessorThread.start();
    }

    @After
    public void stopBackgroundThread() {
        transactionProcessorThread.interrupt();
    }
}
```

These hooks start a TransactionProcessor in a separate thread before each scenario and stop it once the scenario has finished.

## Investigating the Flickering

Our tests are all hooked up to our new architecture, so we're ready to run them and do some investigation into our flickering tests. Run `mvn clean test` and give it a try:

```
-------------------------------------------------------
 T E S T S
-------------------------------------------------------
Running RunCukesTest
Feature: Cash Withdrawal
Listening on http://192.168.1.11:8887/
Server shutdown

  Scenario: Successful withdrawal from an account in credit
    Given my account has been credited with $100.00
    When I withdraw $20
    Then $20 should be dispensed
    And the balance of my account should be $80.00
      java.lang.AssertionError: Incorrect account balance
                                     - expected:<$80.00> but was:<$100.00>
        at org.junit.Assert.fail(Assert.java:88)
        at org.junit.Assert.failNotEquals(Assert.java:743)
        at org.junit.Assert.assertEquals(Assert.java:118)
        at nicebank.AccountSteps.theBalanceOfMyAccountShouldBe$
                                                (AccountSteps.java:32)
        at *.And the balance of my account should be $80.00

1 Scenarios (1 failed)
4 Steps (1 failed, 3 passed)
```

The test has failed and the cause is timing: Cucumber looked in the balance store and found that the balance was zero when it expected it to be 80. That's because we introduced the one-second pause into the transaction processor, meaning it loses its race with Cucumber every time. It didn't get a chance to update the balance before Cucumber checked it and failed the scenario.

Let's swap things around and give the handicap to Cucumber instead of the transaction processor. Remove the `sleep 1` line from the transaction processor and put it into Cucumber's `Then` step instead. Your files should now look like this:

**message_queues/02/src/main/java/nicebank/TransactionProcessor.java**
```java
public void process() {
    do {
        String message = queue.read();

        if (message.length() > 0) {
            Money balance = BalanceStore.getBalance();
```

```
        Money transactionAmount = new Money(message);

        if (isCreditTransaction(message)){
            BalanceStore.setBalance(balance.add(transactionAmount));
        } else {
            BalanceStore.setBalance(balance.minus(transactionAmount));
        }
      }
    } while (true);
}
```

message_queues/02/src/test/java/nicebank/AccountSteps.java
```
@Then("^the balance of my account should be (\\$\\d+\\.\\d+)$")
public void theBalanceOfMyAccountShouldBe$(
                        @Transform(MoneyConverter.class) Money amount)
                                              throws Throwable {

    try {
      Thread.sleep(1000);
    } catch (InterruptedException e) {
      e.printStackTrace();
    }

    Assert.assertEquals("Incorrect account balance -",
                          amount, helper.getMyAccount().getBalance());
}
```

> ## Catching Exceptions from External Services
>
> When you run the code you're testing in the same JVM process that Cucumber is running in, any exception thrown by the code being tested will be caught by Cucumber and displayed in the console. When the error occurs in an out-of-process component, however, Cucumber can't see the error and won't report it to you. This can be confusing because your test fails but you have no idea why.
>
> An easy way to handle this is to write the errors to a log file and then check that log file from your Cucumber tests, perhaps in an After block.

We've moved the sleeps around so that Cucumber loses the race every time, meaning the back-end processor will always finish first. Run mvn clean test now, and you should see the scenario pass.

This illustrates just how fragile tests for asynchronous systems can be to timing issues. We could just leave it like this, but for one thing, it's unnecessarily slow. Even though the transaction processor takes much less than a second to update the balance, our step will always pause for the full second. Also, if we make a change in the future to the transaction processor that means it takes more than one second, the test will start to fail again.

**Joe asks:**

## Should I Show Synchronization Points in My Features?

In this chapter, we've used the JUnit AssertionError method to introduce an implicit synchronization point into our scenario without changing the Gherkin itself. This means that the fact that the behavior is asynchronous remains hidden from anyone reading the scenario. In many situations, asynchronous behavior is a technical detail that doesn't need to be surfaced in the features, but sometimes it's something your readers will want to see in the scenarios.

The key question is whether the nontechnical stakeholders on your project *care* about the asynchronous behavior of the system. Ask them. Perhaps they would prefer to read this:

```
Given my account has been credited with $100
When I withdraw $20
Then $20 should be dispensed
When I wait for all the transactions to be processed
Then the balance of my account should be $80
```

Remember, writing Cucumber features is about communicating the behavior of the system. The right amount of detail will be different for every team and every project, so ask the people on your team what they think.

## Using Sampling to Fix the Flickering

Now that you've seen a flickering test firsthand, let's fix it properly. We need to change the way our Then step behaves so that rather than simply checking the balance once, it checks the balance repeatedly until it reaches the value we expect. Let's write some code that loops until one of the following is true:

- The value is what we expect.

- A time limit is reached.

Here's how we could implement it:

message_queues/03/src/test/java/nicebank/AccountSteps.java
```java
@Then("^the balance of my account should be (\\$\\d+\\.\\d+)$")
public void theBalanceOfMyAccountShouldBe$(
        @Transform(MoneyConverter.class) Money amount) throws Throwable {
    int timeoutMilliSecs = 3000;
    int pollIntervalMilliSecs = 100;

    while (!helper.getMyAccount().getBalance().equals(amount)
                                    && timeoutMilliSecs > 0){
        Thread.sleep(pollIntervalMilliSecs);
```

```
        timeoutMilliSecs -= pollIntervalMilliSecs;
    }

    Assert.assertEquals(
            "Incorrect account balance -",
            amount,
            helper.getMyAccount().getBalance());
}
```

To test this, put the Thread.sleep(1000) line back into the transaction processor and run mvn clean test. You should see the scenario pause for a second as our *eventually* method waits for the system to update the balance and then pass.

**Seb says:**
## That's a Bit of a Mess

Rolling your own sampling (as we've done in this chapter) is fine, but it has left us with some boilerplate code that we'd rather not have to duplicate. If you need to do sampling like this in your application, think about creating your own version of the Assert that provides retries and timeouts. Take a look at the UISpecAssert in the uispec4j[a] project. This project is designed for Swing projects, however, so it isn't directly suitable for our ATM example.

---

a.    http://www.uispec4j.org

### Try This

To satisfy yourself that our new method would fail if there were a problem with the transaction processor, try putting the sleep in the transaction processor up to four seconds. Because the timeout in our polling is only three seconds, the scenario should fail.

## Testing That Nothing Happens

One last thing to consider: Suppose you have a scenario where you credit the account with $100, withdraw $100, and then check that the balance is zero. If the test passes, how can you be sure that the tests have seen the balance *after* the transactions have been processed? It's possible that the transaction processor might not have started processing the transactions or even failed altogether. You'd never know, because the outcome you're looking for to indicate success looks just like the state of the system when you started the scenario.

This kind of problem illustrates the disadvantage of using sampling to synchronize. If you could listen for events from the transaction processor, you could wait until you were sure it had finished its work before checking the balance. Using sampling, you're still left with a potential timing problem.

In these circumstances, you need to introduce an intermediate synchronization point into the scenario to make sure that the system has moved away from the default state. After crediting the account with $100, you need to wait for that credit to have an effect, sampling for the changed balance, before proceeding with the next step.

## What We Just Learned

When you add asynchronous behavior to a system, you need to make a concerted effort to tame the random effects that it can have on your tests. Build your tests with a knowledge of how the system works and introduce synchronization points where timing issues are likely to arise.

Using sleeps in your steps is not a good way to tackle these timing issues, because it makes your tests slow and doesn't solve the reliability problem: if the system changes and becomes slower, your sleep may not be long enough and the test will start to break again. The best solution is to listen for events broadcast by the system and pause at the appropriate points in the scenario until those events have been received. That way, you minimize the amount of time the tests waste waiting for the system.

The next best solution is to use sampling to repeatedly poll the system, looking for an expected change of state. This approach works in most circumstances, but you need to take care, especially when the outcome you're looking for at the end of the scenario looks just the same as at an earlier time in the scenario.

### Try This

Do some more experiments with this code, adding sleeps into the code in different places to make sure you understand how the timing issues affect the reliability of the scenario. Try to draw a sequence diagram[1] of what's going on as the scenario runs.

Think about your own system. Are there any places where there is asynchronous behavior? How do you work around that in the tests at the moment? Could you improve on that using what you've learned in this chapter?

---

1. http://en.wikipedia.org/wiki/Sequence_diagram

# CHAPTER 10

# Databases

Back in Chapter 6, *Keeping Your Cucumbers Sweet*, on page 91 we described the risks associated with *leaky scenarios*, where data left behind by one scenario affects the results of the next. In this chapter we're going to illustrate this problem with an example, and we'll describe the two methods for dealing with it, along with their advantages and disadvantages.

For this final installment of the worked example, we're going to introduce a relational database into our ATM system. Right now, our file-based database can only store the balance of a single customer's account. Let's introduce the capacity to store the balance for several different accounts, using a database table to store each customer's account balance in a separate row.

We'll use a MySql database,[1] although the choice of database is not all that important to this example. That's because we'll be talking to it through an *object relational mapper (ORM)*. Almost every system you'll write Cucumber tests for will have a database of some kind, and it helps to know how to talk to it directly from your test code.

## Iterative Database Development

Many *ORMs* are available to connect your data model to a database, or you could roll your own using JDBC, JPA, or something similar. In this chapter we're going to use ActiveJDBC,[2] which allows us to connect to an existing database with just a few lines of Java code. ActiveJDBC provides the same, consistent interface to every relational database that it talks to and (as of this writing) has drivers for MySQL, PostgreSQL, Oracle, H2, and Microsoft SQL Server databases.

---

1.   http://www.mysql.com
2.   http://code.google.com/p/activejdbc/wiki/GettingStarted

Because we develop our applications iteratively, we also develop our database schemas iteratively. In this chapter we'll use a popular tool called Liquibase[3] to help us manage our database as it evolves. This type of tool becomes particularly useful as your product gets more complicated.

It's useful to have a basic understanding of these database tools, so we'll start with a quick introduction before we plug it into our example.

## Introducing the ActiveJDBC ORM

The ActiveJDBC library is inspired by an implementation found in the Ruby on Rails framework, which is in turn based on the Active Record design pattern.[4] ActiveJDBC is easy to use from Java code to talk to many existing databases. For example, if we had an accounts table with the following data:

| id | number | balance |
|----|--------|---------|
| 1  | 1765   | "80.00" |
| 2  | 2214   | "250.00" |

then we could query that database table using the following Java code:

```
Account account = Account.findFirst("number = 2214");
System.out.println(account.getString("balance"));
```

Similarly, to add a new row to the table, we could do this:

```
Account newAccount = new Account();
newAccount.setInteger("number", 2134);
newAccount.setString("amount", "0.00");
newAccount.saveIt();
```

We still need to define this Account class, but the clever thing is, *we don't need to define the database columns in the code.* Here's how the class is defined:

```
import activejdbc.Model;

public class Account extends Model {}
```

That's it! ActiveJDBC examines the database schema and sprinkles a little bit of Java magic to retrieve the Account class attributes from the database table, providing methods to get and set them by column name. There are also special class methods like where and findFirst for searching for rows by a particular field. All we have to do is inherit from activejdbc.Model, and ActiveJDBC does the rest.

---

3. http://www.liquibase.org
4. http://en.wikipedia.org/wiki/Active_record_pattern

How does it know which table to look at? ActiveJDBC espouses a principle of *convention over configuration*. This means that the expected name for the database table represented by the Account ActiveJDBC class is accounts; if the table were named widgets, we'd call the class Widget. As long as we stick to those conventions, we get a lot of very useful behavior for very little code.

## Tweaking ActiveJDBC for Nonconventional Databases

ActiveJDBC's default conventions are great if you're building a database from scratch, but what if you're working with a legacy system? If your database doesn't fit Active-JDBC's conventions, you can override the default conventions:

```
@Table("tblAccounts")
class Account extends Model {
  int getNumber() {
    return getInteger("intNumber");
  }

  void setNumber(int number){
    setInteger("intNumber", number);
  }
}
```

The @Table annotation tells ActiveJDBC the name of the table you want to use.

## Managing the Schema with Liquibase

It's not enough to have a simple way of connecting your code to your database; you'll also want to control the evolution of your database schema. Several frameworks are available for managing your schema from within the JVM, and we'll use one of the most popular ones, Liquibase.

We define each incremental change to the schema as a *changeset* within a *changelog*. The changelog is a plain XML file, so it can easily be committed to your source control system (along with the code) and managed using normal diff tools. Each changeset is uniquely identified by a combination of ID and author. Liquibase keeps track of which changesets have been applied to your database in a special table (databasechangelog), meaning it can always tell which changesets need to be applied to bring a schema up to date.

Using a Liquibase changelog you can easily create a database from scratch, upgrade a database to the latest schema version, or roll back to a previous version. It's a powerful, well-documented tool, so if you do start using it take some time to read through the features that it provides. For the rest of this chapter we'll use it to create our very simple banking schema, and the examples should be self-explanatory.

Now you have some grounding in ActiveJDBC and Liquibase, let's get our hands dirty and start adding it to our banking system.

# Refactoring to Use a Database

In our current system, the balance of the single account is stored in a file and read and written by the BalanceStore class. In our new design, we will make the Account responsible for reading the balance straight out of a database instead. It's refactoring time again!

## Creating the Database

Once you have installed MySQL[5] you will need to create a database and user. This can be done simply, using the setup-bank.sql script:

databases/00/setup-bank.sql
```
CREATE DATABASE bank;
CREATE USER 'teller'@'localhost' IDENTIFIED BY 'password';
GRANT ALL ON bank.* TO 'teller'@'localhost';
```

As you can see, this script creates a database called bank. It then adds a user teller with password password and grants that user full permissions over the bank database. You can run this script like this:

```
$ mysql -h localhost -u root -p < setup-bank.sql
Enter password:
```

If you set a root password when installing MySQL, enter it when prompted. If you didn't set up a password, remove the -p from the command line and try again.

Now let's configure Liquibase to talk to our new database.

## Configuring Liquibase

To configure Liquibase, we start by adding another plugin to our pom.xml:

databases/00/pom.xml
```
<plugin>
  <groupId>org.liquibase</groupId>
  <artifactId>liquibase-maven-plugin</artifactId>
  <version>3.0.5</version>
  <configuration>
    <changeLogFile>src/main/resources/bank_schema.xml</changeLogFile>
    <driver>com.mysql.jdbc.Driver</driver>
    <url>jdbc:mysql://localhost/bank</url>
    <username>teller</username>
```

---

5.    http://dev.mysql.com/doc/refman/5.7/en/installing.html

```
    <password>password</password>
  </configuration>
  <executions>
    <execution>
      <phase>process-resources</phase>
      <goals>
        <goal>update</goal>
      </goals>
    </execution>
  </executions>
</plugin>
```

Notice that we tell the plugin the name of the database in the url, the user we want to use (username), and the user's password (password). These have to match those created by the setup-bank.sql script.

We also point the plugin at our schema, which we'll create next, in src/main/resources/bank_schema.xml. Liquibase will compare the schema defined by this XML file to the actual schema of the database and perform the necessary actions to ensure that our database is up to date.

We'll create an accounts table shortly with three columns:

id       The primary key, which should be generated automatically.

number   The account number, which serves as a secondary key. This has to be unique.

balance  The current balance of the account.

ActiveJDBC will make all three fields available to each Account instance.

Next, we'll make the Account class an ActiveJDBC class by inheriting from ActiveJDBC::Model. Now it will act on the accounts table we're about to create:

databases/00/src/main/java/nicebank/Account.java
```java
package nicebank;

import org.javalite.activejdbc.Model;

public class Account extends Model {
  private TransactionQueue queue = new TransactionQueue();

  public void credit(Money amount) {
➤     queue.write("+" + amount.toString() + "," + getNumber());
  }

  public void debit(int dollars) {
    Money amount = new Money(dollars, 0);
➤     queue.write("-" + amount.toString() + "," + getNumber());
  }
```

```
    public int getNumber() {
        return getInteger("number");
    }

    public Money getBalance() {
➤       return new Money(getString("balance"));
    }

    public void setBalance(Money amount) {
➤       setString("balance", amount.toString().substring(1));
➤       saveIt();
    }
}
```

Notice that we've changed the getBalance and setBalance methods to use the ActiveJDBC field methods getString and setString. In setBalance we also call the ActiveJDBC method saveIt to commit the balance change to the database.

We've also changed the credit and debit methods to write out the account number as well as the amount so that the TransactionProcessor will know what account a message refers to.

Now let's create our first Liquibase changeset that will create the accounts table if it doesn't exist:

**databases/00/src/main/resources/bank_schema.xml**
```xml
<?xml version="1.0" encoding="UTF-8"?>

<databaseChangeLog
  xmlns="http://www.liquibase.org/xml/ns/dbchangelog"
  xmlns:xsi="http://www.w3.org/2001/XMLSchema-instance"
  xsi:schemaLocation="http://www.liquibase.org/xml/ns/dbchangelog
        http://www.liquibase.org/xml/ns/dbchangelog/dbchangelog-3.0.xsd">

    <changeSet id="1" author="seb">
        <createTable tableName="accounts">
            <column name="id" type="int" autoIncrement="true">
                <constraints primaryKey="true" nullable="false"/>
            </column>
            <column name="number" type="int">
                <constraints nullable="false" unique="true" />
            </column>
            <column name="balance" type="decimal(13,2)" defaultValueNumeric="0.00">
                <constraints nullable="false" />
            </column>
        </createTable>
    </changeSet>

</databaseChangeLog>
```

You'll notice that all the fields are marked nullable="false" because all of them should be set at all times. The id field is marked with autoIncrement="true" (so that the database automatically generates a new id for each account added) and has a primaryKey constraint (to ensure that it is unique and indexed). The number field has a unique="true" constraint (also to ensure uniqueness) and the balance field is a decimal with a default value of 0.00.

## Connecting to the Database

When we run our application we need to get a connection to the database so that we can read and update account balances. We'll do this in the main method of our AtmServer class where we use the Base class to ask ActiveJDBC to open a connection to our MySQL database called bank. Once the call to open completes successfully, the connection is available to all code running *on this thread*.

databases/00/src/main/java/nicebank/AtmServer.java
```java
public static void main(String[] args) throws Exception {
    Base.open(
            "com.mysql.jdbc.Driver",
            "jdbc:mysql://localhost/bank",
            "teller", "password");
    new AtmServer(9988, new CashSlot(), new Account()).start();
}
```

Now we have an Account that can persist itself along with the balance, let's get rid of the BalanceStore class, so we will simply delete the src/main/java/nicebank/BalanceStore.java file. Of course, we now need to modify TransactionProcessor so that it uses the database instead of BalanceStore to access the balance:

databases/00/src/main/java/nicebank/TransactionProcessor.java
```java
public void process() {
    do {
        String message = queue.read();

        if (message.length() > 0) {
➤           String[] parts = message.split(",");
➤           Account account = Account.findFirst("number = ?", parts[1]);
➤           Money transactionAmount = new Money(parts[0]);

            if (isCreditTransaction(message)){
➤               account.setBalance(account.getBalance().add(transactionAmount));
            } else {
➤               account.setBalance(account.getBalance().minus(transactionAmount));
            }
        }
    } while (true);
}
```

We also need to modify src/test/java/hooks/ResetHooks.java, which no longer needs to reference BalanceStore:

databases/00/src/test/java/hooks/ResetHooks.java
```
package hooks;

import cucumber.api.java.Before;

import nicebank.TransactionQueue;

public class ResetHooks {
    @Before
    public void reset() {
        TransactionQueue.clear();
    }
}
```

Before we run Cucumber again, we'll add the ActiveJDBC and MySQL dependencies and configuration to our pom.xml:

databases/00/pom.xml
```
<dependency>
    <groupId>org.javalite</groupId>
    <artifactId>activejdbc</artifactId>
    <version>1.4.1</version>
</dependency>
<dependency>
 <groupId>mysql</groupId>
 <artifactId>mysql-connector-java</artifactId>
 <version>5.1.27</version>
</dependency>
```

databases/00/pom.xml
```
<plugin>
    <groupId>org.javalite</groupId>
    <artifactId>activejdbc-instrumentation</artifactId>
    <version>1.4.1</version>
    <executions>
        <execution>
            <phase>process-classes</phase>
            <goals>
                <goal>instrument</goal>
            </goals>
        </execution>
    </executions>
</plugin>
```

Now let's run mvn clean test:

```
Line 1   [INFO] --- liquibase-maven-plugin:3.0.5:update (default) @ atm-example ---
     2   [INFO] ------------------------------------------------------------------------
     3   [INFO] Executing on Database: jdbc:mysql://localhost/bank
     4   INFO 02/01/14 17:16:liquibase: null: null: Successfully acquired change log lock
     5   INFO 02/01/14 17:16:liquibase: null: null: Reading from DATABASECHANGELOG
     6   INFO 02/01/14 17:16:liquibase: null: null: Reading from DATABASECHANGELOG
     7   INFO 02/01/14 17:16:liquibase: src/main/resources/bank_schema.xml:
     8               src/main/resources/bank_schema.xml::1::seb: Table accounts created
     9   INFO 02/01/14 17:16:liquibase: src/main/resources/bank_schema.xml:
    10               src/main/resources/bank_schema.xml::1::seb:
    11               ChangeSet src/main/resources/bank_schema.xml::1::seb
    12               ran successfully in 13ms
    13   INFO 02/01/14 17:16:liquibase: src/main/resources/bank_schema.xml: null:
    14               Successfully released change log lock
    15   ....
    16   ------------------------------------------------------------
    17    T E S T S
    18   ------------------------------------------------------------
    19   Running RunCukesTest
    20   Feature: Cash Withdrawal
    21
    22     Scenario: Successful withdrawal from an account in credit
    23       Given my account has been credited with $100.00
    24         org.javalite.activejdbc.DBException:
    25           Failed to retrieve metadata from DB, connection:
    26             'default' is not available
    27       at org.javalite.activejdbc.Registry.init(Registry.java:134)
    28       at org.javalite.activejdbc.Model.getMetaModel(Model.java:58)
    29       at org.javalite.activejdbc.Model.getMetaModelLocal(Model.java:946)
    30       at org.javalite.activejdbc.Model.get(Model.java:1021)
    31       at nicebank.Account.get(Account.java)
    32       at org.javalite.activejdbc.Model.getInteger(Model.java:1099)
    33       at nicebank.Account.getInteger(Account.java)
    34       at nicebank.Account.getNumber(Account.java:23)
    35       at nicebank.Account.credit(Account.java:11)
    36       at nicebank.AccountSteps.myAccountHasBeenCreditedWith$
    37       at *.Given my account has been credited with $100.00
    38       When I withdraw $20
    39       Then $20 should be dispensed
    40       And the balance of my account should be $80.00
    41
    42   1 Scenarios (1 failed)
    43   4 Steps (1 failed, 3 skipped)
```

The first thing we see is that the database is automatically migrated—the accounts table is created (at line 8). This technique of letting the application automatically migrate the database when it starts is a handy trick. But then we get a failure further down (at line 24).

It looks like we have some more work to do. Not to worry—the error tells us that we have some sort of problem with our database connection. There's no default connection available when we try to set the initial balance of the account, and we'll work out why in the next section.

## Reading and Writing to the Database

Remember that we opened the connection to the database in *Connecting to the Database*, on page 191, we told you that the connection is available to all code running *on this thread*. The code is failing when our AccountSteps definition tries to set the initial balance of the account directly (without going through the UI or the server). Once you think about it, you'll realize that Cucumber and the server are running on different threads, so we need to open a connection to the database from the Cucumber thread as well.

We'll need to access the database when we set up (or check) the state of our domain entities, so the logical place to open the connection is in KnowsTheDomain:

```
databases/01/src/test/java/support/KnowsTheDomain.java
public KnowsTheDomain() {
    if (!Base.hasConnection()){
        Base.open(
            "com.mysql.jdbc.Driver",
            "jdbc:mysql://localhost/bank",
            "teller", "password");
    }
}
```

Now when we run mvn clean test we get a different error:

```
Given my account has been credited with $100.00
  java.lang.NullPointerException
       at nicebank.Account.getNumber(Account.java:23)
       at nicebank.Account.credit(Account.java:11)
       at nicebank.AccountSteps.myAccountHasBeenCreditedWith$
                                            (AccountSteps.java:23)
       at *.Given my account has been credited with $100.00
                                            (cash_withdrawal.feature:3)
```

This is a problem with our use of ActiveJDBC. We've created an Account instance without setting any values. When we try to access the account number we get a null returned to us, which the ActiveJDBC getInteger method tries to convert to an integer. No wonder it's complaining!

This is actually good news because if we could create an account without an account number, what would the Account write out in the transaction message amount,account_number? Without an account number, how would the Transaction-Processor find the right account in the database to update its balance?

So, let's provide a constructor on the Account class that takes an account number and for good measure, we'll set the balance of a new account to "0.00" too. We need to create a default constructor too, so that ActiveJDBC has a way to create Account instances itself:

databases/02/src/main/java/nicebank/Account.java
```java
public Account() {}

public Account(int number){
    setInteger("number", number);
    setString("balance", "0.00");
}
```

Now we use the non-default constructor when we create the account in KnowsTheDomain:

databases/02/src/test/java/support/KnowsTheDomain.java
```java
public Account getMyAccount() {
  if (myAccount == null){
    myAccount = new Account(1234);
  }

  return myAccount;
}
```

When we run mvn clean test again we get yet another error, which is again due to a thread trying to access the database without having a connection to the database:

```
--------------------------------------------------------
 T E S T S
--------------------------------------------------------
Running RunCukesTest
Feature: Cash Withdrawal
Listening on http://192.168.1.11:8887/
Exception in thread "Thread-9" org.javalite.activejdbc.DBException:
 org.javalite.activejdbc.DBException:
  there is no connection 'default' on this thread, are you sure you opened it?,
    Query: SELECT  * FROM accounts WHERE  number = ? LIMIT 1, params: 1234
        at org.javalite.activejdbc.DB.connection(DB.java:604)
        at org.javalite.activejdbc.DB.find(DB.java:402)
        at org.javalite.activejdbc.LazyList.hydrate(LazyList.java:302)
        at org.javalite.activejdbc.LazyList.size(LazyList.java:528)
        at org.javalite.activejdbc.Model.findFirst(Model.java:1674)
        at nicebank.Account.findFirst(Account.java)
        at nicebank.TransactionProcessor.process(TransactionProcessor.java:14)
        at hooks.BackgroundProcessHooks$1.run(BackgroundProcessHooks.java:16)
```

```
Caused by: org.javalite.activejdbc.DBException:
   there is no connection 'default' on this thread, are you sure you opened it?
        ... 8 more
Server shutdown
```

This time it's the thread running the TransactionProcessor that needs a connection to the database, so let's open a connection in its process method:

databases/03/src/main/java/nicebank/TransactionProcessor.java

```java
public void process() {
    if (!Base.hasConnection()){
        Base.open(
            "com.mysql.jdbc.Driver",
            "jdbc:mysql://localhost/bank",
            "teller", "password");
    }

    do {
        String message = queue.read();

        if (message.length() > 0) {
            String[] parts = message.split(",");
            Account account = Account.findFirst("number = ?", parts[1]);
            Money transactionAmount = new Money(parts[0]);

            if (isCreditTransaction(message)){
                account.setBalance(account.getBalance().add(transactionAmount));
            } else {
                account.setBalance(account.getBalance().minus(transactionAmount));
            }
        }
    } while (true);
}
```

Run mvn clean test again and we now have two errors:

```
Line 1  ---------------------------------------------------------
   2   T E S T S
   3   ---------------------------------------------------------
   4  Running RunCukesTest
   5  Feature: Cash Withdrawal
   6  Listening on http://192.168.1.11:8887/
   7  Exception in thread "Thread-0" java.lang.NullPointerException
   8          at nicebank.TransactionProcessor.process(TransactionProcessor.java:27)
   9          at hooks.BackgroundProcessHooks$1.run(BackgroundProcessHooks.java:16)
  10  Server shutdown
  11
  12    Scenario: Successful withdrawal from an account in credit
  13      Given my account has been credited with $100.00
  14      When I withdraw $20
  15      Then $20 should be dispensed
```

```
16     And the balance of my account should be $80.00
17       java.lang.AssertionError: Incorrect account balance
18                                - expected:<$80.00> but was:<$0.00>
19         at org.junit.Assert.fail(Assert.java:88)
20         at org.junit.Assert.failNotEquals(Assert.java:743)
21         at org.junit.Assert.assertEquals(Assert.java:118)
22         at nicebank.AccountSteps.theBalanceOfMyAccountShouldBe$
23         at *.And the balance of my account should be $80.00
24
25  1 Scenarios (1 failed)
26  4 Steps (1 failed, 3 passed)
```

We'll deal with the first error, which is a NullPointerException. Looking at the stack trace at line 8 we can see this is thrown in the TransactionProcessor class. What's going on here?

databases/03/src/main/java/nicebank/TransactionProcessor.java
```
account.setBalance(account.getBalance().add(transactionAmount));
```

It looks like our Account object is null, so let's take a look in the database to see if there are any clues:

```
$ mysql -h localhost -u teller -p bank
Enter password: password
mysql> select * from accounts;
Empty set (0.00 sec)
```

There's nothing in the accounts table at all. This is because, although we created an instance of the Account class, we never actually told ActiveJDBC to save it to the database. We'll add a call to saveIt to the getMyAccount method of KnowsThe-Domain:

databases/04/src/test/java/support/KnowsTheDomain.java
```
public Account getMyAccount() {
  if (myAccount == null){
    myAccount = new Account(1234);
➤   myAccount.saveIt();
  }

  return myAccount;
}
```

Running mvn clean test one more time shows that we still have to work out why our scenario's assertion is failing:

```
-------------------------------------------------------
 T E S T S
-------------------------------------------------------
Running RunCukesTest
Feature: Cash Withdrawal
Listening on http://127.0.0.1:8887/
```

Server shutdown

```
  Scenario: Successful withdrawal from an account in credit
    Given my account has been credited with $100.00
    When I withdraw $20
    Then $20 should be dispensed
    And the balance of my account should be $80.00
      java.lang.AssertionError: Incorrect account balance
                                    - expected:<$80.00> but was:<$0.00>
        at org.junit.Assert.fail(Assert.java:88)
        at org.junit.Assert.failNotEquals(Assert.java:743)
        at org.junit.Assert.assertEquals(Assert.java:118)
        at nicebank.AccountSteps.theBalanceOfMyAccountShouldBe$
        at *.And the balance of my account should be $80.00


1 Scenarios (1 failed)
4 Steps (1 failed, 3 passed)
```

We expected the balance to be $80, but it looks like it's still $0. Where did the money go? Let's look in the database:

```
mysql> select * from accounts;
+----+--------+---------+
| id | number | balance |
+----+--------+---------+
|  1 |   1234 |   80.00 |
+----+--------+---------+
1 row in set (0.00 sec)
```

Phew! The money is safe in our account. It turns out the step failed because we are still looking at the original instance of the account record—stored in myAccount—from when we created it with a zero balance. Even though the underlying database row has been modified by the TransactionProcessor, Active-JDBC doesn't know that the record we have is out-of-date, so we need to tell it to reload the record from the database, using the refresh method:

databases/05/src/main/java/nicebank/Account.java
```java
public Money getBalance() {
    refresh();
    return new Money(getString("balance"));
}
```

Let's run the scenario again:

```
org.javalite.activejdbc.DBException:
  com.mysql.jdbc.exceptions.jdbc4.MySQLIntegrityConstraintViolationException:
    Duplicate entry '1234' for key 'number', Query:
      INSERT INTO accounts (balance, number) VALUES (?, ?), params: 0.00,1234
      ...
```

```
    at nicebank.Account.saveIt(Account.java)
    at support.KnowsTheDomain.getMyAccount(KnowsTheDomain.java:34)
    ...
```

This time when we run mvn clean test our scenario—which previously only failed because of an incorrect balance—is failing during the first call to KnowsTheDomain.getMyAccount. We have stumbled upon one of the most common problems of automated tests for a system using a database. The previous test run left data in the database, and running it again makes it fail. We can't create an account because the Account number has to be unique, and a row for that Account was left behind by the previous test run. We have a *leaky scenario*!

The good thing about common problems is that there often is a common solution. We have to make sure each scenario starts with a clean database. There are two strategies to achieve this—*transaction* and *truncation*. We'll explore both, starting with transactions.

## Cleaning the Database with Transactions

This is a clever approach that uses the database's transaction support in a somewhat unusual way. Before the scenario starts, we start a new database transaction in a @Before hook. Then, our step definitions and application insert and modify data in the database. However, since this is happening in an uncommitted transaction, nothing gets changed in the database until the transaction is committed. Then, when the scenario is over (in an @After hook), we do the opposite. We roll the transaction back! All the data that was modified during the scenario gets lost, and the database is back in its original state. You can see how this works in Figure 4, *Database transactions*, on page 200.

This is actually what we want. It means that the next scenario that comes along starts with a blank slate, and we don't need to worry about leftovers from the previous scenario.

Unfortunately, the transaction approach doesn't work for our application. Understanding why this doesn't work is essential, so we are going to try it anyway. Seeing it fail and understanding why will save you hours of problem solving in the future. It will also help you understand when to use transactions and when not to use them.

Our previous run would have left a row in the accounts table, so let's remove that before we try to run with transactions:

```
$ mysql -h localhost -u teller -p bank
Enter password: password
mysql> delete from accounts;
mysql> exit
```

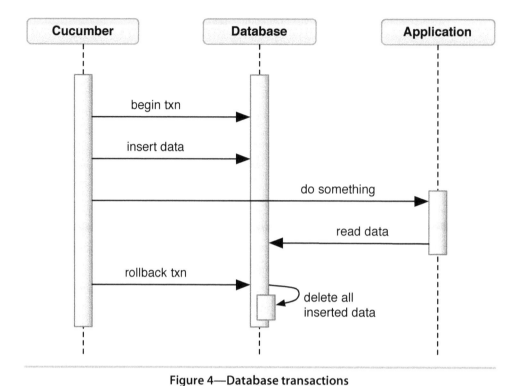

**Figure 4—Database transactions**

Now that we have a clean database, let's configure Cucumber to begin and roll back a transaction. ActiveJDBC is a thin wrapper on top of Java's own JDBC implementation, so we'll turn off transaction auto-completion when we open the connection, and roll back the transaction in an @After hook:

databases/06/src/test/java/support/KnowsTheDomain.java
```java
public KnowsTheDomain() {
    if (!Base.hasConnection()){
        Base.open(
            "com.mysql.jdbc.Driver",
            "jdbc:mysql://localhost/bank",
            "teller", "password");

        try {
            Base.connection().setAutoCommit(false);
        } catch (Exception se){
            // Ignore
        }
    }
}
```

```
databases/06/src/test/java/hooks/ResetHooks.java
@After
public void rollback() {
    Base.rollbackTransaction();
}
```

That's all you need to start a transaction at the beginning of each scenario and roll it back at the end.

We'll also add a bit of helpful diagnostic to the TransactionProcessor:

```
databases/06/src/main/java/nicebank/TransactionProcessor.java
Account account = Account.findFirst("number = ?", parts[1]);
if (account == null) {
    throw new RuntimeException("Account number not found: " + parts[1]);
}
```

Let's see how that works:

```
--------------------------------------------------------
 T E S T S
--------------------------------------------------------
Running RunCukesTest
Listening on http://sebsair13.lan:8887/
Exception in thread "Thread-0" java.lang.RuntimeException:
                                        Account number not found: 1234
        at nicebank.TransactionProcessor.process(TransactionProcessor.java:26)
        at nicebank.BackgroundProcessHooks$1.run(BackgroundProcessHooks.java:16)
```

We told you it wasn't going to work. It's time to find out why. The Transaction-Processor can't find the account we created in our first step, and our scenario fails. Why can't the TransactionProcessor find the account?

One of the properties of database transactions is that they are *isolated*. This means that whatever database activity happens inside a transaction cannot be seen by *any* other database connections. Don't forget that we have several database connections.

The first database connection is made by the process that runs Cucumber. Cucumber begins a database transaction and creates an account.

The second database connection is made by the TransactionProcessor, which is started in a separate process by BackgroundProcessHooks. The TransactionProcessor pops credit and debit messages off a queue, looks up accounts, and updates the balance. However, since the database transaction that Cucumber started never gets committed, the TransactionProcessor can't see the account we created in our first step.

**Aslak says:**
**Browser Testing and Databases**

The problem with transactional cleaning and multiple database connections often occurs when we test web applications. This happens when the web application has a different database connection than Cucumber. The problem typically manifests itself in two situations:

- Cucumber inserts some data, but it isn't displayed in the browser.

- A browser action causes some data to be inserted, but Cucumber can't see it.

If this happens, you need to make sure you are not starting a transaction anywhere. You have to use the *truncation* cleaning strategy instead. If you're logging your database calls, reading the logs can be very useful when diagnosing a problem like this.

In Chapter 12, *Working with Web Applications*, on page 225, you will learn how to drive a browser from Cucumber. Cucumber will start up the web server in a separate thread, so you might think Cucumber and the web server share the same database connection. In fact, they don't—each thread also gets its own database connection, which means transactional cleaning won't work. It obscures data from the other connection.

Of course, we could have committed the transaction after creating the account, but that would defeat our goal of rolling back to get a clean database when the scenario is done. We can't roll back a committed transaction. The rule is simple: when the application has a different database connection than Cucumber, we cannot use transactions to clean the database. We have to use the other strategy instead: *truncation*.

## Cleaning the Database with Truncation

Truncating the database before each scenario is a brute-force technique, and the main drawback is that it's generally slower than rolling back a transaction. This is why the transactional approach is typically preferable if you can get away with it. The advantage of truncation is that it's a cleaning strategy that works reliably when we have more than one database connection, since no transactions are used. Let's modify our cleaning strategy and see how it compares. This is a simple change in our KnowsTheDomain class, shown in the following code.

> **Joe asks:**
> # Why Not Truncate the Database in an @After Hook?
>
> Truncating the database in an @After hook usually works just as well as doing it before the scenario executes, but there is a subtle difference.
>
> First, if the process gets killed before it has time to clean up in the @After hook, it might cause the next test run to fail.
>
> Second, when a scenario fails it might not be evident why it failed, and having the ability to peek inside the database as a postmortem often helps us understand why a scenario is failing.

**databases/07/src/test/java/support/KnowsTheDomain.java**

```java
public KnowsTheDomain() {
    if (!Base.hasConnection()){
        Base.open(
            "com.mysql.jdbc.Driver",
            "jdbc:mysql://localhost/bank",
            "teller", "password");
    }

    Account.deleteAll();
}
```

Running Cucumber again makes the scenario pass again:

```
------------------------------------------------------
 T E S T S
------------------------------------------------------
Running RunCukesTest
Feature: Cash Withdrawal
Listening on http://192.168.1.11:8887/
Server shutdown

  Scenario: Successful withdrawal from an account in credit
    Given my account has been credited with $100.00
    When I withdraw $20
    Then $20 should be dispensed
    And the balance of my account should be $80.00

1 Scenarios (1 passed)
4 Steps (4 passed)
```

That brings us to the end of the worked example. The next part is a series of recipes for using Cucumber in the wild. Good luck out there!

# What We Just Learned

Testing applications that use databases can be difficult. You have to make sure each scenario starts with a clean slate, but cleaning the slate can have its own pitfalls. In this chapter, we learned about the benefits and drawbacks of two strategies—transaction and truncation. To sum it up:

- Liquibase is great for creating and evolving database schema.

- ActiveJDBC is a useful library for quickly connecting to SQL databases.

- Resetting state between scenarios is vital; otherwise, you get weird failures.

- Transaction-based cleaning is preferred because it is fast, but it works only when there is one single-threaded process.

- Truncation-based cleaning is a slower, brute-force technique that works in multiprocess and multithreaded environments.

## Try This

Find an existing database, perhaps somewhere on your network at work, and see if you can connect ActiveJDBC to it. It should only take you a few lines of Java code to set up a Model subclass that can talk to one of the tables in the schema. Read up on ActiveJDBC's API documentation[6] and try running some queries against the database. See how much easier it is to use Active-JDBC to talk to any database!

---

6. http://javalite.io

# CHAPTER 11

# Simplifying Design with Dependency Injection

In *Dependency Injection*, on page 137, we saw how Cucumber uses dependency injection (DI) to share an instance of KnowsTheDomain between our step definitions, but we really only scratched the surface. Now it's time to dig a little bit deeper.

In this chapter we'll discuss how DI can help improve the design of your test code and the various DI containers that are integrated with Cucumber. Then we'll dive in and refactor our ATM example to use DI more effectively, showing you how to do it with four of the popular DI containers.

## DI and Cucumber

You don't *need* to use a DI container when you use Cucumber. When you use Cucumber without one of the DI integrations, it manages the creation of all your hooks and step definitions itself. Cucumber creates fresh instances of each step definition or hook class for each scenario. Of course that means that these classes need to have a default constructor; otherwise Cucumber won't know how to create them. This makes it hard to share state safely between several step definition classes.

DI can make some of your everyday work less tedious and error prone. As soon as you add one of the DI integrations, the DI container takes over the responsibility for creating the hooks and step definitions. All the DI containers can also *inject* objects into our hooks and step definitions when it creates them. Even better, the DI container will create instances of any object that needs to be created so you can easily build networks of dependent objects, leaving the hard work of wiring them all together to the DI container.

The two common ways that DI containers inject objects are *constructor injection* and *field injection*. In the following sections, we'll mainly be using constructor injection, but we'll also show you field injection in action.

## Letting DI Manage Shared State

A DI container is just a tool that creates and manages instances of some classes for us. If you look back at the code we wrote to share a single instance of KnowsTheDomain among all our step definition classes, you'll see that we never create an instance of KnowsTheDomain using new. That's because our DI container, PicoContainer, has been doing it for us. What's more, PicoContainer created a new instance of KnowsTheDomain for each scenario and injected that instance into every step definition class that needed it. This made it easy for us to create a focused step definition class for each domain entity in our application, relying on PicoContainer to share state between them.

If we had done this without DI, it would have meant much more work for us. We could have shared state by creating a static instance of KnowsTheDomain, but that instance would then be shared by all our scenarios. Since we want each scenario to have its own fresh copy of KnowsTheDomain, we would have to add a @Before hook to reset the shared instance. But we don't need to do any of this, because a DI container will do it for us.

Cucumber's use of DI makes our lives much simpler by taking care of the creation of our hook and step definition classes, as well as all the shared state that they depend on. For each step definition that needs access to a scenario's shared state, we define a constructor that takes the shared class as a parameter. If a scenario needs access to instances of several different classes, we simply provide a constructor that has a parameter for each of them:

```
public SomeStepDefinitionOrHooks(Foo sharedFoo, Bar sharedBar) {
  // Store sharedFoo and sharedBar for later use
}
```

You'll want to use DI in most of your Cucumber projects, because it makes sharing state between step definition classes so much simpler. Cucumber has integrations with several DI containers, which we'll take a brief look at next.

## DI Container Integrations

Cucumber ships with integrations to several of the more popular DI containers (as well as some unfamiliar to most people), shown in the following list. The code you write will look slightly different depending on which DI container you choose.

- cucumber-picocontainer—PicoContainer:[1] A lightweight DI container from Aslak Hellesøy, Paul Hammant, and Jon Tirsen

- cucumber-guice—Guice:[2] A lightweight DI container from Google

- cucumber-spring—Spring:[3] A popular framework that includes DI and much more

- cucumber-weld—CDI/Weld:[4] The reference implementation of the CDI (Context and Dependency Injection Framework for the Java EE platform)

- cucumber-openejb—OpenEJB:[5] A stand-alone EJB server from Apache, including a CDI implementation

You choose which framework to use by including the relevant Cucumber JAR in your classpath, but *only one* Cucumber DI JAR should ever be on the classpath. As soon as you put one of these JARs on your classpath, Cucumber will delegate the creation and management of your hooks and step definitions to the DI container you chose. The Cucumber JARs contain only the code to integrate the DI container—you'll also need to add a dependency on the DI container itself.

### Which DI Container Should I Choose?

The various DI containers provide almost exactly the same functionality. Each needs slightly different configuration, but the choice mostly depends on what DI container you're already using in your application. If your application uses Spring, then choose cucumber-spring. If your application uses Guice, then choose cucumber-guice.

If your app isn't using DI at all, PicoContainer is a great choice because it's so simple to use.

Let's to go back to our ATM example and see how DI can improve the structure of our test code. You'll be surprised what a big difference it can make.

## Improving Our Design Using DI

As we've seen, DI can make our lives simpler by doing some of our work for us. At the moment our application is using DI to share some state, but code in KnowsTheDomain is managing the creation of quite a few domain entities. As

---

1. http://picocontainer.codehaus.org
2. https://github.com/google/guice
3. http://projects.spring.io/spring-framework/
4. http://weld.cdi-spec.org
5. http://openejb.apache.org/index.html

our application grows, we're likely to find more domain entities that need to be shared between our step definitions. The temptation would be to put all our shared domain entities into KnowsTheDomain, but this would soon grow huge, exhibiting the Monster Object antipattern.[6]

To keep our step definitions maintainable, it's a good idea to create a step definition class for each domain entity. It's clear that the Cash Slot step definition is going to need to interact with the Cash Slot domain entity, but will it ever need to know about a Customer entity? Probably not, so why would we pass it a helper that has access to the Customer?

Starting with the code from the end of Chapter 10, *Databases*, on page 185, we're going to refactor our ATM example to use DI more effectively. We'll take small steps,[7] looking at the result of each refactoring to see if there is another refactoring that could improve the design further. At the end you'll see a much cleaner application with fewer classes and a clearer architecture.

## Decomposing KnowsTheDomain

We'll start by splitting KnowsTheDomain into several, smaller, cohesive helper classes—one for each domain entity—as as shown in the figure. Then we can make sure that a step definition only has access to entities that it *should* need to interact with by passing them in at construction time.

**Before**

| KnowsTheDomain |
| --- |
| Account getMyAccount()<br>Teller getTeller()<br>CashSlot getCashSlot() |

| CashSlotSteps |
| --- |
| public void CashSlotSteps(KnowsTheDomain helper) {<br>  // ...<br>} |

**After**

| KnowsTheAccount |
| --- |
| Account getMyAccount() |

| KnowsTheTeller |
| --- |
| Teller getTeller() |

| KnowsTheCashSlot |
| --- |
| CashSlot getCashSlot() |

| CashSlotSteps |
| --- |
| public void CashSlotSteps(KnowsTheCashSlot helper) {<br>  // ...<br>} |

---

6.  http://lostechies.com/chrismissal/2009/05/28/anti-patterns-and-worst-practices-monster-objects/
7.  http://c2.com/cgi/wiki?RefactoringInVerySmallSteps

We'll move the functionality that's specific to each domain entity into a separate helper class. Take a look at KnowsTheCashSlot, for example:

```
dependency_injection/pico/02/src/test/java/support/KnowsTheCashSlot.java
package support;
import nicebank.CashSlot;

public class KnowsTheCashSlot {
    private CashSlot cashSlot;

    public CashSlot getCashSlot() {
        if (cashSlot == null){
            cashSlot = new CashSlot();
        }
        return cashSlot;
    }
}
```

Similarly, we can create the KnowsTheTeller and KnowsTheAccount helper classes.

Next we have to change references to KnowsTheDomain, such as in CashSlotSteps:

```
dependency_injection/pico/02/src/test/java/nicebank/CashSlotSteps.java
import support.KnowsTheCashSlot;

public class CashSlotSteps {
  KnowsTheCashSlot cashSlotHelper;

  public CashSlotSteps(KnowsTheCashSlot cashSlotHelper) {
      this.cashSlotHelper = cashSlotHelper;
  }
}
```

Not all changes are quite so simple. Our TellerSteps, for example, interacts with KnowsTheAccount as well as KnowsTheTeller, so we have to pass both in to the constructor. The DI framework can handle multiple parameters, and calls the constructor correctly without any extra work on our part:

```
dependency_injection/pico/02/src/test/java/nicebank/TellerSteps.java
public TellerSteps(KnowsTheTeller tellerHelper, KnowsTheAccount accountHelper) {
    this.tellerHelper = tellerHelper;
    this.accountHelper = accountHelper;
}
```

Once we finish moving functionality into the new helper classes, we notice that there's still some code in KnowsTheDomain that's concerned with creating a shared EventFiringWebDriver. Since this is specific to the technology driving the user interface, it's not logically a concern of any of the KnowsTheXxx classes, so we need to decide where to put it, which we'll do next.

## Extracting a Web Driver

Both AtmUserInterface and WebDriverHooks are dependent on a shared EventFiringWeb-Driver. This used to be managed by KnowsTheDomain but really has nothing to do with the domain. Instead, let's extract a new MyWebDriver class:

dependency_injection/pico/02/src/test/java/support/MyWebDriver.java
```
package support;

import org.openqa.selenium.firefox.FirefoxDriver;
import org.openqa.selenium.support.events.EventFiringWebDriver;

public class MyWebDriver extends EventFiringWebDriver{
    public MyWebDriver() {
        super(new FirefoxDriver());
    }
}
```

There's no code left in KnowsTheDomain, so we can delete it. However, we still have to inject the shared MyWebDriver instance into AtmUserInterface and WebDriver-Hooks by changing their constructors:

dependency_injection/pico/02/src/test/java/support/AtmUserInterface.java
```
private final EventFiringWebDriver webDriver;

public AtmUserInterface(MyWebDriver webDriver) {
    this.webDriver = webDriver;
}
```

(The WebDriverHooks constructor looks the same.)

Now we run mvn clean test to make sure we haven't introduced any defects.

We've improved our design by decoupling the UI from the domain entities. Our DI container now has the responsibility of managing a shared instance of MyWebDriver and injecting it into any constructor that needs it. In the next step, we'll see that most of the helper classes are doing nothing (or very little) that our DI container can't do for us, so we'll refactor them away entirely.

## Replacing the Helper Classes

At this point, we've created smaller, more cohesive helper classes, so now let's take a good look at each of them to see if we're happy with the structure of our test code. Now that we have smaller helper classes it's easier to see exactly what each one does and decide, armed with our deeper understanding of DI, if we could do it better. And if we think that we could improve things further, we still have the safety net of a passing scenario to ensure that we don't break anything while we continue the refactoring.

### KnowsTheCashSlot

Taking a look at the class KnowsTheCashSlot, we can see that all it's doing is managing the creation of the domain entity CashSlot. The reason we're using DI in the first place is to manage the creation of shared objects, so it seems strange that we've ended up with our own class that does just that! What has happened is that by refactoring KnowsTheDomain, and with our new knowledge of how DI works, we can now see that we don't need KnowsTheCashSlot at all. So, let's simplify our codebase by deleting KnowsTheCashSlot and injecting the CashSlot directly into our step definition:

**dependency_injection/pico/03/src/test/java/nicebank/CashSlotSteps.java**
```
CashSlot cashSlot;

public CashSlotSteps(CashSlot cashSlot) {
    this.cashSlot = cashSlot;
}
```

We also need to inject CashSlot into our ServerHooks:

**dependency_injection/pico/03/src/test/java/hooks/ServerHooks.java**
```
private KnowsTheAccount accountHelper;
private CashSlot cashSlot;

public ServerHooks(KnowsTheAccount accountHelper, CashSlot cashSlot) {
    this.accountHelper = accountHelper;
    this.cashSlot = cashSlot;
}
```

Run mvn clean test to make sure we're still green!

### KnowsTheTeller

KnowsTheTeller also only manages the creation of a Teller. If we make exactly the same changes to delete the class, we'll get a runtime error when trying to create TellerSteps. That's because the DI container doesn't know which implementation of the Teller interface to instantiate. We tell it which concrete class to instantiate by changing the signature of the TellerSteps constructor:

**dependency_injection/pico/04/src/test/java/nicebank/TellerSteps.java**
```
KnowsTheAccount accountHelper;
Teller teller;

public TellerSteps(AtmUserInterface teller, KnowsTheAccount accountHelper) {
    this.teller = teller;
    this.accountHelper = accountHelper;
}
```

Run mvn clean test again.

### KnowsTheAccount

Removing KnowsTheAccount is more complicated, because (as is now clear) it has several responsibilities. It does the following:

- Opens a database connection (if necessary)
- Deletes any existing accounts
- Creates an account with a specified account number

Let's start by moving the database connection and account deletion into ResetHooks. We need to ensure that this runs before any other hook that needs a database connection, so we specify a low order number:

```
dependency_injection/pico/05/src/test/java/hooks/ResetHooks.java
public class ResetHooks {
    @Before(order = 1)
    public void reset() {
        if (!Base.hasConnection()) {
            Base.open(
                    "com.mysql.jdbc.Driver",
                    "jdbc:mysql://localhost/bank",
                    "teller", "password");
        }
        Account.deleteAll();
        TransactionQueue.clear();
    }
}
```

Now KnowsTheAccount's only responsibility is to store a test account in the database, so the name no longer makes sense. Rename it TestAccount and have it extend Account:

```
dependency_injection/pico/05/src/test/java/support/TestAccount.java
package support;
import nicebank.Account;

public class TestAccount extends Account {
    public TestAccount() {
        super(1234);
        saveIt();
    }
}
```

Now when we inject a TestAccount directly into our steps, PicoContainer will ensure that they all get a reference to the same, newly created Account object. Try it—it still works fine.

We could have done everything in this section without using DI at all, but you can see how things are made so much simpler when the DI container takes care of managing the creation of our shared entities for us. It's a bit like the way garbage collection in the JVM frees us from having to worry too much about creating and deleting object instances.

So far we've been using PicoContainer as our DI container. Next, let's take a look at how we've integrated it with our application.

## PicoContainer Is Almost Invisible

PicoContainer is probably the simplest DI container on the JVM, which is why we've been using it. It's certainly the simplest to integrate with Cucumber. Some of the other containers have more options, but PicoContainer is sufficient for most applications. The most likely reason to not use PicoContainer is that your application is already using another DI container.

Our use of PicoContainer is so unobtrusive that you may well have forgotten all about it by now. The only evidence that we're even using it at all are two dependencies in our pom.xml:

dependency_injection/pico/01/pom.xml

```
<dependency>
    <groupId>info.cukes</groupId>
    <artifactId>cucumber-picocontainer</artifactId>
    <version>${cucumber.version}</version>
    <scope>test</scope>
</dependency>
```

This dependency puts the cucumber-picocontainer JAR on the classpath, which tells Cucumber to let PicoContainer handle creation of the hooks and step definitions.

dependency_injection/pico/01/pom.xml

```
<dependency>
    <groupId>org.picocontainer</groupId>
    <artifactId>picocontainer</artifactId>
    <version>${picocontainer.version}</version>
    <scope>test</scope>
</dependency>
```

This second dependency puts the *PicoContainer implementation* JAR on the classpath. Without this Cucumber would be unable to find PicoContainer and wouldn't be able to delegate to it.

Apart from adding these dependencies, you can use PicoContainer without adding any code or annotations at all. In the following sections we'll port the example to other DI containers, and we'll see that PicoContainer is the only one that requires so little configuration by us.

# Moving to Guice

Guice is a DI container from Google with many of the same features as Pico-Container. In our opinion it's not as easy to use as PicoContainer, but it does have some extra possibilities, as we'll see. Also, since it's part of the popular Google toolset, you may already be familiar with it.

We'll quickly modify our existing ATM solution to run with Guice, pointing out the differences as we go. Further details can be found on the Guice website.[8] Note that as of this writing Guice 4.0 is in beta, but this example uses Guice 3.0 and cucumber-guice-1.2.0.

## Switching the DI Container

We'll start with the refactored code that we produced at the end of the previous section. The first thing to do is replace the dependencies on cucumber-picocontainer and PicoContainer in pom.xml:

```
dependency_injection/guice/01/pom.xml
<dependency>
    <groupId>info.cukes</groupId>
    <artifactId>cucumber-guice</artifactId>
    <version>${cucumber.version}</version>
    <scope>test</scope>
</dependency>
<dependency>
    <groupId>com.google.inject</groupId>
    <artifactId>guice</artifactId>
    <version>3.0</version>
</dependency>
```

If you run mvn clean test now you'll see a number of errors like this:

```
--------------------------------------------------------
 T E S T S
--------------------------------------------------------
Running RunCukesTest
Feature: Cash Withdrawal
Failure in before hook:ServerHooks.startServer()
Message: com.google.inject.ConfigurationException: Guice configuration errors:

1) Could not find a suitable constructor in hooks.ServerHooks.
   Classes must have either one (and only one) constructor annotated with
    @Inject or a zero-argument constructor that is not private.
  at hooks.ServerHooks.class(ServerHooks.java:19)
  while locating hooks.ServerHooks
```

---

8. https://github.com/google/guice

What this is telling us is that Guice is trying to instantiate an instance of one of our glue classes, but it doesn't know which constructor to use (even though they each have only one constructor).

## @Inject Annotation

To tell Guice which constructor to use, we add the @Inject annotation to the constructor that we want to inject objects into:

**dependency_injection/guice/02/src/test/java/nicebank/CashSlotSteps.java**

```
   CashSlot cashSlot;
➤  @Inject
   public CashSlotSteps(CashSlot cashSlot) {
       this.cashSlot = cashSlot;
   }
```

We also have to annotate the constructors in AtmUserInterface, AccountSteps, ServerHooks, TellerSteps, and WebDriverHooks. When we run mvn clean test both of our scenarios fail but with a different error:

```
--------------------------------------------------------
 T E S T S
--------------------------------------------------------
Running RunCukesTest
Feature: Cash Withdrawal
Listening on http://10.101.1.77:8887/
Failure in after hook:ServerHooks.stopServer()
Message: com.google.inject.ProvisionException: Guice provision errors:

1) Error injecting constructor, org.javalite.activejdbc.DBException:
   com.mysql.jdbc.exceptions.jdbc4.MySQLIntegrityConstraintViolationException:
   Duplicate entry '1234' for key 'number', Query:
   INSERT INTO accounts (number, balance) VALUES (?, ?), params: 1234,0.00
  at support.TestAccount.<init>(TestAccount.java:8)
  while locating support.TestAccount
    for parameter 0 at hooks.ServerHooks.<init>(ServerHooks.java:22)
  while locating hooks.ServerHooks
```

What's going on here? The error being reported is a MySQLIntegrityConstraintViolationException, which is being thrown because we're trying to create more than one account with the same account number. The unique constraint we put on the database won't allow this and that's the cause of the error.

The root cause of this problem is *scope*. We've hit a significant difference between PicoContainer and Guice, which we'll look at next.

## @ScenarioScoped Annotation

The Cucumber-Guice documentation says:

> It is not recommended to leave your step definition classes with no scope as it means that Cucumber will instantiate a new instance of the class for each step within a scenario that uses that step definition.[9]

We have two potential scopes to choose from: @ScenarioScoped and @Singleton. In general we will use @ScenarioScoped, because this ensures that state is reset before each scenario starts to run.

Let's annotate our step definitions and hooks to indicate that we want to create them fresh for each scenario. The classes that need to be annotated are AccountSteps, CashSlotSteps, TellerSteps, BackgroundProcessHooks, ResetHooks, ServerHooks, and WebDriverHooks:

**dependency_injection/guice/03/src/test/java/nicebank/AccountSteps.java**
```
import cucumber.runtime.java.guice.ScenarioScoped;


@ScenarioScoped
public class AccountSteps {
}
```

When we run mvn clean test we get:

```
-------------------------------------------------------
 T E S T S
-------------------------------------------------------
Running RunCukesTest
Feature: Cash Withdrawal
Listening on http://10.101.1.77:8887/
Server shutdown

Scenario: Successful withdrawal from an account in credit
  Given my account has been credited with 1m<b>$100.00</b>
  com.google.inject.ProvisionException: Guice provision errors:

  1) Error injecting constructor, org.javalite.activejdbc.DBException:
     com.mysql.jdbc.exceptions.jdbc4.MySQLIntegrityConstraintViolationException:
     Duplicate entry '1234' for key 'number', Query:
     INSERT INTO accounts (number, balance) VALUES (?, ?), params: 1234,0.00
    at support.TestAccount.<init>(TestAccount.java:8)
    while locating support.TestAccount
      for parameter 0 at nicebank.AccountSteps.<init>(AccountSteps.java:24)
    at nicebank.AccountSteps.class(AccountSteps.java:24)
    while locating nicebank.AccountSteps
```

---

9. http://cukes.info/api/cucumber/jvm/javadoc/cucumber/api/guice/package-summary.html

We've fixed the failure in shutdownServer, but we're still trying to create a duplicate account. That's because, although we've annotated the glue code with @ScenarioScoped, Guice is still creating a new instance of every injected class each time it needs to be injected. Since we are using injection to *share* the same instance between several objects, we need to annotate these classes as well. The classes that need to be annotated are AtmUserInterface, CashSlot, MyWebDriver, and TestAccount.

The only class that presents a problem is CashSlot, because it is part of our production code, and we may not want to add an annotation just to keep our test framework happy. One alternative is to create a TestCashSlot that extends CashSlot, which keeps Guice annotations confined to our test code:

dependency_injection/guice/04/src/test/java/support/TestCashSlot.java
```
package support;

import cucumber.runtime.java.guice.ScenarioScoped;

import nicebank.CashSlot;

@ScenarioScoped
public class TestCashSlot extends CashSlot {
}
```

However, now we need to tell Guice to create an instance of TestCashSlot, not CashSlot. We can do this by changing the signatures of the @Inject-annotated constructors that currently take a CashSlot:

dependency_injection/guice/04/src/test/java/nicebank/CashSlotSteps.java
```
CashSlot cashSlot;

@Inject
public CashSlotSteps(TestCashSlot cashSlot) {
    this.cashSlot = cashSlot;
}
```

Now the test passes!

## @**Singleton** Annotation

In the previous section we applied the @ScenarioScoped annotation indiscriminately to every class that is being managed by Guice. This means that a new instance will be created for every scenario run. That's not a problem for us at the moment because we have only one scenario, but this approach can be wasteful, especially if the objects are expensive to construct.

The other supported scope, @Singleton, tells Cucumber to construct only a single instance for all scenarios that will be run. This strategy should be used only when you're sure that the object stores no state that could allow one scenario to affect the outcome of another scenario. In our case we could apply this to our web driver, MyWebDriver:

dependency_injection/guice/05/src/test/java/support/MyWebDriver.java
```
import javax.inject.Singleton;

@Singleton
public class MyWebDriver extends EventFiringWebDriver{
    public MyWebDriver() {
        super(new FirefoxDriver());
    }
}
```

The test continues to pass, and now when we add more features they'll share the same browser instance.

There are lots more clever things that you can do with Guice, so take a look at the documentation online.

## Spring in Your Steps

Spring is a popular and (very) large framework. Cucumber ships with an integration to Spring for handling step creation and DI, which doesn't require the whole Spring framework on the classpath. The current version of cucumber-spring is built against Spring 4 and is still under active development, so check the release notes online to see the changes in future releases of cucumber-spring.

### Switching the DI Container

We'll start with the code as it was at the end of *PicoContainer Is Almost Invisible*, on page 213. As before, we'll change pom.xml to bring in the minimum dependency on Spring, our chosen DI framework:

dependency_injection/spring/01/pom.xml
```xml
<dependency>
    <groupId>info.cukes</groupId>
    <artifactId>cucumber-spring</artifactId>
    <version>${cucumber.version}</version>
    <scope>test</scope>
</dependency>
<dependency>
    <groupId>org.springframework</groupId>
    <artifactId>spring-context</artifactId>
    <version>${spring.version}</version>
</dependency>
<dependency>
    <groupId>org.springframework</groupId>
    <artifactId>spring-test</artifactId>
```

```
      <version>${spring.version}</version>
      <scope>test</scope>
</dependency>
```

We'll also add a configuration file, cucumber.xml, as a test resource:

dependency_injection/spring/01/src/test/resources/cucumber.xml
```
<?xml version="1.0" encoding="UTF-8"?>
<beans xmlns="http://www.springframework.org/schema/beans"
       xmlns:xsi="http://www.w3.org/2001/XMLSchema-instance"
       xmlns:context="http://www.springframework.org/schema/context"
       xsi:schemaLocation="http://www.springframework.org/schema/beans
            http://www.springframework.org/schema/beans/spring-beans-3.0.xsd
            http://www.springframework.org/schema/context
            http://www.springframework.org/schema/context/spring-context-3.0.xsd">
    <context:annotation-config/>
➤   <context:component-scan base-package="hooks, nicebank, support" />
</beans>
```

Here, we're telling Spring which of the base packages to scan for the classes that we're going to inject using the context:component-scan element. For this example we're interested in the hooks, nicebank, and support packages.

## Some Spring Annotations

Spring uses the annotation @Autowired to identify what should be injected, rather than the @Inject annotation that other DI containers use. Unfortunately, the current cucumber-spring integration only supports no-argument constructors for step definition and hook classes. That means we'll have to use *field injection* instead of the constructor injection that we used in PicoContainer and Guice. Instead of having an annotated constructor that stores the injected objects that are passed to it, the DI container will inject the object directly into the annotated fields:

dependency_injection/spring/01/src/test/java/nicebank/CashSlotSteps.java
```
@Autowired
TestCashSlot cashSlot;
```

Now we just need to tell Spring which of our classes are candidates for injection by marking them with @Component and associating them with the correct scope. The cucumber-spring integration automatically associates all hooks and step definitions with a scope called cucumber-glue, but we'll need to associate any objects that we've created to share state with that scope too:

dependency_injection/spring/01/src/test/java/support/AtmUserInterface.java
```
@Component
@Scope("cucumber-glue")
public class AtmUserInterface implements Teller {
}
```

Now that we've done that, all our support classes are identified as *beans*, and Spring will happily instantiate and inject them on demand.

Run mvn clean test to check it's all working.

## Some Spring Configuration Magic

The Spring configuration file is very powerful. In this section we'll see how we can use the configuration file to specify that a class is a bean without having to modify the Java code at all.

### Beans with No-arg Constructors

Spring provides an alternative way to specify which classes are candidates for injection by configuring them as beans in the configuration file, in our case cucumber.xml. Since we're not saying anything about constructor arguments, these classes need to have a default (or no-arg) constructor:

dependency_injection/spring/02/src/test/resources/cucumber.xml
```
<bean class="support.AtmUserInterface" scope="cucumber-glue" />
<bean class="support.MyWebDriver" scope="cucumber-glue" />
<bean class="nicebank.CashSlot" scope="cucumber-glue" />
```

Now we can remove the annotations from AtmUserInterface and MyWebDriver, and delete TestCashSlot entirely (because we only created it to avoid having to edit the production code). We need to do a bit more to remove TestAccount, though, because we have to pass an account number to its constructor. One solution is to create AccountFactory and configure Spring to use that:

dependency_injection/spring/02/src/test/resources/cucumber.xml
```
<bean class="support.AccountFactory" factory-method="createTestAccount"
                                     lazy-init="true" scope="cucumber-glue" />
```

dependency_injection/spring/02/src/test/java/support/AccountFactory.java
```
package support;

import nicebank.Account;

public class AccountFactory {

    public static Account createTestAccount() {
        Account account = new Account(1234);
        account.saveIt();
        return account;
    }
}
```

Run mvn clean test and the scenario passes as before.

### Bean Constructors with Arguments

In the previous section we saw how we could configure a class as a bean in the cucumber.xml file. That was fine for classes that had default, no-arg constructors. When we needed to call a constructor with an argument for Account we had to create an AccountFactory. Let's see if there's another way to do it. Take a look at MyWebDriver:

dependency_injection/spring/02/src/test/java/support/MyWebDriver.java
```
package support;

import org.openqa.selenium.firefox.FirefoxDriver;
import org.openqa.selenium.support.events.EventFiringWebDriver;

public class MyWebDriver extends EventFiringWebDriver{
    public MyWebDriver() {
        super(new FirefoxDriver());
    }
}
```

As you can see, its only difference from Selenium's EventFiringWebDriver is that the constructor is wired to use a Firefox browser. As a last example, let's use Spring to allow us to get rid of MyWebDriver entirely. We'll start by telling Spring how to create an EventFiringWebDriver for our scenarios to use:

dependency_injection/spring/03/src/test/resources/cucumber.xml
```
<bean class="org.openqa.selenium.support.events.EventFiringWebDriver"
                          scope="cucumber-glue" destroy-method="close">
    <constructor-arg>
        <bean class="org.openqa.selenium.firefox.FirefoxDriver"
                          scope="cucumber-glue"/>
    </constructor-arg>
</bean>
```

Now we need to replace all references to MyWebDriver in our test code with references to EventFiringWebDriver. Here's an example from WebDriverHooks:

dependency_injection/spring/03/src/test/java/hooks/WebDriverHooks.java
```
@Autowired
private EventFiringWebDriver webDriver;
```

Another run of mvn clean test will verify that our scenario still passes.

We'll see more uses of Spring in Chapter 12, *Working with Web Applications*, on page 225.

## CDI with Weld

The Java community have been working on a standardized approach to many of the challenges that software developers have to deal with. One of these is the Contexts and Dependency Injection for Java EE (CDI) standard, of which there are several implementations. Weld and OpenEJB are the two implementations that Cucumber is integrated with, but since they are so similar we'll only show an example using Weld.

Again, we'll start with the code as it was at the end of *PicoContainer Is Almost Invisible*, on page 213. As before we change pom.xml to bring in the minimum dependency on our chosen DI framework:

```
dependency_injection/weld/01/pom.xml
<dependency>
    <groupId>info.cukes</groupId>
    <artifactId>cucumber-weld</artifactId>
    <version>${cucumber.version}</version>
    <scope>test</scope>
</dependency>
<dependency>
    <groupId>javax.enterprise</groupId>
    <artifactId>cdi-api</artifactId>
    <version>${cdi-api.version}</version>
</dependency>
<dependency>
    <groupId>org.jboss.weld.se</groupId>
    <artifactId>weld-se</artifactId>
    <version>${weld.version}</version>
</dependency>
```

In the same way as we have seen with the preceding DI containers, we need to tell Weld/CDI how and where to inject our objects. We show where we want our objects injected using the @Inject annotation and we indicate that we want to share a single instance of each object using the @Singleton annotation. Examples of this can be seen in CashSlotSteps:

```
dependency_injection/weld/01/src/test/java/nicebank/CashSlotSteps.java
CashSlot cashSlot;
➤ @Inject
public CashSlotSteps(TestCashSlot cashSlot) {
    this.cashSlot = cashSlot;
}
```

Both of these annotations come from the javax.inject package, so this code is identical to the Guice version. What is different, however, is that we now need tell the container about the classes that need injected. Guice used the classpath to find candidates for injection, but for Weld/CDI we need to create bean.xml:

```
dependency_injection/weld/01/src/test/resources/META-INF/beans.xml
<?xml version="1.0" encoding="UTF-8"?>
<beans xmlns="http://java.sun.com/xml/ns/javaee"
       xmlns:xsi="http://www.w3.org/2001/XMLSchema-instance"
       xsi:schemaLocation="
    http://java.sun.com/xml/ns/javaee
    http://java.sun.com/xml/ns/javaee/beans_1_0.xsd">
</beans>
```

You'll notice that our bean.xml has almost nothing in it. We could use it to configure our beans in much the same way that we did in *Some Spring Configuration Magic*, on page 220. Since this book is about Cucumber, not Weld/CDI, we're leaving that as an exercise for the reader.

## What We Just Learned

Congratulations, you're ready to inject dependencies!

In this chapter we've seen how Cucumber's use of dependency injection simplifies the management of the graph of objects needed to run our scenarios. We looked at most of the DI containers that Cucumber is integrated with and saw that PicoContainer is probably the simplest to use, if you aren't already using one of the others in your project. Most of the other DI containers require some form of annotation and configuration. Once we choose a DI container, no matter which one, it takes over responsibility for creating all our step definition and hook objects.

As we applied DI to our example we pushed more of the responsibilities for creating and initializing our objects onto the container. That left us with fewer, smaller, more cohesive objects. This style takes a bit of getting used to, but leads to a more *composable* architecture that can be easier to maintain and extend.

### Try This

Using your DI container of choice, try the following:

• If we had more than one scenario, the browser would start up for each one, which takes time. How would you share a single browser session across all scenarios?

• Most of our examples used constructor injection. Change them to use field injection—you should then be able to delete the constructor entirely.

• Choose a DI container and browse its documentation. Experiment with different ways of creating the objects that need to be injected.

# CHAPTER 12

# Working with Web Applications

Our ATM example is a simple web application that has a single feature—withdrawing cash—but even that isn't fully implemented. In this chapter we're going to extend this feature to handle some simple error situations that our stakeholders are concerned about. Along the way we'll learn some techniques for injecting errors into our system and a lot more about how to use Selenium to exercise web applications.

It doesn't take very long to run the single scenario we've written for our ATM example, but as we add more scenarios the time it takes to run Cucumber will get longer. We've already talked about some of the ways to handle slow features in Chapter 6, *Keeping Your Cucumbers Sweet*, on page 91, but in this chapter, after we've added some extra scenarios, we'll take some time to talk about one simple technical approach to managing the problem—browser reuse.

We're also going to discover a user requirement to update our ATM web page while the user types. This will lead us into the realm of JavaScript and Ajax, which are common technologies in almost all modern web applications. We'll learn how to use Cucumber and Selenium to drive out this feature and see that everything is not as simple as we might have hoped.

Before we begin to flesh out some more scenarios, let's take a deeper look at some of the functionality that Selenium provides for interacting with web apps and see how Cucumber fits into the picture.

## Selenium WebDriver

One of the most popular ways to use Cucumber is to automate the development of web applications. Here is a dirty little secret:

Cucumber has no idea how to talk to a web application!

That's right—it's completely useless for that. Still, people keep using it to develop web applications. How come?

Remember, Cucumber isn't much more than a tool that can parse Gherkin feature files and execute step definitions. It doesn't know how to talk to databases, web apps, or any external system. People install other libraries for this and use them in their step definitions and support code to connect to those external systems.

As of this writing, the most popular Java library for programmatically interacting with a web application is Selenium WebDriver. It provides an API for accessing web pages and interacting with them in a way that is similar to how a real user would—entering text in text fields and text areas, checking check boxes, clicking links and buttons, and so on. Selenium WebDriver allows you to plug in different drivers that run those interactions in several different browsers—such as Firefox, Internet Explorer, and Chrome.

We've been using a few pieces of Selenium WebDriver functionality already in the book, but this chapter is going to need more. Therefore, it's time to give you a brief overview of the full power of Selenium so that you're ready for the step definitions we're going to be writing later on. Make sure you consult Selenium's own documentation for more comprehensive details.[1]

## Navigation, WebElements, and Locators

The most basic way of using a web browser is to access a specific URL. Selenium provides the get method, which we've already used earlier, to issue a GET request to the specified URL: driver.get(String path). However, you cannot assume that Selenium will wait for the page to load before returning from this method call.

Once you've loaded a web page, you'll want to do things like enter text into text boxes or click buttons. Selenium calls the components that make up a web page WebElements and provides a number of methods to help you discover them. Most of these methods take a Selenium *locator* as an argument that specifies which element you are interested in, and the simplest is findElement. If more than one element matches the locator you supply, findElement returns the first element that matches the locator. You can also retrieve a list of all elements that match your locator by using findElements.

---

1. http://docs.seleniumhq.org/projects/webdriver/

To construct a locator you'll use one of Selenium's factory methods in the By class. An easy way to find a web control is by its ID, so an example of how you might find a WebElement with the ID dateOfBirth is:

```
driver.findElement(By.id("dateOfBirth"))
```

This makes for a very *fluent*[2] interface that reads like an English sentence: "find element by ID dateOfBirth."

The id factory method is only one of many provided. Others include xpath, linkText, name, cssSelector, className, and inputFieldName—check the Selenium documentation for more. All the method names are self-explanatory and help to keep your steps easy to read (and maintain).

Once you've got hold of the WebElement that you're interested in, you'll want to do things with it. You have plenty of methods to choose from, all with descriptive, self-explanatory names like click, sendKeys, and submit. The actual behavior of the HTML control behind a WebElement instance depends on what type of control it is. For example, calling click on a check box will change its selected state, whereas calling it on a button will cause a button press to occur.

## Switching Windows

Of course not all web apps have a single browser window, so you may need to switch between windows or frames. Selenium provides the switchTo method for this purpose. For example, you can switch to another window by name: driver.switchTo().window("myOtherWindow"). Once this method has been called, the driver will direct all further Selenium calls to the named window.

As well as the window methods, frame and alert are available to direct calls to a specified iFrame or alert box, respectively.

## Cookie Management

The Selenium driver also has the manage method to give you direct access to the current browser session. You'll need to use this to manage cookies if your web app uses them. Selenium provides methods with descriptive names, such as addCookie, deleteAllCookies, and getCookieNamed, which you use like this: driver.manage().getCookieNamed("my-cookie");

---

2.    http://en.wikipedia.org/wiki/Fluent_interface

Selenium also provides the Cookie class as a wrapper to make working with cookies easy. If you want to add a cookie to your browser session, it's as simple as this:

```
Cookie cookie = new Cookie("name", "value");
driver.addCookie(cookie);
```

Even if our web application used cookies, we probably wouldn't have needed to manage them yet, because our browser restarts for each scenario and we only have a single scenario anyway. By the end of this chapter we'll have several scenarios running in a single browser session, so if our application used cookies we would need to start managing them carefully.

## Managing Timeouts

Another useful piece of functionality available through the Selenium driver's manage interface is the timeout, which is used to alter the various timeouts that Selenium will wait for before signaling an error. This can be used, for example, to ensure a page has time to load before looking for a specific WebElement on it: driver.manage().timeout().pageLoadTimeout(10, TimeUnit.SECONDS).

You can also tell the driver to poll the DOM for a certain period of time while looking for a particular WebElement—for example: driver.manage().timeout().implicitlyWait(10, TimeUnit.MILLISECONDS). This can help when some of the elements on the page may take a certain amount of time to be rendered and is Selenium's own implementation of exactly what we did in *Synchronization by Sampling*, on page 172.

The downside of using these timeouts is that they apply globally to all Selenium calls, which can make failing scenarios fail very slowly. You'll learn a more focused approach later in *Synchronization in Selenium*, on page 242.

This section has given you more of a taste of the automation possibilities that Selenium has to offer. We'll use some of these features when we write step definitions in the following sections. We'll be particularly grateful for the timeout functionality when we begin using Ajax toward the end of the chapter. We've got a lot to do, so let's get started.

# Handling Failure

We've delivered a working scenario and shown it to our stakeholders. They're happy with what we've done so far, but they want to discuss how we're going to handle some common error cases. Once we've had these discussions, it'll be time to extend our web app, and we'll see some examples of how to write scenarios that force an error to happen so that we can drive out our error handling functionality.

Our running scenario describes the situation where a customer who has money in his account successfully withdraws some of it using the ATM. What happens if the mechanism that counts and dispenses the money malfunctions? Or if the ATM doesn't contain enough money to fulfill the customer's request? We're sure you can think up plenty of other situations that need to be considered, but that's enough to give you an idea.

Now we'll implement the scenarios that you captured while working with your stakeholders. Since Spring is such a popular DI container, we'll start from the code that we wrote in *Spring in Your Steps*, on page 218. We won't spend a lot of time describing the code, because you learned most of this earlier in the book, but we will describe new Selenium functionality as we use it. You can always jump ahead to *Reusing the Browser*, on page 233 if you want to skip the development phase.

## A Faulty ATM

The first scenario we decide to handle is where the ATM develops a fault after the user tries to withdraw money but before that money is dispensed. Working with our stakeholders, we capture this scenario as follows:

**fast/01/src/test/resources/cash_withdrawal.feature**
```
Scenario: Unsuccessful withdrawal due to technical fault
  Given my account has been credited with $100.00
  But the cash slot has developed a fault
  When I withdraw $20
  Then I should see an out-of-order message
  And $0 should be dispensed
  And the balance of my account should be $100.00
```

There are two new steps in this scenario: one that injects a fault into the cash slot and another that checks that the correct error message is displayed to the user. We'll look at both of these before seeing if we can do anything to improve how the scenario reads.

### Injecting a Fault

We'd like to make sure that our software behaves correctly when something goes wrong with the ATM mechanism, represented by our CashSlot. We wouldn't want to change our production code, so instead we create a TestCashSlot (that extends CashSlot) to allow us to simulate a fault:

```
fast/01/src/test/java/support/TestCashSlot.java
package support;

import nicebank.CashSlot;

public class TestCashSlot extends CashSlot {
    private boolean faulty;

    public void injectFault() {
        faulty = true;
    }

    public void dispense(int dollars){
        if (faulty) {
            throw new RuntimeException("Out of order");
        } else {
            super.dispense(dollars);
        }
    }
}
```

Since we're using Spring, we can make a simple change to the configuration file cucumber.xml to inject our test class into our application:

```
fast/01/src/test/resources/cucumber.xml
<bean class="support.AtmUserInterface" scope="cucumber-glue" />
<bean class="support.TestCashSlot" scope="cucumber-glue" />
```

Now when our scenarios run, Spring will create a single instance of TestCashSlot and inject it anywhere that we need a TestCashSlot or CashSlot. When we try to withdraw cash from a faulty ATM, dispense will throw an exception. For the time being we're using Java's RuntimeException, but we'd want to replace this with something more meaningful if this was more than an example.

We can inject a fault into our TestCashSlot at any time using the injectFault method. We call this from our new step "But the cash slot has developed a fault":

```
fast/01/src/test/java/nicebank/CashSlotSteps.java
@Given("^the cash slot has developed a fault$")
public void theCashSlotHasDevelopedAFault() throws Throwable {
    cashSlot.injectFault();
}
```

Remember that by the time this step definition gets executed, the TestCashSlot will already have been created by Spring and wired into our application. We're simply changing a flag to indicate that for all future calls we want it to behave as if it was faulty.

## Checking for Text

If the ATM develops a fault, we want a helpful message to be displayed to the user. We'll use Selenium WebDriver to check that the correct message is being displayed. To do this we add the following step definition:

```
fast/01/src/test/java/nicebank/TellerSteps.java
@Then("^I should see an out-of-order message$")
public void iShouldSeeAnOutOfOrderMessage() throws Throwable {
    Assert.assertTrue(
        "Expected error message not displayed",
        teller.isDisplaying("Out of order"));
}
```

All this step definition is doing is delegating responsibility to the Teller implementation to check that the required "Out of order" message is being displayed. We don't do any complicated work in the step definition itself, because as we've already explained we want to keep this layer of glue code as thin as possible. We do the actual work of checking the text displayed on the UI in AtmUserInterface:

```
fast/01/src/test/java/support/AtmUserInterface.java
public boolean isDisplaying(String message) {
    List<WebElement> list = webDriver
        .findElements(By.xpath("//*[contains(text(),'" + message + "')]"));
    return (list.size() > 0);
}
```

Of course, the first time we run this it'll fail, because we haven't made any change to our production code yet. To handle the exception thrown when we try to use a faulty CashSlot, we've modified the doPost on WithdrawalServlet. It now extracts the message from the caught exception and displays it to the user:

```
fast/01/src/main/java/nicebank/WithdrawalServlet.java
    protected void doPost(HttpServletRequest request, HttpServletResponse response)
                                            throws ServletException, IOException
    {
        Teller teller = new AutomatedTeller(cashSlot);
        int amount = Integer.parseInt(request.getParameter("amount"));

        try {
            teller.withdrawFrom(account, amount);

            response.setContentType("text/html");
            response.setStatus(HttpServletResponse.SC_OK);
            response.getWriter().println(
                "<html><head><title>ATM</title></head>" +
                "<body>Please take your $" + amount + "</body></html>");
        }
        catch (RuntimeException e) {
```

```
        response.setContentType("text/html");
        response.setStatus(HttpServletResponse.SC_OK);
        response.getWriter().println(
            "<html><head><title>ATM</title></head>" +
            "<body>" + e.getMessage() + "</body></html>");
    }
}
```

At this point we can run mvn clean test and our new scenario will pass.

### Rewriting the Scenario

Take a look at our new scenario. Does it read well to you? Are there any details in it that are *incidental* to the behavior being described? Remember, this scenario is about handling a technical fault. We aren't interested in how much money is in the account to start with, how much money the customer is trying to withdraw, or what the balance is after the fault occurs. What we want to be sure of is that the correct error message is displayed, that no money is dispensed, and that the customer's balance is not affected.

After we discuss this with our stakeholders, we rewrite the scenario as:

**fast/02/src/test/resources/cash_withdrawal.feature**
```
Scenario: Unsuccessful withdrawal due to technical fault
  Given my account is in credit
  But the cash slot has developed a fault
  When I request some of my money
  Then I should see an out-of-order message
  And $0 should be dispensed
  And the balance of my account should be unchanged
```

This scenario has been stripped of several incidental details, allowing us to use natural language to focus our attention on the things that are really important.

## Insufficient Funds in ATM

The next scenario we'll tackle is where the ATM contains less cash than the user tries to withdraw. Working with our stakeholders, we capture this scenario as follows:

**fast/03/src/test/resources/cash_withdrawal.feature**
```
Scenario: Unsuccessful withdrawal due to insufficient ATM funds
  Given my account is in credit
  And the ATM contains $10
  When I withdraw $20
  Then I should see an ask-for-less-money message
  And $0 should be dispensed
  And the balance of my account should be unchanged
```

This scenario introduces the idea that an ATM contains a limited amount of money. We'll need to implement a way to specify how much money to load into the ATM, and check that we have sufficient funds before we attempt to dispense money to the customer:

fast/03/src/main/java/nicebank/CashSlot.java
```
public void load(int dollars){
    available = dollars;
}

public void dispense(int requested){
    if (available >= requested) {
        contents = requested;
        available -= requested;
    } else {
        throw new RuntimeException("Insufficient ATM funds");
    }
}
```

We also need to make sure that our original, successful withdrawal scenario keeps working. We could do this by adding an extra step to it to load the ATM, but this would be an incidental detail. Instead we add a constructor to our TestCashSlot that makes sure there's plenty of cash available for any scenarios that aren't specifically interested in how much money is in the machine:

fast/03/src/test/java/support/TestCashSlot.java
```
public TestCashSlot() {
    super.load(1000);
}
```

We can now run mvn clean test and see all three scenarios pass.

We added only two extra scenarios, but already our feature takes longer to run. If we don't do something, it won't be long before the team stops running the scenarios. Next we'll take a look at the simplest way to speed things up.

## Reusing the Browser

Each of our scenarios is exercising our application through our web UI and so needs to use a browser. At the moment we start a new instance of Firefox for each scenario, which takes a fair amount of time. Is it really necessary, or could our scenarios all use the same instance of Firefox?

It's important that each scenario is *isolated* from all other scenarios, but the browser itself holds very little context. In most situations it is quite safe to reuse the same browser instance for all your scenarios as long as you clear out any cookies. In this example it's even simpler—we have no cookies.

## Sharing a Browser Using Spring

We're using a Spring configuration file, cucumber.xml, to define our EventFiringWeb-Driver. It just takes a tiny modification to keep the browser instance alive for the whole run of Cucumber. In the XML that follows, we've simply removed the attribute scope="cucumber-glue" from the definition of the bean:

**fast/04/src/test/resources/cucumber.xml**
```xml
<bean class="org.openqa.selenium.support.events.EventFiringWebDriver"
                                          destroy-method="quit">
    <constructor-arg>
        <bean class="org.openqa.selenium.firefox.FirefoxDriver" />
    </constructor-arg>
</bean>
```

Now when Spring creates an instance of the web driver, it's associated with the default scope that lives for the entire Cucumber run. Try running mvn clean test and you'll see that this makes the feature run much quicker overall, because we don't have to wait for the browser to start up for each scenario.

If you needed to delete cookies as well, you'd need to write a hook that does this programmatically, which we'll see next.

## Using a Shutdown Hook

There's a more general way to do some cleanup when a JVM is closing down that doesn't rely on Spring: using Java's addShutdownHook. The following code comes from the Webbit-Websockets-Selenium example in the Cucumber project:[3]

```java
Line 1  public class SharedDriver extends EventFiringWebDriver {
    -       private static final WebDriver REAL_DRIVER = new FirefoxDriver();
    -       private static final Thread CLOSE_THREAD = new Thread() {
    -           @Override
    5           public void run() {
    -               REAL_DRIVER.close();
    -           }
    -       };
    -
    10      static {
    -           Runtime.getRuntime().addShutdownHook(CLOSE_THREAD);
    -       }
    -
    -       public SharedDriver() {
    15          super(REAL_DRIVER);
    -       }
```

---

3. https://github.com/cucumber/cucumber-jvm/blob/master/examples/java-webbit-websockets-selenium/src/test/
   java/cucumber/examples/java/websockets/SharedDriver.java

```
  -
  -        @Override
  -        public void close() {
 20            if (Thread.currentThread() != CLOSE_THREAD) {
  -                throw new UnsupportedOperationException(
  -                    "You shouldn't close this WebDriver. " +
  -                    " It's shared and will close when the JVM exits.");
  -            }
 25            super.close();
  -        }
  -
  -        @Before
  -        public void deleteAllCookies() {
 30            manage().deleteAllCookies();
  -        }
  -    }
```

We create a single driver instance and store it in a static variable (line 2). This will be shared by all instances of SharedDriver. We also create a static Thread (line 3) and add it to the JVM's list of hooks that should be called when the JVM is shutting down (line 11).

If you try to close the driver manually, SharedDriver will check whether the call is coming from the registered CLOSE_THREAD (line 20). If it isn't, SharedDriver will report the error through an exception. This protects you from inadvertently closing the browser midway through executing your Cucumber features.

This example also shows how you can use a hook to clear cookies before each scenario runs (line 29). The method manage is part of the EventFiringWebDriver API provided by Selenium.

While driving out some fault handling features in our ATM, we've learned a general way to call cleanup code at the end of a Cucumber run. We've also used Selenium to ensure that each scenario cleans up any cookies that the previous scenario might have saved. Now we need to show what we've done to our users and see whether they like it!

## Ajax

During usability testing sessions, we discover that users don't like being told that the amount of money they request isn't available. They'd prefer it if we could display a message that the ATM has insufficient funds while they are typing the amount into the ATM *before* they press the Submit button. This is described by a new scenario:

**fast/05/src/test/resources/cash_withdrawal.feature**
```
Scenario: Unsuccessful withdrawal due to insufficient ATM funds
  Given my account is in credit
  And the ATM contains $10
  When I type $20
  Then I should see an ask-for-less-money message
```

There is a subtle but essential difference in our When step here. We're only *typing* text, and unlike the When step in our previous scenario, we are not submitting the form by clicking the button or pressing the Enter/Return key. We have an idea about how to implement this feature—we'll issue an Ajax request whenever the user types a character, and when the response comes back, we'll display a message on the same page without doing a submit.

## Entering an Amount

When we run mvn clean test, Cucumber exits with a missing step definition. We need to tell it how to enter text in a field without submitting the form. That's easy! We'll implement the undefined step definition almost like the one we used in our previous scenario, except this time we won't press the Submit button—we are only going to fill in the field:

**fast/05/src/test/java/support/AtmUserInterface.java**
```java
public void type(int amount) {
    webDriver.get("http://localhost:" + hooks.ServerHooks.PORT);
    WebElement input = webDriver.findElement(By.id("amount"));
    String amountString = String.valueOf(amount);
    input.sendKeys(amountString);
}
```

If you run the feature again and look carefully, you'll see that the amount field is populated with the amount requested from our Gherkin scenario before the browser is closed when the scenario is done. Neat! This leaves us with only one more failing step—the one where we need to verify that the error message is being displayed. It's time to take a little break and think about how we are going to implement this with Ajax and dynamic HTML.

## Designing Our Live Messages

When the user types in the amount field and waits a short time, the browser will issue an Ajax GET request to ask if the ATM contains sufficient funds. There's one important difference about this request—it will have an additional Accepts HTTP header, indicating to the server that we want the response as JSON (instead of HTML). When the response comes back to the browser, we'll iterate over the JSON we get back and create the notification message (if necessary) dynamically with JavaScript.

Implementing this in JavaScript, even with the help of jQuery, will require somewhere between twenty and sixty lines of code, depending on your style. This is not an insurmountable amount of code, but running Cucumber every time you make a small change to this code is something we recommend against because the feedback loop will be too slow. So, how do we proceed now? There are two main directions you can take from here: TDD or not.

## JavaScript TDD

Developing JavaScript with TDD used to be hard to do because of a lack of good tools, but this is a thing of the past. Unfortunately, Cucumber is not one of those tools—it's too high level. Low-level TDD with JavaScript is beyond the scope of this book, but if you want to give it a try, we can recommend QUnit[4] or Jasmine.[5] *Test-Driven JavaScript Development [Joh10]* is an excellent book that treats the topic really well. It's also well worth having a look at Jim Shore's "Let's code JavaScript" screencasts.[6]

## Without JavaScript TDD

This is how we all started programming. Write the code; test it manually! Since JavaScript TDD is a big topic that we are not going to cover in this book, we're going to cheat a little and "just write the code." We'll start up the web server with a limited amount of cash in the ATM and code until we have something that works, testing it manually in the browser. When we think we have something that works, we can run Cucumber to get a final verification.

This approach is not ideal—on real projects we would use TDD for our Java-Script as well. Still, our Cucumber scenario will serve as validation and will protect us against regressions should someone change the JavaScript in the future. So, without further ado, we'll just give you some JavaScript code that we developed exactly this way. Create a new file in src/main/webapp/js called notifications.js with the following content:

```
fast/06/src/main/webapp/js/notifications.js
function Validate(form) {
    this.form = form;
}

Validate.prototype.queue = function (amount) {
    if (this.timer) {
        clearTimeout(this.timer);
    }
```

4.   http://docs.jquery.com/QUnit/
5.   http://pivotal.github.com/jasmine/
6.   http://www.letscodejavascript.com/

```
    var self = this;
    this.timer = setTimeout(function () {
        self.checkAmount(amount);
    }, 150);
};

Validate.prototype.checkAmount = function (amount) {
    var self = this;
    jQuery.ajax({
        url: '/validate',
        type: 'GET',
        data: {'amount': amount},
        success: function(results) {self.render(results)},
        contentType: 'application/json',
        dataType: 'json',
    });
}

Validate.prototype.render = function (notifications) {
    var html ="";
    if (notifications.content.length > 0) {
        html = "<li>" + notifications.content + "</li>";
    }
    jQuery(this.form).find('ol.notifications').html(html);
}

jQuery.fn.setupValidation = function () {
    this.each(function () {
        var validator = new Validate(this);
        var input = jQuery(this).find("input[type=text]");
        input.bind('keyup', function () {
            validator.queue(this.value);
        });
    });
};

jQuery(function() { jQuery('#withdrawalForm').setupValidation();});
```

This code defines a jQuery checkAmount plug-in and activates it on the input
element with a DOM ID of withdrawalForm. Whenever a user (or Selenium!) enters
a character, the browser fires the keyup event, and this starts a timer. If a
delay of 150ms elapses without any more characters being typed, it issues
an Ajax request with the amount. We use the delay so that we don't hammer
our server with search requests if the user is a really fast typist. This request
also indicates that it would like to have the response back as JSON. When
the response successfully comes back with the search results in a JSON
array, we iterate over them and render any notifications we've received.

## Making the Web App Return JSON

As we mentioned earlier, we want the response from the search request to contain JSON when the client explicitly says it wants JSON. To do this, we create a new ValidationServlet that returns a JSON payload that contains any notifications we want to show to the user:

fast/06/src/main/java/nicebank/ValidationServlet.java
```java
package nicebank;

import java.io.IOException;
import javax.servlet.ServletException;
import javax.servlet.http.HttpServlet;
import javax.servlet.http.HttpServletRequest;
import javax.servlet.http.HttpServletResponse;

public class ValidationServlet extends HttpServlet
{
    private CashSlot cashSlot;

    public ValidationServlet(CashSlot cashSlot) {
        this.cashSlot = cashSlot;
    }

    protected void doGet(HttpServletRequest request, HttpServletResponse response)
                                        throws ServletException, IOException
    {
        response.setContentType("application/json");
        response.setStatus(HttpServletResponse.SC_OK);

        int amount = Integer.parseInt(request.getParameter("amount"));

        if (cashSlot.canDispense(amount)) {
            response.getWriter().println("{\"content\":\"\"}");
        } else {
            response.getWriter().println(
                "{\"content\":\"Insufficient ATM funds\"}");
        }
    }
}
```

Now, not only do we need to wire in our ValidationServlet to our server, we also need to arrange to serve our static JavaScript resources. We use Jetty's ResourceHandler to serve the JavaScript and ContextHandlerCollection to allow us to serve both static resources and servlets. The ResourceHandler gets first option to serve the request—if it doesn't know how to, then the request passes to our ServletContext.

Finally, we've also added an autocomplete="off" attribute to our input field in AtmServlet to prevent the browser itself from suggesting values as we type.

That's a lot of code all of a sudden, and it's high time we ran Cucumber again!

```
Scenario: Unsuccessful withdrawal due to insufficient ATM funds
  Given my account is in credit
  And the ATM contains $10
  When I type $20
  Then I should see an ask-for-less-money message
    java.lang.AssertionError: Expected error message not displayed
        at org.junit.Assert.fail(Assert.java:88)
        at org.junit.Assert.assertTrue(Assert.java:41)
        at nicebank.TellerSteps.iShouldSeeAnAskForLessMoneyMessage
        at *.Then I should see an ask-for-less-money message
```

Our other features are still passing, but our new one testing the Ajax isn't. The output indicates that the expected notification did not show up on the page. This is going to take a bit of detective work, which we'll dive into next.

## Selenium sendKeys Misbehavior

We debug our Jetty server and find that our ValidationServlet isn't receiving any requests at all. Investigating further, we discover that our JavaScript method queue is never being called either, which means that our ATM web page is never receiving any keyup events. What's going on?

A quick search on the Internet turns up the little known fact that the Selenium sendKeys method doesn't result in keyup or keydown events if you pass it a string,[7] but it does if you pass it members of the Keys enumeration.

So, we do the simplest thing, which is to convert our integer amount into a sequence of keystrokes:

```
fast/07/src/test/java/support/AtmUserInterface.java
public void type(int amount) {
    webDriver.get("http://localhost:" + hooks.ServerHooks.PORT);
    WebElement input = webDriver.findElement(By.id("amount"));
    String amountString = String.valueOf(amount);
    for (int i = 0; i<amountString.length(); i++) {
        input.sendKeys(convertToKey(amountString.charAt(i)));
    }
}
```

---

7.   https://code.google.com/p/selenium/issues/detail?id=5786

```java
private Keys convertToKey(char digit) {
    switch (digit){
        case '0': return Keys.NUMPAD0;
        case '1': return Keys.NUMPAD1;
        case '2': return Keys.NUMPAD2;
        case '3': return Keys.NUMPAD3;
        case '4': return Keys.NUMPAD4;
        case '5': return Keys.NUMPAD5;
        case '6': return Keys.NUMPAD6;
        case '7': return Keys.NUMPAD7;
        case '8': return Keys.NUMPAD8;
        case '9': return Keys.NUMPAD9;
        default: throw new RuntimeException("Invalid keypress in test");
    }
}
```

Sadly the scenario still fails when we run mvn clean test, but our ValidationServlet is now receiving requests. It looks like we'll need to dig even deeper.

## Pausing Selenium

It can often be quite frustrating watching Selenium's browser flash past something that you want to take a closer look at. This feels like it might be one of those situations, so we'd like to find a way to slow things down. One easy trick to get Cucumber, and therefore Selenium, to pause during a step is to bring up a Java Swing JOptionPane in the step definition.

To do this, we add the following code to AtmUserInterface:

**fast/08/src/test/java/support/AtmUserInterface.java**
```java
public void type(int amount) {
    webDriver.get("http://localhost:" + hooks.ServerHooks.PORT);
    WebElement input = webDriver.findElement(By.id("amount"));
    String amountString = String.valueOf(amount);
    for (int i = 0; i<amountString.length(); i++) {
        input.sendKeys(convertToKey(amountString.charAt(i)));
    }

    ask("Ready to continue");
}

public void ask(String question) {
  JOptionPane.showMessageDialog(
    null,
    question,
    "Ask for response",
    JOptionPane.PLAIN_MESSAGE);
}
```

Now when we run mvn clean test the ask method puts up a dialog box when we expect the notification method to be visible. And sure enough, there it is: "Insufficient ATM funds"! It looks like we have yet another issue to sort out in the next section.

### Synchronization in Selenium

What's missing? It can be a little hard to tell at this point. Pausing the scenario using ask has helped us understand that the notification we expect is being displayed—eventually.

In our step, we are typing the amount to be withdrawn and then verifying that we have the expected notification on the page. The problem is—we are looking for the results too soon, before the Ajax query has a chance to complete! As we discussed in Chapter 9, *Message Queues and Asynchronous Components*, on page 169, we need to introduce a *synchronization point* so that we can be sure the validation request has completed before we proceed in checking what it has returned.

Luckily, Selenium has a number of different ways to deal with this situation in a simple way.[8] In this case we'll use the helper class WebDriverWait to poll the page every 30 milliseconds for up to 2 seconds:

```
fast/09/src/test/java/support/AtmUserInterface.java
public boolean isDisplaying(String message) {
    By locator = By.xpath("//*[contains(text(),'" + message + "')]");

    WebDriverWait wait = new WebDriverWait(webDriver, 2, 30);
    WebElement element = wait.until(
        ExpectedConditions.presenceOfElementLocated(locator));

    List<WebElement> list = webDriver.findElements(locator);
    return (list.size() > 0);
}
```

This will make the scenario pass, and what's more, we have covered the essential parts of the Selenium API. Selenium has more to offer, but it's mostly variations of what we have already seen.

## What We Just Learned

We've covered a lot of ground in this chapter. We started by taking a quick tour of some of the most useful parts of the Selenium WebDriver API, and we used some of them when we came to implement basic fault handling in our

---

8.   http://assertselenium.com/2013/01/29/webdriver-wait-commands/

ATM. When we added the fault handling scenarios, we saw the feature runtime start to get longer, so we applied a simple technique to reduce it by sharing a single browser session among all our scenarios. And then we extended our ATM using Ajax to give live feedback to our customer, which taught us another way to provide synchronization using Selenium.

There are a lot more features that we would want to implement in our ATM, and that would lead to lots more scenarios. Sharing a single browser session between them all will certainly help control the runtime, but we'll need to consider other techniques as well if we want to be able to run hundreds (or thousands) of scenarios in an acceptable amount of time. This is what we'll be looking at in the next chapter.

## Try This

Selenium can be used outside of Cucumber too. A handy way to get to grips with Selenium is to automate some dull, repetitive task that you have to do on the Web, such as filling in timesheets or downloading your bank statement.

We've provided a plain old Java project that you can flesh out with whatever you'd like it to automate. The heart of it is this simple Java class:

robot/01/src/main/java/WebRobot.java
```java
import javax.swing.JOptionPane;
import org.openqa.selenium.firefox.FirefoxDriver;
import org.openqa.selenium.support.events.EventFiringWebDriver;

public class WebRobot {
    public static void main(String[] args){
        FirefoxDriver firefoxDriver = new FirefoxDriver();
        EventFiringWebDriver webDriver = new EventFiringWebDriver(firefoxDriver);

        webDriver.get("http://www.google.com");
        // .... etc
        ask("Click to finish");
        webDriver.quit();
    }

    private static void ask(String question) {
      JOptionPane.showMessageDialog(null, question, "Ask for response",
        JOptionPane.PLAIN_MESSAGE);
    }
}
```

Once you've downloaded the project, you can run it by typing mvn clean compile exec:java -Dexec.mainClass="WebRobot".

Now flesh out the robot to do your bidding!

# CHAPTER 13

# Keeping Your Features Fast

We've driven out some new functionality in our CashSlot to handle errors that might arise when the ATM tries to dispense money to the customer. We also implemented functionality that lets users know if the ATM doesn't hold enough money to satisfy their request before they even press the Submit button. The scenarios are all running through the ATM UI in a single browser session, which seems fast enough at the moment.

However, we'll want to develop hundreds, if not thousands, more scenarios before we ship our application so the runtime of our features will continue to increase. Many of the scenarios that we write will exercise the same parts of the UI over and over again, not because it gives us any extra confidence in the application, but because that's the only way we are able to demonstrate the behaviors we're interested in. Before you know it, you'll be waiting hours rather than minutes for feedback. This is what we refer to in Chapter 6, *Keeping Your Cucumbers Sweet*, on page 91 as *Lots of Scenarios*, on page 108.

In this chapter you'll learn a new way to think about your specifications and what they test. By the end of this chapter, you'll be able to maintain comprehensive living documentation in your feature files without sacrificing the quick feedback that is so valuable while developing and maintaining your application. But first we're going to show you a very simple technique that you can use as first-aid to help control the growing runtime of your test suite.

## Partitioning Features and Scenarios

One of the simplest ways to reduce your Cucumber runtime is to run fewer scenarios. Tag your scenarios, and you can choose a subset of the scenarios to run, covering the area that you're currently working on. Once the work is checked in, a larger, but still reduced, subset of faster tests might run in our continuous integration (CI) server. Larger subsets might run in subsequent steps of a continuous delivery pipeline, or at scheduled intervals (such as overnight or weekly). Finally, the full set of scenarios could run on demand as part of a release or QA process.

## Possible Classifications

To facilitate this way of working, we need to agree on a set of tags to be applied to our scenarios. Here are some typical tags that we've seen used:

| Partitioning Type | Description | Examples |
| --- | --- | --- |
| Speed | An arbitrary classification of the time the scenario takes to run. Lets us to exclude slower scenarios. | @fast, @slow, @glacial |
| Release | Execute scenarios that only apply to particular releases. | @release_1_04, @hot-fix_2014_3_27, @version_2 |
| Defect | Execute scenarios that verify defects. | @defect, @defect_10983 |
| Purpose | A categorization of where the test is most useful. | @regression, @smoke_test |
| Risk | An arbitrary grouping of the risk mitigated by the scenario, so we can run scenarios with certain risk profiles. | @High, @Medium, @Low, @CurrentSprint, @WIP |

Remember that tags are just free-form text, so Cucumber can't know, and won't warn us, if we misspell one.

## Tag Expressions

As we explained in *Running a Subset of Scenarios*, on page 261, we can build logical expressions of tags to specify which scenarios we want Cucumber to execute. We can put tags on features, scenarios, scenario outlines, or example blocks, and we can have as many tags as we like on each. For example, take a look at the following feature file:

```
@high_risk
@first_released_2_0
Feature: Retain card when instructed by authentication system

@fast
@regression
Scenario: Dispenser retains cancelled card
  Given a cancelled bank card
  When authentication is sought
  Then the card is retained
```

```
@slow
@smoke_test
Scenario: Incorrect credentials submitted too many times
  Given a valid bank card
  When invalid credentials are submitted repeatedly
  Then the card is retained

@slow
Scenario Outline: Customer uses ATM with bank card
  Given a valid bank card
  When the customer is <customer-action>
  Then the card is <card-action>

  @regression
  Examples: Common customer behaviors
    | customer-action          | card-action |
    | does nothing for 30 seconds | retained    |
    | presses cancel           | returned    |
    | enters PIN               | authorized  |

  @defect
  @defect_12345
  Examples: Unexpected behavior
    | customer-action         | card-action |
    | inserts card incorrectly | returned    |
```

Tags on the feature apply to every scenario and scenario outline within the feature. Tags on a scenario outline apply to every example that is associated with it (in addition to any tags applied to the feature). And tags on an example block apply to all examples in that block (in addition to any tags applied to the feature and the scenario outline).

If we run this feature file without any tag expression, six scenarios will be run (two scenarios + a scenario outline with four examples). If we wanted to run just the regression or defect scenarios, we'd tell Cucumber to run @regression or @defect, and only five scenarios from this feature would be run. If instead we specified that we wanted to run scenarios that were high-risk regressions, we'd use @high_risk and @regression and four scenarios from this feature would be run. That's because the whole feature is tagged with @high_risk, but only one scenario and three examples are tagged with @regression. Finally, if we run only scenarios that are not marked as @slow, only one scenario would be run. The syntax for combining tags is explained in *Running a Subset of Scenarios*, on page 261.

Using tags, we can build subsets of scenarios that we can run at different times in our development process to control how long it takes before the development team gets feedback. As our application evolves, we can add or remove tags from our feature file. For example, a feature that is classified as high risk today might be seen as less risky in six months once we've ironed out all the technical problems.

Now that we've explored this simple technique, it's time to tackle the problem of slow tests from another angle. To do this, we'll need to go back to the fundamental question of what we're testing and why.

# What Sort of Tests?

Both BDD and TDD ask us to write examples before we write the code to help us drive out just the functionality that our customers want, and no more. When we write these scenarios and tests, they guide our emerging design. Once the functionality has been implemented, their purpose is to give us confidence when we refactor or add new behavior to protect us from regressions.

Many people assume that when using a tool like Cucumber—where the test is a business-readable *acceptance test*—we must exercise all layers of the solution. That's not the case! The choice between using a natural language tool or a more technical tool, such as JUnit, to run the tests depends on who is interested in reading the specification. How much of the application that the test should exercise is a completely separate decision.

We're going to introduce a new model to help you think about this, but let's start by looking at a recognized model used in the Agile community.

## The Testing Pyramid

In his book, *Succeeding with Agile: Software Development Using Scrum [Coh09]*, Mike Cohn introduced the concept of the testing pyramid to emphasize that you should have more unit tests than full-stack tests. The figure that follows is inspired by his ideas and shows that unit tests are the foundation of your automated test suite. They help drive out the implementation and specify the precise behavior of individual components. Integration or component tests validate the interactions between subsystems or units. Finally, the full-stack tests ensure that the whole application "hangs together."

Unit tests are preferable to full-stack tests because they are faster, and when they fail, they give us a clear indication of where we need to go to fix the problem. Additionally, unit tests are often less brittle and easier to understand than full-stack tests.

Using BDD, we encourage the team to specify the application's behavior in business language. When thinking about the application from a user's per-

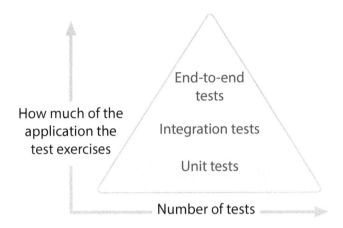

spective, we often write a large number of full-stack tests, exercising the application the same way a user would—through the UI. In the extreme case, you end up with an inverted pyramid (known as the Ice Cream Cone antipattern[1]).

One of the solutions that has been proposed when features take too long to run is to *push* some scenarios down into the unit test suite. This can work, but because less behavior is now specified in the features, it can make our *living documentation* less complete and less useful. We need a new way to think about this problem.

The pyramid image is often drawn with a cloud around the summit labeled "Manual and exploratory testing" to emphasize that we still need human testers to apply their skill, experience, and intuition. Automated testing is ideal for repetitious, scriptable behaviors, but is, by its very nature, less useful for discovering the more unlikely ways in which an application can fail. Liz Keogh captured this idea perfectly in her talk,[2] which describes the value that a tester (wearing the Evil Hat) brings to the team.

## The Testing Iceberg

The decision about whether or not a behavior should be specified in the feature files should be based on whether your business stakeholders are interested in it, not on how long it takes to run or how much of the application it exercises. Imagine the Testing Pyramid became a Testing Iceberg floating in water.

1. http://watirmelon.com/2012/01/31/introducing-the-software-testing-ice-cream-cone/
2. http://www.infoq.com/presentations/Learning-and-Perverse-Incentives

Above the water are all the tests that are business readable. Below the water are all the tests that only the technical people on the team can read.

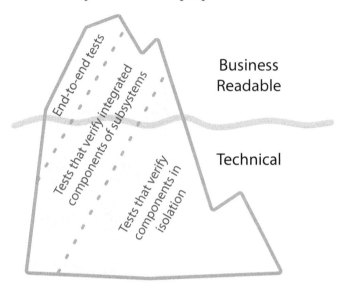

As the iceberg settles in the water, it tilts to one side. Some of the unit tests appear above the waterline, becoming business readable. Some full-stack tests disappear beneath the water, as they are specifying behavior that only a technical audience would be interested in.

With this understanding of the distribution of tests between business-readable and technical, we are in a position to modify many of our step definitions to exercise components directly through their Java API, rather than through the UI. Our step definitions could also work with test doubles[3] (mocks, fakes, stubs) of some components—the database or file system, for example.

The testers and the business often find this difficult to accept, especially if code quality has, historically, not been very good. So let's look at three techniques for trying to keep our living documentation complete and our feedback fast while building trust between developers, testers, and the business.

## Environment-Specific Step Definitions

A common request is to run the scenarios differently depending on the environment they're running in. For example, we may not have access to external web services or production databases from our CI environment, so we'll want to use test doubles when we run our scenarios there. On the other hand, we'll

---

3.   http://xunitpatterns.com/Test%20Double.html

use the real systems when we run our scenarios in system integration test (SIT) or user acceptance test (UAT) environments.

We'll pass Cucumber an environment variable to let our step definitions know how to behave. It's up to us to build the conditional logic that implements that behavior, using standard software development techniques.

## Creating the Seam

Michael Feathers introduces the concept of a *seam* in his seminal book *Working Effectively with Legacy Code [Fea04]*. He defines a seam like this:

> A seam is a place where you can alter behavior in your program without editing in that place.

One way of introducing a seam is to create a factory that creates different implementations of an interface depending on the environment. The first thing we do is extract an AtmInterface that offers the functionality that our TellerSteps depends on:

fast/10/src/test/java/support/AtmInterface.java
```
package support;
import nicebank.Teller;
public interface AtmInterface extends Teller {
    void type(int amount);
    boolean isDisplaying(String message);
}
```

We then modify AtmUserInterface to implement AtmInterface and change TellerSteps to use AtmInterface:

fast/10/src/test/java/nicebank/TellerSteps.java
```
@Autowired
private AtmInterface teller;
```

Now we need to tell Spring to use a factory to create an instance of AtmUserInterface whenever an implementation of AtmInterface is needed:

fast/10/src/test/resources/cucumber.xml
```
<bean class="support.AtmInterfaceFactory" factory-method="createAtmInterface"
    lazy-init="true" scope="cucumber-glue" />
```

Finally we create a factory that creates the object we need:

fast/10/src/test/java/support/AtmInterfaceFactory.java
```
package support;
public class AtmInterfaceFactory {
    public static AtmInterface createAtmInterface() {
        return new AtmUserInterface();
    }
}
```

What we've done is create a *seam* where we can make a decision about what sort of AtmInterface we want to create. At the moment we're just creating a AtmUserInterface as before, but we can add logic to the factory to make a decision to use a different implementation.

## Varying the Implementation

Now let's create a new implementation of AtmInterface. This one won't go through the UI but will interact directly with Teller, CashSlot, and Account:

**fast/11/src/test/java/support/AtmProgrammaticInterface.java**

```java
package support;

import java.util.List;

import nicebank.Account;
import nicebank.AutomatedTeller;
import nicebank.CashSlot;

import org.springframework.beans.factory.annotation.Autowired;

public class AtmProgrammaticInterface implements AtmInterface {
    @Autowired
    private CashSlot cashSlot;

    RuntimeException runtimeException;

    public void withdrawFrom(Account account, int amount) {
        try {
            AutomatedTeller.withdrawFrom(cashSlot, account, amount);
        } catch (RuntimeException e){
            runtimeException = e;
        }
    }

    public void type(int amount) {
        // NOTHING TO BE DONE
    }

    public boolean isDisplaying(String message) {
        // SHOULD THIS BE true OR false OR throw new NotImplementedException();?
        return true;
    }
}
```

We decide that when the test runs in an environment that has the variable CUCUMBER_ENVIRONMENT defined with the value DEVELOPMENT, we want the factory to create an instance of AtmProgrammaticInterface. If the variable has a different value, or is not set, it will create an instance of AtmUserInterface:

fast/11/src/test/java/support/AtmInterfaceFactory.java
```java
package support;

public class AtmInterfaceFactory {

    public static AtmInterface createAtmInterface() {
        String cucumberEnvironment = System.getenv("CUCUMBER_ENVIRONMENT");

        if (cucumberEnvironment != null
                && cucumberEnvironment.equalsIgnoreCase("DEVELOPMENT")) {
            return new AtmProgrammaticInterface();
        } else {
            return new AtmUserInterface();
        }
    }
}
```

Now we can modify the behavior of our steps, depending on what environment variables we've set:

- *nix: export CUCUMBER_ENVIRONMENT=DEVELOPMENT

- Windows: set CUCUMBER_ENVIRONMENT=DEVELOPMENT

When we run the feature now, we'll see that the steps don't exercise the UI. This technique allows us to vary the behavior of our steps depending on the environment they're running in, which can be useful in a CI pipeline. We can even use our CI tool to control the behavior of our scenarios.

## Changing Step Definitions Using Tags

This section builds on the techniques of the previous section to use Gherkin tags to modify the behavior of our step definitions. The advantage of using tags, rather than environment variables, is that the number of layers exercised by the test is documented in the feature file for the whole team to see.

### Using Tagged Hooks

In the previous sections we put a seam in place that allowed AtmInterfaceFactory to decide whether our step definitions were going to interact with the Teller through the web UI or its Java API. We're going to reuse that seam in this section, but we'll use Gherkin tags to modify the factory's behavior, instead of the environment variable that we used previously.

The Cucumber feature that we're going to use is *tagged hooks*, which we saw in *Tagged Hooks*, on page 157. We'll use the tag @bypass_teller_ui to mark scenarios that we want to run directly against the Java API, and write a tagged hook to record that we've made this decision:

fast/12/src/test/java/hooks/TaggedHooks.java
```java
@ContextConfiguration("classpath:cucumber.xml")
public class TaggedHooks {
    @Before("@bypass_teller_ui")
    public void bypassTellerUI() {
        AtmInterfaceFactory.bypassTellerUI();
    }
}
```

We'll modify our factory to take account of this tag:

fast/12/src/test/java/support/AtmInterfaceFactory.java
```java
package support;

public class AtmInterfaceFactory {

    private static boolean bypassTellerUI = false;

    public static void reset() {
        bypassTellerUI = false;
    }

    public static void bypassTellerUI() {
        bypassTellerUI = true;
    }

    public static AtmInterface createAtmInterface() {
        if (bypassTellerUI) {
            return new AtmProgrammaticInterface();
        } else {
            return new AtmUserInterface();
        }
    }
}
```

And, because the factory flag is static, we need to remember to reset the flag before we run each scenario:

fast/12/src/test/java/hooks/ResetHooks.java
```java
public class ResetHooks {
    @Before(order = 1)
    public void reset() {
        AtmInterfaceFactory.reset();
    }
}
```

Now we can simply annotate selected features with our @bypass_teller_ui tag and they will run directly against the Java API, rather than through the web UI. We're now in a position to choose how much of the application stack each scenario exercises just by adding tags to our feature file, without modifying the text of the scenarios or the Java implementation of our step definitions. This technique is a powerful tool that allows us to control the runtime of our features while preserving their comprehensive nature and helps us build trust that our software does what the customer expects.

Remember that Gherkin tags are simply free-form text. You can use any text you like, so you should choose words that convey meaning to your team. In this example we've used the string bypass_teller_ui, but there's nothing magic about these words. You may choose to use NO-UI, DirectToTeller, or something entirely different. It's up to you.

## Building Trust

As we saw in *Three Amigos*, on page 101 , the tester, the programmer, and the product owner collaborate to discover examples that illustrate how the application should work. These examples become scenarios, and the development team uses them to drive out the implementation. Meanwhile, because they are written using business domain language, they are also used by testers and business stakeholders as automated acceptance tests. We want to run them regularly to assure ourselves that the application still delivers the functionality that our customers require. This helps build trust between customers, developers, and testers that we understand each other's needs.

We also want our scenarios to run relatively quickly so that we can run them often and get feedback quickly. We can use the technique presented in the previous section to focus in and exercise the part of the application where the behavior specified by the scenario is implemented. Since the scenarios started out exercising the whole application stack, we win the trust of our customers. Using tags in this way makes it a better test without compromising the *specification*.

Lots of scenarios will exercise the same UI elements as others, because that's the only way that we can vary the paths through our application's business logic. So we can introduce tags to reduce the amount of application being exercised without seeing a reduction in the coverage of our scenarios. We just have to leave enough scenarios untagged so that every UI element is exercised, but this will be a fraction of all our scenarios.

By exercising the whole application when we first write our scenarios, we build the trust that the application is correct. Once this trust has been established, we can use tags and unit test techniques to minimize the cost of running all our scenarios. Without trust this wouldn't be possible, so it's important to remember how easy it is to lose the trust of other parts of the organization and remain focused on delivering software that reliably delivers value to our customers.

In this chapter, we've seen techniques that can help you control the runtime of your scenarios. The example that we have used focused on bypassing the UI to reduce the amount of web automation required. These techniques are not limited to our UI and can be used anywhere in our application. Instead of calling a service over the network, we could use these techniques to switch to using a local test double that could return canned data to speed up the scenarios. Or we could switch between using a real database for our persistent store and an in-memory data structure. The possibilities are endless. Our executable specifications remain comprehensive and our scenarios deliver consistently high coverage, but they continue to run quickly and deliver fast, reliable feedback.

## What We Just Learned

We began this chapter by reviewing the recommended distribution of test depth as described by the Testing Pyramid. We then looked at the separate concern of who the tests should be readable by, as captured by the Testing Iceberg. This led us into a discussion of how we can keep our scenarios running quickly, while still keeping their documentation of our application complete. Finally, we looked at concrete techniques that allow us to vary the amount of the application that our steps exercise without changing the scenarios themselves.

### Try This

The example in this chapter focused on switching between the web UI and the business logic. Try to introduce a similar choice somewhere else in our application. For instance, you could implement a switch that lets you replace the asynchronous processing of the message file and TransactionProcessor with a synchronous, in-memory test double. Or you could try to switch between using the database and using an in-memory account balance.

When you try this, consider how the design decisions that we made earlier affect the ease of the change. Have some of them made the introduction of a seam harder? Would it have been better to implement the seam from the start?

# Part III

# More Techniques

*In this final part of the book, we'll show you how to fine-tune your control of Cucumber. This material will be of use whether you're running Cucumber from the command line or through one of the many continuous integration (CI) servers.*

*You'll also learn techniques for using Cucumber in situations that weren't covered in the previous worked example. We'll work through a simple REST web service example that will let you practice interacting with an application that doesn't have a user interface. And to finish off, we'll give you advice about how to use BDD and Cucumber with legacy applications.*

# CHAPTER 14

# Controlling Cucumber

We have done our best to make Cucumber work out of the box without complex configuration. It doesn't require us to provide a configuration file or pass a lot of complex command-line options to work. However, there are times when we want to tweak how Cucumber behaves.

Sometimes the default output can be too verbose, or perhaps we need it in a format that's easier to share with others. We might want to run just a subset of scenarios or perhaps organize the location of our Gherkin features and step definitions a little differently. In this chapter, we're going to take a closer look at what options Cucumber has to offer and how they can help us achieve some of these goals.

The most basic way of running Cucumber is by using the cucumber.api.cli.Main class. We started using this class in the examples in Part I of the book. We can control some aspects of how Cucumber behaves by passing arguments to Main.main. We've seen some of these already, but let's take a look at what's available.

## Cucumber's Runtime Options

Let's start by exploring the runtime options. Cucumber provides a --help option, which you can invoke from the command line (you'll need to have cucumber-core.jar and gherkin.jar on your classpath):

```
$ java cucumber.api.cli.Main --help

Usage: java cucumber.api.cli.Main [options] [ [FILE|DIR][:LINE[:LINE]*] ]+

Options:

    -g, --glue PATH
            Where glue code is loaded from.
```

```
-p, --plugin PLUGIN[:PATH_OR_URL]
        Register a plugin.
        Built-in PLUGIN types: junit, html, pretty, progress, json, usage,
        rerun. PLUGIN can also be a fully qualified class name, allowing
        registration of 3rd party plugins.
-f, --format FORMAT[:PATH_OR_URL]
        Deprecated. Use --plugin instead.
-t, --tags TAG_EXPRESSION
        Only run scenarios tagged with tags matching TAG_EXPRESSION.
-n, --name REGEXP
        Only run scenarios whose names match REGEXP.
-d, --[no-]-dry-run
        Skip execution of glue code.
-m, --[no-]-monochrome
        Don't colour terminal output.
-s, --[no-]-strict
        Treat undefined and pending steps as errors.
    --snippets
        Snippet name: underscore, camelcase
-v, --version
        Print version.
-h, --help
        You're looking at it.
    --i18n LANG
        List keywords for in a particular language
        Run with "--i18n help" to see all languages
```

That's quite a few options, and it may not be obvious when each one is useful. Let's look at situations when you'd use some of them.

## How Cucumber Finds Our Step Definitions

Cucumber calls our step definitions *glue* code, because they glue the *feature* to the *application*. Hooks (@Before and @After hooks and all our tagged hooks) are also considered to be glue code.

We use the --glue option to tell Cucumber which package(s) our glue code is in, and if there are step definitions in them (or hooks), they get loaded. It's important to understand that Cucumber treats the packages you specify as a root from which to scan for glue code. Once you understand this, you'll save yourself from a common source of confusion and frustration. Let's illustrate that with an example. Assume we've organized our features and step definitions as follows:

```
├── features
│   └── stuff.feature
└── step_definitions
    └── widgets
        └── MyWidgetSteps.java
```

We can run all the scenarios in our feature with this:

```
$ java cucumber.api.cli.Main -g step_definitions.widgets features
```

Then, one day we add a new scenario to our stuff.feature and find that we need to create a hook:

```
├── features
│   └── stuff.feature
└── step_definitions
    ├── hooks
    │   └── MyHooks.java
    └── widgets
        └── MyWidgetSteps.java
```

Now when we run the same command, Cucumber tells us that all our hook definitions are undefined. We could add the new package, step_definitions.hooks, to our command line:

```
$ java cucumber.api.cli.Main -g step_definitions.widgets
                             -g step_definitions.hooks features
```

That would work fine, but the command line is getting long and there's a more compact way of getting the same result:

```
$ java cucumber.api.cli.Main -g step_definitions features
```

Now Cucumber will search the classpath for *all* glue code beneath the root package step_definitions. And if we need to add more packages beneath step_definitions, we won't have to change the glue option when we run Cucumber.

## Running a Subset of Scenarios

As the number of features and scenarios grows, we'll frequently run into situations where we want to run only a single (or maybe a couple) of scenarios to get faster feedback. This might be the case if we're working on a new scenario or if we've broken an existing one. Let's take a closer look at how this works.

### Filtering with Tag Expressions

The simplest way to use the --tags option is to give it a single tag to run. Here's an example:

```
$ java cucumber.api.cli.Main --tags @focus features
```

This would cause Cucumber to run just the scenarios tagged with @focus. It's quite common to temporarily tag a scenario or feature with a unique tag like this for filtering purposes.

In some situations, we may want a little more control over the tag filtering. Imagine that we've made some changes to a piece of our application that sends out emails. What if we want to run all scenarios tagged with @focus or @email? Here's how:

```
$ java cucumber.api.cli.Main --tags @focus,@email features
```

The comma is interpreted as a logical OR statement. It's not uncommon to have scenarios that run fast and others that run slowly. If we've applied a tag to the fast scenarios or features, such as @fast, we can apply a logical AND to say we want to run scenarios that are tagged as @fast and either @focus or @email:

```
$ java cucumber.api.cli.Main --tags @fast --tags @focus,@email features
```

Here we're using --tags twice. Each of them will be logically ANDed together. Ideally, most of our scenarios are fast, and only a few are slow. So, instead of tagging most of our scenarios with @fast, it makes more sense to tag the few that are slow with @slow. If we want to run the scenarios that are *not* slow (and at the same time @focus or @email), we can use negation (the tilde):

```
$ java cucumber.api.cli.Main --tags ~@slow --tags @focus,@email features
```

Let's look at another way to run a subset of scenarios—line numbers.

### Filtering on Lines

You don't need to tag your scenarios or features to run just a subset of them. Cucumber also provides a convenient way to specify the line number of the scenario you want to run. As you've probably noticed, Cucumber prints out the location of a feature file with the line number in error messages.

If you want to rerun the scenario that failed, just select the text and paste it:

```
$ java cucumber.api.cli.Main features/something.feature:45
```

If the feature file has more than one scenario, it will run only the one on line 45. The line number can be anywhere in the feature, ranging from a comment line to the last step (including a step table or doc string).

The colon notation also lets you specify several line numbers, allowing you to specify several scenarios to run:

```
$ cucumber features/something.feature:45:89:107
```

### Filtering on Names

If tag filtering doesn't meet your needs, you can filter scenarios based on name. Say, you want to run all scenarios that have the text *logout* in their name and that they're scattered around several feature files without a particular tag to identify them. Running them is just a matter of the following:

```
$ java cucumber.api.cli.Main --name logout
```

The argument to the --name option is a regular expression, so you can use the usual special characters.

## Changing Cucumber's Output

Cucumber's default behavior is to output results using the progress plugin, which produces a minimal report with a single character per step (as we've seen already):

```
$ java cucumber.api.cli.Main features
..U--..F..
```

Each character represents the status of each step:

- . means passing.
- U means undefined.
- - means skipped (or a Scenario Outline step).
- F means failing.

Cucumber can also produce a more verbose report that's similar to the Gherkin source text—with a little extra information such as colors, locations of matched step definitions, highlighting of arguments, and so on—using the pretty plugin:

```
$ java cucumber.api.cli.Main --plugin pretty features
```

Cucumber also has built-in plugins that output html, json, and junit. The latter is handy if you're running Cucumber in a CI environment since most CI servers know how to interpret JUnit reports. More on that in a minute.

### Other Plugins

In addition to the plugins we've seen so far, Cucumber bundles a few that create output that isn't meant to be read as a report of the run. These plugins serve as a development aid.

The usage plugin lists all the step definitions in our project, as well as the steps that are using it. It shows you unused step definitions, and it sorts the step definitions by their average execution time. The output from the usage plugin is useful for quickly finding slow parts in your code but also a great way to get an overview of your step definitions.

Finally, there's the rerun plugin. This is a special plugin that creates output like this:

```
$ java cucumber.api.cli.Main --plugin rerun features
features/one.feature:367 features/another.feature:91:117
```

Does this look familiar? This is the same kind of information that you give to Cucumber when you want to run a subset of your scenarios using line filtering (which we described earlier).

If all scenarios are passing, the rerun plugin doesn't output anything at all. However, if one or more scenarios fail, it will output their location so that you can copy and paste the output to rerun just those scenarios. Being able to do this saves you a lot of time when fixing broken scenarios.

### Outputting to File and Using Multiple Output Plugins

By default, all bundled plugins will print their output to STDOUT. So, what do you do if you want to see the usual pretty output but also have an html and rerun report? This is where you have to tell Cucumber to direct the output to a file instead of STDOUT. Here's an example:

```
$ java cucumber.api.cli.Main -p pretty -p html:cukes.html
                                     -p rerun:rerun.txt features
```

This tells Cucumber to write the HTML report to the file cukes.html and the rerun output to rerun.txt, and display the pretty plugin's output in the console.

## Miscellaneous Options

There are a couple of other options that we feel are worth mentioning.

### Snippet Name Format

The format of your variable names can cause a lot of friction in some development teams, so Cucumber allows you to choose whether it generates snippets with CamelCase[1] or underscores[2] method names (the default is underscores):

```
# snake_case
$ java cucumber.api.cli.Main --snippets underscore features
```

```
# CamelCase
$ java cucumber.api.cli.Main --snippets camelcase features
```

---

1. http://en.wikipedia.org/wiki/CamelCase
2. http://en.wikipedia.org/wiki/Snake_case

### Color or Monochrome Output

By default, the bundled plugins will produce colored output to help emphasize the outcome of each step. This is done by inserting control characters into the output, but sometimes this is not what you want. Simply supply the --monochrome option and the output will be plain text.

## Overriding Cucumber Options

There are several ways you can set the options used to control how Cucumber runs your features. Learning how they interact is useful if you want Cucumber to behave differently depending on how you invoke it. Let's look at the various ways you can supply options to Cucumber and how they interact.

### How Cucumber Overrides

Cucumber options initially get set by the arguments you provide to your runner—either directly on the command line for cucumber.api.cli.Main or using a @CucumberOptions annotation for the JUnit or TestNG runners.

Cucumber then looks to see if any option overrides have been provided. It looks in the following three places:

1. The OS environment variable CUCUMBER_OPTIONS

2. The Java system property cucumber.options

3. The Java resource bundle cucumber.properties with a cucumber.options property

Overrides are provided in a variable (or property) called cucumber.options or CUCUMBER_OPTIONS. Cucumber searches for this variable in the order shown here and uses the first value it finds. It will not continue to search other locations once it has found an override.

Except for the plugin argument, values found in the override replace any values already set. Arguments not mentioned in the override will not affect any value already supplied for that argument.

The plugin option is handled slightly differently. The list of plugins specified by the override is combined with any plugins already specified. This can cause a problem if Cucumber ends up with more than one plugin trying to output to STDOUT, in which case you'll get this error: Only one plugin can use STDOUT.

The plugin option is also the only one for which Cucumber provides a default. If no plugin is specified, then Cucumber will always use the progress plugin to output to STDOUT.

## Formatting the Override

When overriding Cucumber's options, use exactly the same format as you did on the command line in *Cucumber's Runtime Options*, on page 259. For example:

```
$ java cucumber.api.cli.Main -g step_definitions features
```

can be rewritten as a Java system property:

```
$ java -Dcucumber.options="-g step_definitions features" cucumber.api.cli.Main
```

This could also be set in an OS environment variable:

```
export CUCUMBER_OPTIONS="-g step_definitions features"
```

Or you might choose to place it in the cucumber.properties resource bundle:

```
cucumber.options=-g step_definitions features
```

As you can see, to override options simply copy what you would have written on the command line.

# Automating Cucumber

Throughout this book we've been running Cucumber from the command line using Maven and JUnit. Although this is very common, you may use other unit test or build frameworks. In the following sections, we'll look at some of the most popular alternatives. Even if you choose to use another framework entirely, the examples will give you the understanding you'll need to integrate Cucumber with your environment.

## Cucumber Integration with Unit Test Frameworks

We've seen how to invoke Cucumber from the command line, but most of us will be using an existing framework to run our automated unit tests. Cucumber integrates with JUnit[3] and TestNG[4] so that we can run our scenarios using the same tooling as our unit tests. Let's take a look at how Cucumber integrates with each framework.

### Running Cucumber from JUnit

Cucumber ships with a JUnit runner cucumber.api.junit.Cucumber. To get JUnit to run our scenarios, we'll create a simple JUnit test class like this (of course the name of the class is irrelevant):

---

3.  http://junit.org
4.  http://testng.org/doc/index.html

```
import cucumber.api.junit.Cucumber;
import org.junit.runner.RunWith;

@RunWith(Cucumber.class)
public class RunCukesTest {
}
```

This class should not contain any code. All it does is tell JUnit to invoke the Cucumber JUnit runner. It will search for feature files and run them, providing the output back to JUnit in a format that it understands. As always, we can control how Cucumber runs by annotating the test class with the options that we've been discussing. For example:

```
import cucumber.api.CucumberOptions;
import cucumber.api.junit.Cucumber;
import org.junit.runner.RunWith;

@RunWith(Cucumber.class)
@CucumberOptions(plugin={"pretty", "html:out.html"}, glue="nicebank",
                            features ="src/test/resources/nicebank")
public class RunCukesTest {
}
```

Remember that the options provided in the @CucumberOptions annotation may be overridden in all the ways described previously in this chapter.

## Running Cucumber from TestNG

TestNG support was added to the Cucumber project in 2013, and it's very similar to JUnit integration:

```
import cucumber.api.CucumberOptions;
import cucumber.api.testng.AbstractTestNGCucumberTests;

@CucumberOptions(plugin = "json:target/cucumber-report.json")
public class RunCukesTest extends AbstractTestNGCucumberTests {
}
```

The TestNG runner uses the same @CucumberOptions annotation as the JUnit runner to control Cucumber.

## Using the @CucumberOptions Annotation

Often, you'll be running Cucumber using JUnit or TestNG, so you'll want to supply your options to the runner classes using an @CucumberOptions annotation. Although the options that you can set are exactly the same, the structure is different and could do with some explanation.

The simple example that we've been using so far is easy to put into a @CucumberOptions annotation:

```
@CucumberOptions(glue="step_definitions", features="features")
```

### Supplying Multiple Values for a Property

If you want to specify multiple values for a property, you can use a list. Here we're specifying a list of two plugins we want to use:

```
@CucumberOptions(glue="step_definitions", features="features",
                 plugin={"pretty", "html:out"})
```

You can use lists of strings for features, glue, plugin, and tags.

### Snippets

The snippets option is typed, so you'll need to use one of the constants provided, SnippetType.CAMELCASE or SnippetType.UNDERSCORE:

```
@CucumberOptions(glue="step_definitions", features ="features",
                 snippets=SnippetType.CAMELCASE)
```

Remember: You must add import cucumber.api.SnippetType; to your class.

### Tag Expressions

To run all scenarios tagged with a specific tag, use the following:

```
@CucumberOptions(tags="@TagA", glue="step_definitions", features ="features")
```

Tag terms can still be combined to form logical expressions as described earlier. So, to run all our scenarios tagged with either @TagA or @TagB, we'd write:

```
@CucumberOptions(tags="@TagA,@TagB", glue="step_definitions", features ="features")
```

To run all scenarios tagged with both @TagA and @TagB, we'd write:

```
@CucumberOptions(tags={"@TagA", "@TagB"},
                              glue="step_definitions", features ="features")
```

We can use the negation (NOT) operator (~) as well.

## Running Cucumber from Build Tools

As part of your development environment you'll have set up an automated build script of some sort. In the old days, people might have used make,[5] but JVM developers are more likely to be using Ant,[6] Maven,[7] or Gradle.[8] We'll take a look at how Ant and Maven integrate with Cucumber.

5.  http://www.gnu.org/software/make/
6.  http://ant.apache.org
7.  http://maven.apache.org
8.  http://www.gradle.org

### Running Cucumber from Maven

The simplest way for Maven to run your scenarios is to run them at the same time as your unit tests. You'll have already created an empty test class as shown in *Cucumber Integration with Unit Test Frameworks*, on page 266. If you were already running unit tests, there's nothing more to do—your scenarios would be run by the Surefire[9] plugin that ships with Maven.

Of course, the trouble with running your scenarios as unit tests is that they may become indistinguishable from unit tests. Occasionally you'll want to run scenarios independently of your unit tests. There are ways of doing this with Maven, one of which (using the Maven Failsafe[10] plugin) is described in detail in a blog by Sébastien Le Callonnec.[11]

Another way of separating your unit tests from your scenarios is to run them explicitly using cucumber.api.cli.Main. To do this within Maven, you'd use the exec-maven-plugin[12] (an example of which was posted in the Cucumber mailing list[13]).

```
<build>
    <plugins>
     <plugin>
          <groupId>org.codehaus.mojo</groupId>
          <artifactId>exec-maven-plugin</artifactId>
          <version>1.2.1</version>
          <executions>
           <execution>
                <phase>integration-test</phase>
                <goals>
                 <goal>java</goal>
                </goals>
                <configuration>
                 <classpathScope>test</classpathScope>
                 <mainClass>cucumber.cli.Main</mainClass>
                 <arguments>
                        <argument>--plugin</argument>
                        <argument>pretty</argument>
                        <argument>--glue</argument>
                        <argument>nicebank</argument>
                        <argument>src/test/resources/nicebank</argument>
                 </arguments>
                </configuration>
```

---

9. http://maven.apache.org/surefire/maven-surefire-plugin/
10. http://maven.apache.org/surefire/maven-failsafe-plugin/
11. http://www.weblogism.com/item/334/integration-tests-with-cucumber-selenium-and-maven
12. http://mojo.codehaus.org/exec-maven-plugin/
13. https://groups.google.com/forum/#!topic/cukes/ye5JJoTFqfs

```
            </execution>
          </executions>
        </plugin>
      </plugins>
</build>
```

Maven is a powerful piece of software, and fully describing its functionality is beyond the scope of this book. The examples in this section demonstrated some approaches for using Cucumber from Maven, but there are other ways of achieving similar results.

### Running Cucumber from Ant

Ant is an older build tool, but it's still very common. It doesn't ship with dependency management tooling, so many people use it in conjunction with Ivy,[14] which can use the Maven infrastructure to manage dependencies.

### Using Test Runners

JUnit[15] and TestNG[16] Ant tasks are available that will run your scenarios via the test runners described in *Cucumber Integration with Unit Test Frameworks*, on page 266. As always, you can control the execution of Cucumber using options that are defined as annotations on the test class or passed to the Ant task as system properties (using the nested sysproperty tag). Here's an example:

```
<junit>
  <sysproperty key="cucumber.options" value="plugin='pretty'" />
</junit>
```

### Using cucumber.api.cli.Main

You can also run the scenarios using the java task and the cucumber.api.cli.Main runner, passing the options directly as command-line arguments:

```
<target name="runcukes" depends="compile-test">
  <java classname="cucumber.cli.Main" fork="true"
    failonerror="false"
    resultproperty="cucumber.exitstatus">
      <classpath refid="classpath"/>
      <arg value="--plugin"/>
      <arg value="pretty"/>
      <arg value="--glue"/>
      <arg value="nicebank"/>
      <arg value="src/test/resources"/>
  </java>
```

---

14. http://ant.apache.org/ivy/
15. https://ant.apache.org/manual/Tasks/junit.html
16. http://testng.org/doc/ant.html

```
    <fail message="Cucumber failed">
        <condition>
            <not>
                <equals arg1="${cucumber.exitstatus}" arg2="0"/>
            </not>
        </condition>
    </fail>
</target>
```

Now that you know how to run Cucumber both by hand and from Ant and Maven, you can also make your CI server run it. Cucumber exits with a status code of 1 if any scenarios fail, so your CI server can properly detect failure.

## Running Cucumber in Continuous Integration

Many teams set up their continuous integration[17] (CI) server to run Cucumber every time someone shares changes with the rest of the team. Since it's a command-line tool, you don't have to do anything fancy—just plop the build command you're using into the CI project's configuration.

You may want to use slightly different command-line options for CI than you use on your own workstation. You can do this by providing different options, as described earlier.

### Being Strict

It's common to have missing or pending steps while we're working on a new scenario. Some teams strive to keep the mainline (trunk) of the source repository pristine, without any pending or missing steps.

CI systems detect failure by inspecting the exit status of the processes they are running, and by default Cucumber exits with an error status (a nonzero value) only if there are one or more *failing* steps. If you're running Cucumber in a CI environment, you may want to set it up to fail if anyone checks in *missing* or *pending* steps.

If you pass the --strict option to cucumber, it will exit with a nonzero value if there are any *missing* or *pending* steps as well as *failing* ones. You can inspect the exit status after running Cucumber:

```
# OS X or Linux
$ echo $?

# Windows
$ echo %ERRORLEVEL%
```

---

17. http://martinfowler.com/articles/continuousIntegration.html

### Sharing Reports

Earlier in this chapter we saw how to use the --plugin option to change Cucumber's output. If we pass --plugin junit:JUNIT_DIR to Cucumber, we can configure our CI server to pick up those reports from JUNIT_DIR and analyze them. Some CI servers can generate a trend chart showing how healthy our build stays over time. This is a great way to get an indicator of whether the project is improving or decaying.

We can also pass the -p html:HTML_FILE to get a full HTML report of the results. This is particularly handy if we're using a browser automation tool, because we can embed screenshots of the browser right into the HTML report, as we did in *Building the User Interface*, on page 161.

## What We Just Learned

Cucumber has a rich set of options that give us full control over how it behaves. We now know how to choose which features and/or scenarios to run, based on tags, names, and line numbers. Using the special rerun plugin, we can even choose to only run scenarios that failed the last time the features were executed. A wealth of other plugins ship with Cucumber, and we've learned how to control their output as well as how to use several of them at the same time.

We've looked at some of the other options that control Cucumber, especially the glue option (which gives us the freedom to structure our solution in the way that we want) and the snippets option (which gives us control of the formatting of our snippet names).

We've also looked at some of the unit test and build frameworks that Cucumber integrates with, so that you can use it in your project today. And with the knowledge of how you can use your OS or your build environment to override Cucumber options, you have the power to customize what Cucumber does in a flexible way.

### Try This

Here are some exercises you can try:

- Modify one of the examples from Part II to use cucumber.api.cli.Main instead of the JUnit integration.

- How many different ways can you find to get the Cucumber version number? Think about all the places you could provide a --version override.

# CHAPTER 15

# Working with a REST Web Service

Sometimes the user of the system we're developing isn't a human being but another computer program. For systems like these, the user interface is often a REST[1] web service. To automate scenarios against it, we need to make our Cucumber step definitions talk to the web service as though they were a regular client application.

Your application doesn't have to be written in Java (or any other JVM language) in order to be developed using Cucumber. Applications written in Ruby, .NET, PHP, or any other programming language can be tested by starting your application before Cucumber runs and then having Cucumber talk to it using an HTTP client library.

We'll be dealing with a very simple REST API for storing and retrieving fruit. It's probably not the most useful system in the world, but it should allow us to illustrate the fundamentals of REST and Cucumber. We're going to build our web service from scratch. Here's our first scenario:

```
rest_web_services/00/src/test/resources/fruit_list.feature
Feature: Fruit list
  To make a great smoothie, I need some fruit
  Scenario: List fruit
    Given the system knows about the following fruit:
      | name       | color  |
      | banana     | yellow |
      |strawberry  | red    |
    When the client requests GET /fruits
    Then the response should be JSON:
      """
      [ {"name": "banana",     "color": "yellow"},
        {"name": "strawberry", "color": "red"}    ]
      """
```

---

1.  http://en.wikipedia.org/wiki/Representational_state_transfer

In the rest of this section, we'll implement this feature. We'll see how Cucumber can issue HTTP requests to our application.

## Structure Your Step Definitions

When we run our List fruit feature with mvn clean test, we'll see the usual snippets:

```
@Given("^the system knows about the following fruit:$")
public void theSystemKnowsAboutTheFollowingFruit(DataTable arg1) throws Throwable {
    // Write code here that turns the phrase above into concrete actions
    // For automatic transformation, change DataTable to one of
    // List<YourType>, List<List<E>>, List<Map<K,V>> or Map<K,V>.
    // E,K,V must be a scalar (String, Integer, Date, enum etc)
    throw new PendingException();
}


@When("^the client requests GET /fruits$")
public void theClientRequestsGETFruits() throws Throwable {
    // Write code here that turns the phrase above into concrete actions
    throw new PendingException();
}


@Then("^the response should be JSON:$")
public void theResponseShouldBeJSON(String arg1) throws Throwable {
    // Write code here that turns the phrase above into concrete actions
    throw new PendingException();
}
```

Before we go ahead and paste the previous snippets into a Java file and fill in the blanks, let's look at each one. The first snippet is a domain-specific step definition—it's about our fruit system. The last two seem like more general-purpose step definitions for HTTP REST operations. As discussed in *Organizing the Code*, on page 134, we'll put each of them in a file that describes the domain concept they're related to. This makes it easier in the future to find our step definitions. Paste the first one in an src/test/java/fruit/FruitSteps.java file and the last two in an src/test/java/fruit/RestSteps.java file.

Now when we run mvn clean test, our scenario is marked as Pending.

What should we do to make the first step pass? We need some way for Cucumber to tell our web service—which is going to be running in a different process from the web service—what fruits we have available. There are many ways to make this happen, but the essence of it is that we need to make our application's data store accessible from a different process.

One option would be to expose a method over our HTTP API that allowed a client (like our Cucumber scenarios) to add new fruit to the system with an HTTP POST. POSTing to a special URL to reset a database is not an uncommon approach. If you do this, make sure that the URL is disabled in your production environment. Another route would be to build our application to use a data store such as MySQL or MongoDB and use a database library to insert data. If we did that, our step definition could put fruit in the system by talking directly to the same database as our web application.

## Storing Some Fruit

For the sake of simplicity, let's use the second simplest data store after memory—a file. Let's get our step definition to write out the fruit information to a file:

rest_web_services/02/src/test/java/fruit/FruitSteps.java

```
Line 1  package fruit;
    -
    -   import com.google.gson.Gson;
    -
    5   import cucumber.api.java.en.*;
    -
    -   import java.io.PrintWriter;
    -   import java.util.List;
    -
    10  public class FruitSteps {
    -       @Given("^the system knows about the following fruit:$")
    -       public void theSystemKnowsAboutTheFollowingFruit(List<Fruit> fruitList)
    -                                                       throws Throwable {
    -           Gson gson = new Gson();
    15          PrintWriter writer = new PrintWriter("fruit.json", "UTF-8");
    -           writer.println(gson.toJson(fruitList));
    -           writer.close();
    -       }
    -   }
```

There are a couple of things that are new in this step definition. First, you'll see that we've changed the signature of the step definition to accept List<Fruit> (on line 13). This means that Cucumber will try to convert each row of the data table to a Fruit object (matching the column headings to members of the Fruit class).

We're also using the Gson library from Google for the first time. This is a handy utility that does all the hard work of converting objects to and from JSON. You can see from our use of it (on line 16) that it can be trivially simple to use. We'll use some more advanced features of Gson later, but for now all we need to do is add a dependency to pom.xml:

rest_web_services/02/pom.xml

```
<dependency>
  <groupId>com.google.code.gson</groupId>
```

```
    <artifactId>gson</artifactId>
    <version>${gson.version}</version>
</dependency>
```

The last thing we need to do to get the first step to pass is to define the Fruit class:

rest_web_services/02/src/main/java/fruit/Fruit.java
```
package fruit;

public class Fruit {
    private String name;
    private String color;

    public String getName() {
        return name;
    }

    public void setName(String name) {
        this.name = name;
    }

    public String getColor() {
        return color;
    }

    public void setColor(String color) {
        this.color = color;
    }
}
```

Now when we run mvn clean test the first step passes and the file fruit.json is created in the project root:

rest_web_services/02/fruit.json
```
[{"name":"banana","color":"yellow"},{"name":"strawberry","color":"red"}]
```

The contents of the file are, as you'd expect, a JSON representation of the data defined in the first step of our scenario. Next we need to create a web server for our step definitions to talk to.

## Building a Skeleton Web Server

Now it's time to build a walking skeleton that we can "hang" our functionality on. Initially our web server needs to be able to respond to a simple request so that we can be sure our scenarios can talk to the server successfully. This allows us to check that whatever frameworks we choose to use are working for us and try different frameworks if they're not. By doing this early in the project we avoid nasty surprises later.

## Creating the Server with Jersey

We're going to implement our little REST web service with the Jersey[2] web framework because it makes it so easy to create a very simple web service from scratch. If we did this without using a web framework, the feature and step definition files would be exactly the same, but there would be much more application code for us to include in the book. Let's start by adding the dependencies we'll need to pom.xml:

```
rest_web_services/03/pom.xml
<dependency>
  <groupId>org.eclipse.jetty</groupId>
  <artifactId>jetty-webapp</artifactId>
  <version>${jetty.version}</version>
</dependency>
<dependency>
  <groupId>com.sun.jersey</groupId>
  <artifactId>jersey-server</artifactId>
  <version>${jersey.version}</version>
</dependency>
<dependency>
  <groupId>com.sun.jersey</groupId>
  <artifactId>jersey-client</artifactId>
  <version>${jersey.version}</version>
</dependency>
<dependency>
    <groupId>com.sun.jersey</groupId>
    <artifactId>jersey-json</artifactId>
    <version>${jersey.version}</version>
</dependency>
```

We need jetty-webapp to run our web server, jersey-client to deploy a JAX-RS web service, jersey-client to let our step definitions talk to the web service, and jersey-json for automatic conversion of our domain objects to JSON.

With that out of the way, we can get on with building our web server. Create a file named FruitServer.java in the src/main/java/fruit directory. Add the following code to that file:

---

2.    https://jersey.java.net/

rest_web_services/03/src/main/java/fruit/FruitServer.java

```
Line 1  package fruit;

   -    import org.eclipse.jetty.server.Server;
   -    import org.eclipse.jetty.servlet.ServletContextHandler;
   5    import org.eclipse.jetty.servlet.ServletHolder;

   -    import com.sun.jersey.spi.container.servlet.ServletContainer;

   -    public class FruitServer
  10    {
   -        private final Server server;

   -        public FruitServer(int port) {
   -            ServletHolder sh = new ServletHolder(ServletContainer.class);
  15            sh.setInitParameter("com.sun.jersey.config.property.resourceConfigClass",
   -                                "com.sun.jersey.api.core.PackagesResourceConfig");
   -            sh.setInitParameter("com.sun.jersey.config.property.packages", "fruit");
   -            sh.setInitParameter("com.sun.jersey.api.json.POJOMappingFeature", "true");

  20            server = new Server(port);
   -            ServletContextHandler context =
   -                new ServletContextHandler(server, "/", ServletContextHandler.SESSIONS);
   -            context.addServlet(sh, "/");
   -        }
  25
   -        public void start() throws Exception {
   -            server.start();
   -            System.out.println("Listening on " + server.getURI());
   -        }
  30
   -        public void stop() throws Exception {
   -            server.stop();
   -            System.out.println("Server shutdown");
   -        }
  35
   -        public static void main(String[] args) throws Exception {
   -            new FruitServer(9988).start();
   -        }
   -    }
```

This is very similar to our AtmServer from the ATM example, but this time instead of adding servlets to the app explicitly, we tell it to look for services in the fruit package (on line 17). This is followed by setting the property POJOMappingFeature to true (on line 18), which tells Jersey to automatically convert Plain Old Java Objects (POJO) to JSON whenever possible.

We'll create hooks (in exactly the same way as in the ATM example) to start and stop the web service in src/test/java/hooks/ServerHooks.java. And we'll need to delete the fruit.json before each scenario, using a hook defined in src/test/java/hooks/ResetHooks.java.

Now it's time to get the second step to pass, which will need us to issue a GET request:

```
rest_web_services/03/src/test/java/fruit/RestSteps.java
@When("^the client requests GET /fruits$")
public void theClientRequestsGETFruits() throws Throwable {
    try {

        Client client = Client.create();

        WebResource webResource = client
                .resource("http://localhost:" + ServerHooks.PORT + "/fruits");

        response = webResource.type("application/json")
                .get(ClientResponse.class);
    } catch (RuntimeException r) {
        throw r;
    } catch (Exception e) {
        System.out.println("Exception caught");
        e.printStackTrace();
    }

    Assert.assertEquals("Did not receive OK response: ",
        HttpURLConnection.HTTP_OK, response.getStatus());
}
```

Unfortunately, when we run mvn clean test the second step fails with a set of stack traces and a failed assertion that says expected:<200> but was:<500>. This HTTP status code indicates a server error, and looking at the beginning of the stack trace gives us a clue as to what went wrong: The ResourceConfig instance does not contain any root resource classes. It's not a great error message, but what Jetty is trying to tell us is that we have created a server without any services. In the next section we'll see just how easy it is to add a service.

## Creating the Service Using JAX-RS

Creating the service using JAX-RS[3] is really easy. Take a look at this simple implementation of FruitService:

```
rest_web_services/04/src/main/java/fruit/FruitService.java
package fruit;

import javax.ws.rs.GET;
import javax.ws.rs.Path;
```

---

3.   https://jax-rs-spec.java.net/

```
import javax.ws.rs.Produces;
import javax.ws.rs.core.MediaType;

import java.util.List;
import java.util.ArrayList;

@Path("/")
public class FruitService {
    @GET
    @Path("/fruits")
    @Produces(MediaType.APPLICATION_JSON)
    public Fruit[] getAllFruits() {
        List<Fruit> fruits = new ArrayList<Fruit>();
        return fruits.toArray(new Fruit[]{});
    }
}
```

The @GET annotation indicates that this method should be called when a GET request is sent to the URI described by the @Path annotation. Finally, the @Produces annotation specifies what format of data this service can provide. JAX-RS allows you to create much more complex services than this one, but that's outside the scope of this book, so take a look at the documentation.[4]

At the end of theClientRequestsGETFruits, you'll notice that we're asserting that the GET request returns an HTTP status of OK. This is similar to when we check the balance of the account during the deposit step of the ATM example—it helps us validate that the step actually is doing what we expect.

Run mvn clean test one more time and you'll see that the second step is now passing, which means that our web service is returning a status of OK. Just one more step to go!

## The Fruits of Our Labor

Now it's time to get the third, and final, step of the scenario to pass. Before changing anything in our service, we should implement the step so that it compares the JSON we receive to the JSON we expect. Then, once we have moved our third step from Pending to Failing, it's time to write the code in the service and get the scenario to pass.

### Putting It All Together

JSON is generally represented as text, so it is really easy to compare our expected JSON by comparing the String that we expect to the String that we receive from our web service:

---

4.    https://jersey.java.net/documentation/latest/user-guide.html#d0e1657

rest_web_services/05/src/test/java/fruit/RestSteps.java
```java
@Then("^the response should be JSON:$")
public void theResponseShouldBeJSON(String jsonExpected) throws Throwable {
    Assert.assertEquals("Incorrect JSON representation.",
                        jsonExpected, response.getEntity(String.class));
}
```

When we run mvn clean test, the scenario fails as expected with an error:

```
Scenario: List fruit
  Given the system knows about the following fruit:
  When the client requests GET /fruits
  Then the response should be JSON:
    """
    [
      {"name": "banana", "color": "yellow"},
      {"name": "strawberry", "color": "red"}
    ]
    """
    org.junit.ComparisonFailure: Incorrect JSON representation. expected:<[[
      {"name": "banana", "color": "yellow"},
      {"name": "strawberry", "color": "red"}
    ]]> but was:<[[]]>
      at org.junit.Assert.assertEquals(Assert.java:115)
      at RestSteps.theResponseShouldBeJSON(RestSteps.java:44)
      at *.Then the response should be JSON:(fruit_list.feature:11)


1 Scenarios (1 failed)
3 Steps (1 failed, 2 passed)
```

This is telling us that our service is returning an empty list, which should come as no surprise, because that's what we're creating in our current implementation. What we need to do is read fruit.json and return that list of fruit to our caller:

rest_web_services/06/src/main/java/fruit/FruitService.java
```java
private List<Fruit> getFruitsFromFile() {
    String fruitJson = readJsonFruitFile();
    return buildListFromJson(fruitJson);
}


private String readJsonFruitFile() {
    try {
        java.nio.file.Path path = FileSystems.getDefault().getPath("fruit.json");
        return new String(Files.readAllBytes(path));
    }
    catch (IOException ioe) {
        return "[]";
    }
}
```

```
private List<Fruit> buildListFromJson(String fruitJson) {
    final TypeToken<List<Fruit>> token = new TypeToken<List<Fruit>>() {};
    final Type type = token.getType();
    final Gson gson = new Gson();

    return gson.fromJson(fruitJson, type);
}
```

The first method, getFruitsFromFile, simply delegates to the two other methods. The next method, readJsonFruitFile, opens fruit.json and reads its contents. If the file doesn't exist, then it returns "[]", the empty list. The third method, buildListFromJson, takes a JSON representation and uses Gson to construct a List<Fruit> from it. Because of the way Java handles generic types, we need to use Gson's TypeToken to tell Gson how to turn the JSON into Java objects. We won't go into the details here, but you can read about it in the Gson documentation.[5]

The third step is still failing. In the next section we'll find out why.

 **Joe asks:**
**I Thought Scenarios Should Avoid Technical Terms like JSON**

It's always important to ensure that the scenarios are readable by the stakeholders, so you should consider who your stakeholders actually are. If the scenarios are only going to be read by other programmers writing a client for the REST interface, it may be fine to expose technical details. For systems that involve collaboration with nontechnical stakeholders, you should use nontechnical terms.

## Only Compare Strings if You Have To

The scenario is failing simply because the actual JSON has a different layout than the JSON from our scenario. Of course, we could try to make the scenario pass by making the JSON in our scenario match that returned by our web service, but that would make it very hard to read. Remember, our features are supposed to serve as documentation too, not only automated tests. In any case, it's the data that's significant in this scenario, not the layout. What we really want to do is to parse the two JSON strings into an object structure and compare them. This is just a small change:

5. https://sites.google.com/site/gson/gson-user-guide#TOC-Collections-Limitations

```
rest_web_services/07/src/test/java/fruit/RestSteps.java
@Then("^the response should be JSON:$")
public void theResponseShouldBeJSON(String jsonExpected) throws Throwable {
    JsonParser parser = new JsonParser();
    Assert.assertEquals("Unexpected JSON.",
        parser.parse(jsonExpected), parser.parse(response.getEntity(String.class)));
}
```

Finally, our first REST feature is passing!

 **Matt says:**
### Comparing Data Is Less Brittle than Comparing Strings

The lesson we learn in this chapter about parsing both strings into JSON documents before comparing them is a useful one to remember for other situations. When you compare two strings in a test, you're often leaving yourself open to brittle failures that aren't telling you anything useful. Parsing the string from the Gherkin feature into more meaningful data can often mean you have more robust tests that fail only when they should.

## What We Just Learned

When developing a REST web service with Cucumber, we need to keep in mind that the service is running in a different process than Cucumber. This means that we need to remember to start the service *before* we can run our features.

Although our example used the Jersey JAX-RS library, the techniques used in this chapter can be applied to any other web services technology. And because we're accessing the service's functionality through its web interface, the service can be written in any language—Cucumber doesn't care what language the application you're developing is written in, as long as there's an API that it can talk to.

Often our services will "talk" in JSON, and this may surface in our features. You can make this easier to read by using indented JSON documents in your scenarios, as long as you ignore whitespace when you compare them to documents produced by your API.

## Try This

Our Fruit application is very simple. It doesn't provide an API to store fruit, and the file-based database is not complex. Here are some new features you can try to express with Cucumber and then implement:

- Add a scenario that starts with one fruit in the database, adds another one via an HTTP POST, and then verifies that you now have two fruit.

- Refactor your code to use a proper database, like MySQL or MongoDB, to store fruit. Make sure all scenarios are still passing and that you can run each of them individually. Hint: Remember to make sure each scenario starts with a blank database.

# CHAPTER 16

# Working with Legacy Applications

In the real world, you don't always get the luxury of working on shiny new code. Reading a book like this can be a little bit frustrating because the examples all deal with nice, simple problems, usually in a new codebase.

We all know that software development isn't really like that.

Even in the best teams we've worked on, there have always been a few dark and ugly corners of the codebase where nobody wanted to go. People would sometimes disappear into there for days at a time and emerge exhausted and confused, blinking in the bright sunlight.

Like an old abandoned mine, those areas of the codebase are dangerous. The code is fragile, and the slightest change can cause other parts of the code to collapse and stop working. Everyone knows this, and that's why people are reluctant to go in there; it's stressful work.

If you had to go down an old mine tunnel, what would you do to make it safer? You'd probably build some scaffolding to hold the roof of the tunnel up so that it didn't collapse—just enough to help you get in and get out again safely.

You can think of automated tests like this. When you have to make a change to an area of the code that you know is brittle, it's scary. What is the thing that you're most afraid of?

*Breaking something.*

Automated tests can help you keep this fear at bay. If you make a change and other parts of the code start to collapse, the tests will give you a warning while you still have a chance to do something to correct it. But what if you don't have any tests?

Even if you have recognized that automated testing can help your team write better code, the prospect of adding tests to a large legacy codebase can seem overwhelming. In this chapter, we'll show you some simple techniques you can use to help to solve the problem gradually, giving you added benefit each step of the way.

This isn't a technical chapter, but it will give you some useful techniques and encouragement if you're facing this situation.

Let's start with the first tool you'll need when you enter the mine: a flashlight.

## Characterization Tests

In his excellent book *Working Effectively with Legacy Code [Fea04]*, Michael Feathers talks about two different types of tests, which he calls *specification tests* and *characterization tests*.

Specification tests are the ones we've been talking about throughout this book. They check that the code does what it's supposed to. Ideally you write them before you write the code itself and use them as a guide to help you get the code into the right shape.

Characterization tests are different. You can think of them more like a science experiment, where you test the properties of a mysterious substance by boiling it or mixing it with other substances to see how it reacts. With characterization tests, the aim is just to understand what the system currently does.

Characterization tests apply perfectly to legacy code that has limited or no tests and where the code is hard to read and understand. Here is our approach, adapted from Michael Feathers's book, for creating a Cucumber characterization test:

1. Write a scenario that exercises some interesting—but mysterious— behavior of your system.

2. Write a Then step that you know will fail.

3. Wire up the step definitions and run the scenario. Let the failure in the Then step tell you what the actual behavior is.

4. Change the failing Then step so that it describes the actual behavior of the system.

5. Repeat.

As an example, let's suppose we're making some changes to the checkout system for a supermarket. We've been asked to add a new special offer to the system, which was developed a couple of years ago by a firm of expensive management consultants, who are sadly no longer with us. We've grabbed the source code, managed to get the system to spin up on our development machine, and have been poking around through the user interface. The code is pretty gnarly and it's hard to tell exactly what's going on, but we noticed something about shampoo. It looks like there might be an existing special offer on shampoo bottles already baked into the code, but it's hard to tell exactly what the rules are. Let's write a test:

```
Scenario: Buy Two Bottles of Shampoo
  Given the price of a bottle of shampoo is $2
  When I scan 2 bottles of shampoo
  Then the price should be $0
```

We know that's going to fail; they're not going to give us the shampoo for free, are they (steps 1 and 2)?

So, we wire up the step definitions to the system and run the scenario. Here's what happens:

```
-------------------------------------------------------
 T E S T S
-------------------------------------------------------
Running RunCukesTest
Feature:

  Scenario: Buy Two Bottles of Shampoo
    Given the price of a bottle of shampoo is $2
    When I scan 2 bottles of shampoo
    Then the price should be $0
      java.lang.AssertionError: expected:<0> but was:<2>
        at org.junit.Assert.fail(Assert.java:88)
        at org.junit.Assert.failNotEquals(Assert.java:743)
        at org.junit.Assert.assertEquals(Assert.java:118)
        at org.junit.Assert.assertEquals(Assert.java:555)
        at org.junit.Assert.assertEquals(Assert.java:542)
        at legacy.Steps.thePriceShouldBe$(Steps.java:19)
        at *.Then the price should be $0(bogof.feature:5)

1 Scenarios (1 failed)
3 Steps (1 failed, 2 passed)
```

A-ha! Now we know what price the system is charging for two $2 bottles of shampoo: $2 (step 3).

Now we update the Then step of our scenario to reflect our new understanding of what the system does (step 4):

```
Scenario: Buy Two Bottles of Shampoo
  Given the price of a bottle of shampoo is $2
  When I scan 2 bottles of shampoo
  Then the price should be $2
```

We run the scenario again, and this time it passes. Great! We've added our first characterization test. It's not much, but it's a start, and we know that whatever we do to the code from now on, we'll always have this scenario to tell us whether we break this particular aspect of its behavior.

It looks like there's a buy-one-get-one-free offer on shampoo, but we can't be sure from this single example. We now need to repeat steps 1 to 4 and add some more scenarios to give us some more clues as to what the system is doing.

We can refactor the scenario into a scenario outline (see Chapter 5, *Expressive Scenarios*, on page 69) to allow us to try different amounts and prices:

```
Feature: Special Offers

  Scenario Outline: Shampoo
    Given the price of a bottle of shampoo is $2
    When I scan <number> bottles of shampoo
    Then the price should be <total>

    Examples:
      | number | total |
      | 1      | $0    |
      | 2      | $2    |
```

We can now add examples into the table, one at a time. Each time, we start with a silly value for the total price and then run the scenario and let it tell us what the real total is. Then we update the scenario to document that behavior.

## Squashing Bugs

Our legacy application is big and mysterious, and we could spend an awfully long time writing characterization tests if we just started adding them aimlessly. So, assuming that we do want to grow our suite of automated tests, where should we start?

One of the best ways to start practicing with Cucumber is when you have a bug to fix. Bug reports generally come to you in the form of an example, so they're nice and easy to translate into Cucumber scenarios. Using a bug report, work through the steps on the following list:

1. Translate the bug report into a Cucumber scenario. Show the scenario to the person who reported the bug, and ask that person whether it accurately describes what he or she was doing.

2. Wire up the step definitions and run the scenario. It should fail in the same way as the real system did when the bug was first discovered. The bug is trapped!

3. Examine the defective code, and think about what you'll need to change. If you're unsure or worried about breaking some existing behavior, write one or more characterization test scenarios for it.

4. Fix the code so that the bug report scenario passes.

5. Run the characterization tests to check that you didn't break anything.

You'll find that the bug report scenario acts as a driving force, helping you focus on the code instead of having to keep running a manual test to see whether the fix has worked.

Despite your new characterization tests, you may still find that you missed something and introduced a new bug. That happens sometimes, and it would have happened just the same if you hadn't used any automated tests. If you use the same recipe to fix that new bug and each new bug that comes along, then gradually, over time, you'll build up a solid suite of Cucumber scenarios. Not only will those scenarios prevent any of these bugs from recurring, but they'll start to document the behavior of the system for anyone doing maintenance on it in the future.

## Adding New Behavior

When you think about it, the process of adding new behavior to a system isn't so different from fixing a bug. The overall goal is to change some aspect of how the system behaves, without breaking anything else.

Just as with bug fixing, we can use characterization tests to pin down the surrounding behavior of the system to make sure it isn't dislodged by our work. Characterization tests can also be useful before that, while the new feature is first being considered. You can use them to help understand how much work is involved in the new feature by clarifying exactly what the system currently does.

Here's our approach for adding new behavior to a legacy system:

1. Examine the new feature. If needed, write a few characterization scenarios to examine and clarify the current behavior of the system in that area.

**Matt says:**
## Features for Bug Fixes

We've just told you to use Cucumber to help you reproduce and trap bugs, so it's quite likely that you might end up writing a new feature and calling it something like features/verify_bugfix_52553.feature. We've done this ourselves, and trust us—it doesn't make for great documentation!

There are two ways around this problem. If you judge that the scenario is relevant enough to keep as business-facing documentation, then just talk to your team about where to file it away tidily in your features. If you're adding features to a legacy system, that might well mean creating a new empty feature file about a whole big area of the system and then just adding a single scenario to describe one aspect of its behavior. That's OK; you've created a space where other people can add more scenarios as they come up. Try not to mention the bug itself as you write the scenario—just describe the behavior you want as though it's always been there.

On the other hand, if you decide that it's such an obscure edge case that it isn't interesting enough to remain as business-facing documentation, you can just delete the scenario once you've fixed the bug. That's assuming you've used a unit test to cover the changes you've made to make the fix, so you can be safe in the knowledge that the bug won't reappear.

2. Now, with the new feature in mind, modify those scenarios or write new ones to specify the desired new behavior.

3. Run through the scenarios with your team's stakeholder representative to check that you're about to build the right thing. Correct the scenarios with them if necessary.

4. Run the scenarios. For each failing scenario, examine the code you'll need to change to make it pass, but work on only one failing scenario at a time.

5. Write any extra characterization tests you need to give you the confidence to change that code.

6. Change the code to make the scenario pass.

7. Repeat from step 4 until all the scenarios pass.

Sometimes we find that when we're about to implement the change (step 6), we see that the code we're about to change is responsible for doing things that we hadn't anticipated when we wrote the original characterization tests in step 1. At this point, we'll stop and add some new characterization tests (step 5) first if we think there's a significant risk we could break something.

Just as with bug fixing, following this process means that you quickly get the benefits of automated testing in the areas of the system where you most need them: the ones that are most prone to change and instability.

As you gradually build up your suite of Cucumber scenarios for your legacy application, you'll find you have more confidence to refactor and clean up the code. This becomes a virtuous cycle, with cleaner code causing less bugs.

## Are Your Scenarios Sufficient?

Often it's difficult to tell whether the characterization tests that you've written cover enough of the functionality of the application to give you confidence to go in and make changes safely. There are some tools that can help you decide how safe you should really be feeling. The last thing we want is a false sense of security leading to uncaught regressions being delivered to our customer.

### Code Coverage

Code coverage tools allow us to discover which specific lines of code in the system were executed during a test. When you are starting to add tests to a legacy application, it can be useful to know your code coverage:

- If you know that a line of code isn't covered by your tests yet, you can see more clearly what kind of a characterization test you need to write.

- If you know that a line of code is covered by your tests, you can be more confident in refactoring or changing it.

### Mutation Testing

Code coverage tools tell us what lines get executed when we run our tests, but don't tell us whether we're testing the right things. You might think that there's no substitute for human analysis when it comes to checking that your tests are sufficient, but mutation testing tools, like pitest (http://pitest.org) can help.

The theory behind mutation testing is quite simple. The tool takes your application and creates a *mutant* version by automatically injecting a bug. It then runs your tests, and if one or more fails, then the mutant is killed. But if they all pass, the mutant survives. Any mutant that survives indicates a gap in our tests. We might choose to go back and fill that gap, either by writing a new test or by modifying an existing test.

As you can imagine, a huge number of bugs could be injected into any reasonably sized application, so mutation testing can be quite slow. A lot of work

## Track Your Code Coverage for Team Encouragement

Code coverage is a much misused metric of code quality. We've heard of managers who've demanded that their teams achieve 100 percent code coverage. We've also heard of teams that, under those circumstances, simply wrote a load of tests with no assertions in them. All the code was run, but it wasn't tested!

As a source of internal feedback for the team, though, code coverage can be useful, especially when you're embarking on a long-term project to bring a legacy system under the control of automated tests. Start measuring your code coverage today, and come back every few weeks to measure it again. You should be pleased to see the number is climbing all the time.

Another great related metric to track, which your manager might be more impressed with, is the defect rate (number of new bugs discovered per week). If your Cucumber tests are going to add any value to your customers, this is the most likely place it will surface. As you add more test coverage, your team will make fewer and fewer mistakes, and you should see your defect rate drop.

has gone into the development of tools like pitest to minimize the time it takes to run them on your application, but they are still relatively slow compared to our scenarios and unit tests. Used as part of your development process and integrated into your CI pipeline, mutation testing can be a cost-effective way of confirming the quality of your automated testing.

## What We Just Learned

Working with legacy code is always a challenge, but you can use Cucumber scenarios to help make it a much more enjoyable challenge. Be pragmatic! Don't exhaust yourself trying to retrofit a complete set of Cucumber features for everything the system already does. Instead, add them gradually, one at a time, as you need them.

You'll use characterization tests to help understand what the system is already doing and to give you some security before you make a change. Similarly, every time you discover a bug, you'll trap it with a new Cucumber scenario. And, every time you add new behavior to the system, start by describing it with a Cucumber feature.

Code coverage can give you and your team feedback and encouragement about your progress in getting the system under test.

Enjoy the newfound confidence with which you can refactor and clean up the code that's covered by the tests.

# Installing Cucumber

Cucumber for Java is packaged as a series of JAR files. You can install it simply by downloading the relevant JAR files and placing them on the Java classpath, which is what we did in Chapter 2, *First Taste*, on page 11. More likely you'll be using some dependency management tool in your build process, such as Maven or Ivy, but this still requires you to specify the leaves of the dependency tree. This can be confusing, and that's what this appendix will explain.

## Choosing Your JARs

The current release of Cucumber for Java contains nineteen JARs, which split into four groups, described in the following sections. You will need to select the JARs that are relevant to your environment. As you'll see, some choices are optional, whereas others are required. Full details are outlined below and further information can be found online.[1]

### Core JARs

The core JAR cucumber-core is always needed. As its name suggests, it implements the core functionality of Cucumber.

If you're using a dependency management tool, then you'll never need to specify cucumber-core because the other Cucumber JARs that you have to specify (specifically the Programming Language Module) depend on it, and so it will always be present in the dependency graph. If you're downloading JARs manually, then you'll need to download it.

---

1.    http://cukes.info/install-cucumber-jvm.html

## Backend Modules

The choice of Backend module specifies which language you are going to write your glue (step definitions and hooks) in. The modules define the format of the snippets that are generated when Cucumber discovers a missing step definition and may also control how Cucumber searches for your glue code.

| Language | JAR |
| --- | --- |
| Java | cucumber-java |
| Clojure | cucumber-clojure |
| Groovy | cucumber-groovy |
| Ioke | cucumber-ioke |
| JRuby | cucumber-jruby |
| Jython | cucumber-jython |
| Rhino | cucumber-rhino |
| Scala | cucumber-scala |
| Java for Android | cucumber-android |

You must choose one, and only one, of these modules and have it on the Java classpath. Without a Backend module, Cucumber will fail with this error:

```
Exception in thread "main" cucumber.runtime.CucumberException:
  No backends were found.
  Please make sure you have a backend module on your CLASSPATH.
```

With more than one Backend module, Cucumber will not run correctly. Also, if you use cucumber-android you'll need the Android development environment correctly installed.

## Runners

The cucumber-core JAR provides a class that offers a command-line interface. If, however, you want to run your features from within an IDE or from a continuous integration (CI) server, you may want to interact with the features via a more common test API, such as JUnit.

These runners are currently supported by Cucumber:

| Runner | JAR |
| --- | --- |
| JUnit | cucumber-junit |
| TestNG | cucumber-testng |

You only need to include these JARs on the Java classpath if you want to run your features using these tools. Including both cucumber-junit and cucumber-testng on the classpath will not stop Cucumber from running.

### Dependency Injection Modules

As described in Chapter 11, *Simplifying Design with Dependency Injection*, on page 205, you can optionally choose to use one of several dependency injection (DI) containers in your glue code.

| DI Container | JAR |
| --- | --- |
| Guice | cucumber-guice |
| Weld | cucumber-weld |
| PicoContainer | cucumber-picocontainer |
| OpenEJB | cucumber-openejb |
| Spring | cucumber-spring |
| Needle | cucumber-needle |

You may choose not to use a DI container, but you must not place more than one Dependency Injection Module on the classpath.

If you do include one of these DI modules on the classpath, you'll also need to ensure that the corresponding DI container is available since the modules only include the binding between Cucumber and the container, not the container itself.

### Version Numbers

Each time Cucumber is released, the version number is incremented. You should never mix different version numbers together. As of this writing, the latest released version is 1.2.0.

Some of the JARs that Cucumber-JVM depends on are not part of the release, and their version numbers are not directly linked to the version of Cucumber-JVM you are using. Specifically cucumber-jvm-deps and gherkin are released as required and have their own version numbers.

## External Dependencies

As described in the previous section, there are some JARs that Cucumber depends on that are not part of a specific Cucumber release. You won't need to concern yourself with these if you use a dependency manager, but if you're downloading JARs manually you will.

## Gherkin

Gherkin is the name of the dialect that we use to write our feature files. It includes the keywords, and their translations into other languages. Obviously Cucumber depends on Gherkin to make sense of our feature files, but it is a separate project that is released independently.

The relevant gherkin JAR is available from the cukes portion of the public Maven repo.[2] As of this writing, the released version is 2.12.2.

## Cucumber Dependencies

Cucumber makes use of some other tools as well, such as the XStream utility from Thoughtworks (for marshaling data from your features through to your step definitions) and difflib for comparing tables.

These, and others, are packaged in the cucumber-jvm-deps JAR, also available from the cukes portion of the public Maven repo. As of this writing, the released version is 1.0.3.

# Console Colors on Windows

Cucumber uses ANSI escape codes to print colored output to the console. This isn't supported natively in Windows, so you have to install a tool called ANSICON to see colors.

Download and unzip the latest version.[3] Open a command prompt and cd to the folder where you unzipped it. Now, cd into either x86 or x64 (depending on your machine's processor) and install it globally on your machine:

```
C:\somewhere\ansi140\x64> ansicon -i
```

Any program that prints ANSI colors will now display properly on your machine.

If you don't want (or aren't allowed) to install ANSICON, then you can use the --monochrome option to make the output text only.

---

2. http://repo1.maven.org/maven2/info/cukes/
3. https://github.com/adoxa/ansicon/downloads

# Cucumber and Other JVM Languages

Cucumber comes in several flavors—it has been ported from Ruby to Java-Script, C#, Java, PHP, and others. The choice of which flavor of Cucumber you use essentially comes down to what language you want to write your step definitions in. Since most languages offer libraries that let you drive web browsers or interact with web services, you can use any implementation of Cucumber if you want to drive these sorts of applications from the outside. You should therefore choose the Cucumber that offers the language that your team will be most comfortable writing the step definitions in.

However, if you want your steps to interact directly with the code of the system under test, it's best to choose the version of Cucumber that allows you write the step definitions in the same language. So, for Ruby applications, choose Cucumber for Ruby; for JavaScript applications, choose Cucumber-JS: and so on.

Cucumber for Java is written in Java and is an obvious choice when using Cucumber with Java applications. However, Java runs on the JVM and interoperates seamlessly with other JVM languages. This opens up the possibility of writing your step definitions in the JVM language of your choice. You can choose to write your step definitions in one JVM language and your application in another.

As described in *Backend Modules*, on page 294, there are many languages to choose from. The functionality they offer is all built on top of the same Cucumber functionality (implemented in cucumber-core), but due to the differing paradigms of these languages the mechanisms used to make the functionality available varies from language to language.

Since there are a large number of JVM languages integrated with Cucumber, with varying popularity, we have chosen to focus on the Java back end in this book. In this appendix we'll show you some simple examples of using Cucumber directly with step definitions written in Groovy, Scala, and Clojure. For each language, we'll show a simple Checkout example, similar to the one we started developing in Chapter 2, *First Taste*, on page 11.

Combined with the knowledge you have gained from this book (and other examples available in the cucumber-jvm repository[1]), this should be sufficient for you to start using any of the other JVM languages for which Cucumber provides an integration.

# Groovy

Our favorite source of truth has this to say about Groovy:[2]

> Groovy is an object-oriented programming language for the Java platform. It is a dynamic language with features similar to those of Python, Ruby, Perl, and Smalltalk. It can be used as a scripting language for the Java Platform, is dynamically compiled to Java Virtual Machine (JVM) bytecode, and interoperates with other Java code and libraries. Groovy uses a Java-like curly-bracket syntax. Most Java code is also syntactically valid Groovy.

So, Groovy is quite like Java, but it has some of the ease-of-use features more commonly found in languages (often used for scripting) like Ruby. What's more, Groovy (like other JVM languages) has access to any library written in any JVM language.

To demonstrate how you might use Groovy, we've implemented the Checkout application—once with the production code written in Groovy and again with the production code written in Java. But we've used the same Groovy step definitions to drive both our implementations. In the next two sections we'll take a look at these implementations and discuss the differences.

## Groovy All the Way Down

If you have a look at the project, you'll see that it looks remarkably similar to the Java examples that we've been working with throughout the rest of the book. However, there are some notable differences, which we'll tackle one by one.

### The POM

The first thing we need to do is change pom.xml, as you can see in this extract:

---

1.   https://github.com/cucumber/cucumber-jvm/tree/master/examples
2.   http://en.wikipedia.org/wiki/Groovy_(programming_language)

**appendix/groovy/01/pom.xml**

```
Line 1  <dependencies>
   -        <dependency>
   -            <groupId>info.cukes</groupId>
   -            <artifactId>cucumber-groovy</artifactId>
   5            <version>${cucumber.version}</version>
   -            <scope>test</scope>
   -        </dependency>
   -        <dependency>
   -            <groupId>info.cukes</groupId>
  10            <artifactId>cucumber-junit</artifactId>
   -            <version>${cucumber.version}</version>
   -            <scope>test</scope>
   -        </dependency>
   -        <dependency>
  15            <groupId>junit</groupId>
   -            <artifactId>junit</artifactId>
   -            <version>${junit.version}</version>
   -            <scope>test</scope>
   -        </dependency>
  20        <dependency>
   -            <groupId>org.codehaus.groovy</groupId>
   -            <artifactId>groovy-all</artifactId>
   -            <version>${groovy.version}</version>
   -            <scope>provided</scope>
  25        </dependency>
   -    </dependencies>
   -
   -    <build>
   -        <plugins>
  30            <plugin>
   -                <groupId>org.codehaus.gmaven</groupId>
   -                <artifactId>gmaven-plugin</artifactId>
   -                <version>${gmaven-plugin.version}</version>
   -                <executions>
  35                    <execution>
   -                        <goals>
   -                            <goal>generateStubs</goal>
   -                            <goal>compile</goal>
   -                            <goal>generateTestStubs</goal>
  40                            <goal>testCompile</goal>
   -                        </goals>
   -                    </execution>
   -                </executions>
   -            </plugin>
  45        </plugins>
   -    </build>
```

On line 4, we've specified cucumber-groovy as the Cucumber back end. Then on line 21, we add a dependency on Groovy itself. Finally, in the plugins section, starting on line 30 we tell Maven to use the gmaven plugin.[3]

Notice that we're still referencing cucumber-junit and junit, and we can still run the project by executing mvn clean test.

### The World

The original version of Cucumber was written in Ruby and introduced the concept of a *World*. Step definitions can share context by adding objects, functions, and data to the World. The World is re-created before each scenario is run to make sure that you don't end up with *Leaky Scenarios*, on page 103.

In Chapter 11, *Simplifying Design with Dependency Injection*, on page 205 we discussed how Cucumber for Java uses various dependency injection containers to allow us to easily share state between our step definitions. The Cucumber Groovy integration takes a different approach, borrowed from the original Ruby version of Cucumber. Before each scenario is run, cucumber-groovy creates a new World, which is the shared context that all your hooks and step definitions will use. You can provide your own implementation of this by implementing the World hook:

appendix/groovy/01/src/test/groovy/checkout/World.groovy
```
this.metaClass.mixin(cucumber.api.groovy.Hooks)

class CheckoutWorld {
  def priceList = new PriceList()
  def checkout = new Checkout(priceList)
}

World {
  new CheckoutWorld()
}
```

Now the World contains an instance of CheckoutWorld and any step definition has access to its members. Notice that we need to mix in the cucumber.api.groovy.hooks package. This *mixin* also gives us access to @Begin and @After hooks when we need them.

### Step Definitions

Step definitions in Groovy are similar to their counterparts in Java. Take a look at CheckoutSteps:

---

3.   http://gmaven.codehaus.org/

appendix/groovy/01/src/test/groovy/checkout/CheckoutSteps.groovy

```
package checkout

this.metaClass.mixin(cucumber.api.groovy.EN)

When(~/^I scan a "(.*?)"$/) { String itemName ->
    checkout.scan(itemName)
}

Then(~/^the total is (\d+)c$/) { int expectedTotal ->
    assert expectedTotal == checkout.getTotal()
}
```

Notice that instead of Java annotations, the Groovy implementation uses classes mixed in from cucumber.api.groovy.EN. The language identifier in the Groovy mixin package is capitalized (for example, cucumber.api.groovy.EN), unlike the equivalent Java package (e.g. cucumber.api.java.en).

Maybe the most noticeable difference is that access to members of the world is so concise. In the code shown we can access the shared instance checkout directly, without any qualification, even though it is a member of an instance of CheckoutWorld.

## Groovy Driving a Java Application

It has been said that you'd be crazy to write your step definitions in Java when developing a Java application.[4] We don't necessarily agree, but just to show how easy it is to use Groovy and Java together, this project includes a Java implementation as an example. All you have to do is change which import statement is commented out in World.groovy:

appendix/groovy/01/src/test/groovy/checkout/World.groovy

```
/*
 * Change which import below is commented out to switch between the
 * Java and Groovy implementations of the checkout code.
 */
//import checkout.java.*
import checkout.groovy.*
```

Now when you run mvn clean test exactly the same, Groovy step definitions drive the Java implementation. Simple!

---

4.   https://twitter.com/cowspassage/status/507284159505895424

## Scala

Wikipedia describes Scala like this:[5]

> Scala is an object-functional programming language for general software applica-
> tions. Scala has full support for functional programming and a very strong static
> type system. This allows programs written in Scala to be very concise and thus
> smaller in size than most general purpose programming languages. Many of Scala's
> design decisions were inspired by criticism over the shortcomings of Java.

The cucumber-scala back end has neither integrations with DI containers (like
cucumber-java) nor a World hook like Groovy. You have to roll your own context-
sharing mechanism and ensure that it gets reset before each scenario. This
example shows one way to do it:

appendix/scala/01/src/test/scala/checkout/CheckoutWorld.scala
```
package checkout

import cucumber.api.Scenario
import cucumber.api.scala.{ScalaDsl, EN}

object CheckoutWorld extends ScalaDsl with EN {

  var priceList: PriceList = _
  var checkout: Checkout = _

  Before(){ scenario : Scenario =>
    priceList = new PriceList
    checkout = new Checkout(priceList)
  }
}
```

Here, we've created our own CheckoutWorld object to store data that needs to be
shared. The contents get reset for each scenario, using a @Before hook. This
object can be accessed easily by our step definitions, which also extend ScalaDsl:

appendix/scala/01/src/test/scala/checkout/CheckoutSteps.scala
```
package checkout

import cucumber.api.scala.{ScalaDsl, EN}
import org.junit.Assert._

class CheckoutSteps extends ScalaDsl with EN {

  When("""^I scan a "(.*?)"$"""){ (itemName:String) =>
    CheckoutWorld.checkout.scan(itemName)
  }
```

---

5.   http://en.wikipedia.org/wiki/Scala_(programming_language)

```
Then("""^the total is (\d+)c$"""){ (expectedTotal:Int) =>
  assertEquals(expectedTotal, CheckoutWorld.checkout.getTotal)
}
}
```

Notice that we've imported the JUnit package, so we can use the same assert statements in Scala that we could in Java.

## Clojure

The Clojure website describes Clojure like this:[6]

> It is designed to be a general-purpose language, combining the approachability and interactive development of a scripting language with an efficient and robust infrastructure for multithreaded programming. Clojure is a compiled language—it compiles directly to JVM bytecode, yet remains completely dynamic. Every feature supported by Clojure is supported at runtime. Clojure provides easy access to the Java frameworks, with optional type hints and type inference, to ensure that calls to Java can avoid reflection.

The profusion of parentheses might confuse a Java programmer, but they should come as no surprise, because Clojure is a dialect of Lisp—which of course means that Clojure is a functional language.

Managing state in a functional language can be confusing for programmers not used to it—not because it's difficult, but because these languages encourage idempotence, and hence stateless functions. In this example our step definitions test functions defined in the production code. No state is stored in the production code, which leaves this responsibility to our step definitions.

There are two common approaches taken when using Cucumber with Clojure: use the traditional Java infrastructure or use Leiningen.[7] We'll show you both.

### Maven and JUnit

This project uses Maven, so the folder structure should look familiar to Java programmers. There's no support from the cucumber-clojure integration for managing or resetting state, so we have to do it ourselves:

**appendix/clojure-java/01/src/test/clojure/checkout/world.clj**
```
(require '[checkout.checkout :refer [empty-cart empty-price-list]])
(import '[org.junit Assert])
```

---

6.  http://clojure.org/
7.  http://leiningen.org/

```clojure
(def cart (atom (empty-cart)))
(def price-list (atom (empty-price-list)))

(defn- force-long
  [maybe-str]
  (Long. maybe-str))

(defn- assert-equals [expected actual]
  (Assert/assertEquals expected actual))

(Before []
        (reset! cart (empty-cart))
        (reset! price-list (empty-price-list)))
```

As you can see, we use a @Before hook to reset the state of the world before each scenario runs. You'll also notice that we've defined a function, force-long, to make sure that we treat the argument passed from the feature as a number —this is something that cucumber-java handles for us.

Our step definitions should be recognizable:

**appendix/clojure-java/01/src/test/clojure/checkout/checkout_steps.clj**
```clojure
(require '[checkout.checkout :refer :all])

(load-file "src/test/clojure/checkout/world.clj")

(When #"^I scan a \"(.*?)\"$" [item-name]
      (swap! cart scan @price-list item-name))

(Then #"^the total is (\d+)c$" [expected-total]
      (assert-equals (force-long expected-total) (checkout @cart)))
```

We've made the shared state available to our step definitions using a load-file expression. And we've made the JUnit assertEquals available by using an import statement.

## Leiningen

Now we'll show you how to use Leiningen to build this example. Leiningen is a build tool developed expressly for Clojure development, and it allows projects to be configured using Clojure—no XML is needed. The file structure is quite different from the one Java programmers are used to, so it's worth having a look at the example project.

Apart from the folder structure, the most noticeable difference is that the pom.xml has been replaced by project.clj:

**appendix/clojure-lein/01/project.clj**
```clojure
(defproject clojure-cucumber "0.1.0-SNAPSHOT"
```

```
  :description "A checkout example tested using Cucumber"

  :dependencies [[org.clojure/clojure "1.6.0"]]

  :plugins [[lein-cucumber "1.0.2"]]

  :cucumber-feature-paths ["test/features/"])
```

We've also replaced the use of JUnit with the more idiomatic clojure.test:

appendix/clojure-lein/01/test/features/step_definitions/checkout_steps.clj
```
(require '[clojure-cucumber.core :refer :all])
(require '[clojure.test :refer [is]])

(load-file "test/features/step_definitions/world.clj")

(When #"^I scan a \"(.*?)\"$" [item-name]
      (swap! cart scan @price-list item-name))

(Then #"^the total is (\d+)c$" [expected-total]
      (is (= (force-num expected-total) (checkout @cart))))
```

You can build and test this example by typing lein do clean, cucumber. This uses the lean-cucumber plugin,[8] which works well but doesn't expose all of Cucumber's options. For example, the output to the console always uses the progress plugin, whereas the pretty output gets written to target/test-reports/cucumber.out—there's nothing you can do about this.

We've had a brief look at Cucumber's integration with the three most popular non-Java JVM languages. They, and the other integrations, are under active development by the Cucumber community, so check the documentation online for the latest details. And if you'd like to see other features in these integrations, then why not implement them yourself and submit a pull request? The Cucumber team needs YOU!

---

8.  https://github.com/nilswloka/lein-cucumber

# Bibliography

[Ad 11]    Gojko Adžić. *Specification by Example*. Manning Publications Co., Greenwich, CT, 2011.

[Bec00]    Kent Beck. *Extreme Programming Explained: Embrace Change*. Addison-Wesley Longman, Reading, MA, 2000.

[Bec02]    Kent Beck. *Test Driven Development: By Example*. Addison-Wesley, Reading, MA, 2002.

[Bro95]    Frederick P. Brooks Jr. *The Mythical Man-Month: Essays on Software Engineering*. Addison-Wesley, Reading, MA, Anniversary, 1995.

[CADH09]  David Chelimsky, Dave Astels, Zach Dennis, Aslak Hellesøy, Bryan Helmkamp, and Dan North. *The RSpec Book*. The Pragmatic Bookshelf, Raleigh, NC and Dallas, TX, 2009.

[CG08]     Lisa Crispin and Janet Gregory. *Agile Testing: A Practical Guide for Testers and Agile Teams*. Addison-Wesley, Reading, MA, 2008.

[Coc04]    Alistair Cockburn. *Crystal Clear: A Human-Powered Methodology for Small Teams*. Addison-Wesley Professional, Boston, MA, 2004.

[Coh05]    Mike Cohn. *Agile Estimating and Planning*. Prentice Hall, Englewood Cliffs, NJ, 2005.

[Coh09]    Mike Cohn. *Succeeding with Agile: Software Development Using Scrum*. Addison-Wesley, Reading, MA, 2009.

[Eva03]    Eric Evans. *Domain-Driven Design: Tackling Complexity in the Heart of Software*. Addison-Wesley Longman, Reading, MA, First, 2003.

[FBBO99]   Martin Fowler, Kent Beck, John Brant, William Opdyke, and Don Roberts. *Refactoring: Improving the Design of Existing Code*. Addison-Wesley, Reading, MA, 1999.

[Fea04]    Michael Feathers. *Working Effectively with Legacy Code*. Prentice Hall, Englewood Cliffs, NJ, 2004.

[FP09]     Steve Freeman and Nat Pryce. *Growing Object-Oriented Software, Guided by Tests*. Addison-Wesley Longman, Reading, MA, 2009.

[GHJV95]   Erich Gamma, Richard Helm, Ralph Johnson, and John Vlissides. *Design Patterns: Elements of Reusable Object-Oriented Software*. Addison-Wesley, Reading, MA, 1995.

[HT00]     Andrew Hunt and David Thomas. *The Pragmatic Programmer: From Journeyman to Master*. Addison-Wesley, Reading, MA, 2000.

[Joh10]    Christian Johansen. *Test-Driven JavaScript Development*. Addison-Wesley Professional, Boston, MA, 2010.

[Mes07]    Gerard Meszaros. *xUnit Test Patterns*. Addison-Wesley, Reading, MA, 2007.

[Ohn88]    Taiichi Ohno. *Toyota Production System: Beyond Large Scale Production*. Productivity Press, New York, NY, USA, 1st, 1988.

# Index

# Explore Testing and Cucumber

Explore the uncharted waters of exploratory testing and beef up your automated testing with more Cucumber.

## Explore It!

Uncover surprises, risks, and potentially serious bugs with exploratory testing. Rather than designing all tests in advance, explorers design and execute small, rapid experiments, using what they learned from the last little experiment to inform the next. Learn essential skills of a master explorer, including how to analyze software to discover key points of vulnerability, how to design experiments on the fly, how to hone your observation skills, and how to focus your efforts.

Elisabeth Hendrickson
(160 pages) ISBN: 9781937785024. $29
*https://pragprog.com/book/ehxta*

## Cucumber Recipes

You can test just about anything with Cucumber. We certainly have, and in *Cucumber Recipes* we'll show you how to apply our hard-won field experience to your own projects. Once you've mastered the basics, this book will show you how to get the most out of Cucumber—from specific situations to advanced test-writing advice. With over forty practical recipes, you'll test desktop, web, mobile, and server applications across a variety of platforms. This book gives you tools that you can use today to automate any system that you encounter, and do it well.

Ian Dees, Matt Wynne, Aslak Hellesøy
(272 pages) ISBN: 9781937785017. $33
*https://pragprog.com/book/dhwcr*

# Be Agile

Don't just "do" agile; you want to *be* agile. We'll show you how, for new code and old.

## Your Code As a Crime Scene

Jack the Ripper and legacy codebases have more in common than you'd think. Inspired by forensic psychology methods, this book teaches you strategies to predict the future of your codebase, assess refactoring direction, and understand how your team influences the design. With its unique blend of forensic psychology and code analysis, this book arms you with the strategies you need, no matter what programming language you use.

Adam Tornhill
(190 pages) ISBN: 9781680500387. $36
*https://pragprog.com/book/atcrime*

## The Nature of Software Development

You need to get value from your software project. You need it "free, now, and perfect." We can't get you there, but we can help you get to "cheaper, sooner, and better." This book leads you from the desire for value down to the specific activities that help good Agile projects deliver better software sooner, and at a lower cost. Using simple sketches and a few words, the author invites you to follow his path of learning and understanding from a half century of software development and from his engagement with Agile methods from their very beginning.

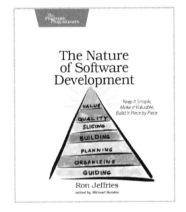

Ron Jeffries
(150 pages) ISBN: 9781941222379. $24
*https://pragprog.com/book/rjnsd*

# Seven in Seven

From Web Frameworks to Concurrency Models, see what the rest of the world is doing with this introduction to seven different approaches.

## Seven Web Frameworks in Seven Weeks

Whether you need a new tool or just inspiration, *Seven Web Frameworks in Seven Weeks* explores modern options, giving you a taste of each with ideas that will help you create better apps. You'll see frameworks that leverage modern programming languages, employ unique architectures, live client-side instead of server-side, or embrace type systems. You'll see everything from familiar Ruby and JavaScript to the more exotic Erlang, Haskell, and Clojure.

Jack Moffitt, Fred Daoud
(302 pages) ISBN: 9781937785635. $38
*https://pragprog.com/book/7web*

## Seven Concurrency Models in Seven Weeks

Your software needs to leverage multiple cores, handle thousands of users and terabytes of data, and continue working in the face of both hardware and software failure. Concurrency and parallelism are the keys, and *Seven Concurrency Models in Seven Weeks* equips you for this new world. See how emerging technologies such as actors and functional programming address issues with traditional threads and locks development. Learn how to exploit the parallelism in your computer's GPU and leverage clusters of machines with MapReduce and Stream Processing. And do it all with the confidence that comes from using tools that help you write crystal clear, high-quality code.

Paul Butcher
(296 pages) ISBN: 9781937785659. $38
*https://pragprog.com/book/pb7con*

# The Pragmatic Bookshelf

The Pragmatic Bookshelf features books written by developers for developers. The titles continue the well-known Pragmatic Programmer style and continue to garner awards and rave reviews. As development gets more and more difficult, the Pragmatic Programmers will be there with more titles and products to help you stay on top of your game.

# Visit Us Online

### This Book's Home Page
*https://pragprog.com/book/srjcuc*
Source code from this book, errata, and other resources. Come give us feedback, too!

### Register for Updates
*https://pragprog.com/updates*
Be notified when updates and new books become available.

### Join the Community
*https://pragprog.com/community*
Read our weblogs, join our online discussions, participate in our mailing list, interact with our wiki, and benefit from the experience of other Pragmatic Programmers.

### New and Noteworthy
*https://pragprog.com/news*
Check out the latest pragmatic developments, new titles and other offerings.

# Save on the eBook

Save on the eBook versions of this title. Owning the paper version of this book entitles you to purchase the electronic versions at a terrific discount.

PDFs are great for carrying around on your laptop—they are hyperlinked, have color, and are fully searchable. Most titles are also available for the iPhone and iPod touch, Amazon Kindle, and other popular e-book readers.

Buy now at *https://pragprog.com/coupon*

# Contact Us

| | |
|---|---|
| Online Orders: | *https://pragprog.com/catalog* |
| Customer Service: | *support@pragprog.com* |
| International Rights: | *translations@pragprog.com* |
| Academic Use: | *academic@pragprog.com* |
| Write for Us: | *http://write-for-us.pragprog.com* |
| Or Call: | +1 800-699-7764 |